FINANCIAL CRISES AND THE WORLD BANKING SYSTEM

Also by Forrest Capie

THE INTER-WAR ECONOMY: A Statistical Abstract (*with M. Collins*)
DEPRESSION AND PROTECTIONISM
A MONETARY HISTORY OF THE UNITED KINGDOM, 1870–1982 (*with Alan Webber*)

Also by Geoffrey E. Wood

THE FINANCING PROCEDURES OF BRITISH FOREIGN TRADE (*with Stephen Carse and John Williamson*)
MONETARY TARGETS (*editor with Brian Griffiths*)
EXCHANGE RATE POLICY (*editor with Roy A. Batchelor*)
MONETARISM IN THE UNITED KINGDOM (*editor with Brian Griffiths*)

Financial Crises and the World Banking System

Edited by

Forrest Capie

Reader in Monetary History, The City University

and

Geoffrey E. Wood

Reader in Banking and International Finance, The City University

MACMILLAN

in association with
Centre for Banking and International Finance
The City University
London

First published 1986

Published by
THE MACMILLAN PRESS LTD
Houndmills, Basingstoke, Hampshire RG21 2XS
and London

Companies and representatives
throughout the world

Printed in Hong Kong

British Library Cataloguing in Publication Data
Financial crises and the world banking system.
1. Banks and banking, International 2. Depressions
I. Capie, Forrest II. Wood, Geoffrey E.
III. City University. *Centre for Banking and International Finance.*
332.1'5 HG3881
ISBN 0–333–35129–0

Contents

Acknowledgements

The conference at which these papers were first presented would not have been possible without the financial support of: Union Discount Company of London plc; L. Messel & Co.; and the Water Authorities Superannuation Fund.

Notes on the Contributors

Roy A. Batchelor is a Senior Research Fellow and Director of Research at the Centre for Banking and International Finance at the City University. A graduate of Glasgow University, he has worked in government and in the National Institute of Economic and Social Research. He is co-author of *Industrialisation and the Basis for Trade*, co-editor of *Exchange Rate Policy* (with Geoffrey E. Wood) and author of numerous papers in applied economics and econometrics.

Michael D. Bordo is Professor of Economics at the University of South Carolina and a Research Associate of the National Bureau of Economic Research. He has been Assistant Professor from 1969 to 1976 and Associate Professor from 1976 to 1981 at Carleton University. He has also been a Visiting Professor at the London School of Economics, University of California, Los Angeles, Lund University, Sweden, and Erasmus University, Rotterdam; a visiting scholar at the Federal Reserve Bank of St Louis; and consultant to the Executive Director of the Congressional Gold Commission. His publications include co-editorship of the NBER conference volume, *A Retrospective on the Classical Gold Standard, 1821–1931*, and numerous journal articles.

Forrest Capie is a Reader in Monetary History at the Centre for Banking and International Finance at the City University, London. He has also taught at the Universities of Warwick and Leeds and was British Academy Overseas visiting Fellow to the USA in 1978. He is author of *Depression and Protectionism* and co-author of *The Inter-War Economy: A Statistical Abstract* and *Monetary History of the United Kingdom* and over twenty journal articles.

Tim Congdon has been economics partner of L. Messel & Co. since 1980 and is economics leader-writer and a weekly economic columnist for *The Times*. A frequent contributor to the financial press and bank journals, he is also author of a dictionary of economics, *Monetary*

Control in Britain, *Monetarism: an Essay in Definition*, *Against Import Controls* and *Trade and Financial Liberalization in Latin America.*

John Standish Fforde is an Economic Adviser at the Bank of England. From 1951 to 1956 he was a research and official Fellow in economics at Nuffield College, Oxford. He joined the Bank of England in 1957 and was Chief Cashier from 1966 to 1970, Executive Director (Home Finance) from 1970 to 1982 and Adviser to the Governor from 1982 to 1984. He is currently working on the official history of the Bank of England for the period 1945 to 1961.

Alec G. Ford is Professor of Economics at the University of Warwick and has been Pro-Vice-Chancellor since 1977. He was previously on the staff at the University of Leicester. He has research interests and publications in the areas of recent British, Argentine and international economic history and in macroeconomics.

Charles Goodhart is Professor of Banking and Finance at the London School of Economics and was formerly a Chief Adviser at the Bank of England. He previously taught at Cambridge University and has been an Economic Adviser in the Department of Economic Affairs in London. He was Lecturer in Monetary Economics at the London School of Economics from 1966 to 1968. He is the author of *Money, Information and Uncertainty*, and other books and articles, mostly on monetary economics and monetary history.

Lars Jonung is Research Director at the National Institute of Economic Research (Konjunkturinstitutet), Stockholm, and Lecturer at the University of Lund, Sweden. He has published several articles on Swedish monetary policy and Swedish stabilisation policy. His main field of research is Swedish monetary history.

Allan H. Meltzer is John M. Olin Professor of Political Economy and Public Policy at Carnegie-Mellon University and has been Visiting Professor at Harvard, the Universities of Chicago and Rochester, and in Yugoslavia, Austria, Brazil and London. His reputation in the field of money and capital markets has brought frequent assignments with Congressional committees, as a consultant to the President's Council of Economic Advisers, the US Treasury Department, the Board of Governors of the Federal Reserve System and to foreign governments and central banks. His writings have appeared in numerous journals and his career includes experience as a self-employed businessman, management adviser, corporate director and consultant to banks and financial institutions. He is a founder and co-chairman of the Shadow Open Market Committee. In 1983 he received a medal for distinguished professional achievement from the University of California.

Terence C. Mills is Lecturer in Economics at the School of Economic Studies, University of Leeds. From 1980 to 1984 he was also an economist at the Bank of England. He has published articles in numerous journals.

D. E. Moggridge is Professor of Economics and Dean for the Social Sciences in the School of Graduate Studies, University of Toronto. A graduate of the Universities of Toronto and Cambridge, he previously lectured in Cambridge from 1971 to 1975, where he was a Fellow of Clare College from 1967 to 1975 and from 1979 to 1981. His publications include *British Monetary Policy, 1924–1931: The Norman Conquest of $4.86*; *Keynes*; and as editor with Sir Austin Robinson, *The Collected Writings of John Maynard Keynes*.

L. S. Pressnell has had appointments in several universities, most recently at the University of Kent from 1977 to 1982. He was Specialist Adviser to the House of Commons Select Committee on Nationalised Industries for the inquiry into the Bank of England from 1969 to 1970 and has been Official Historian at the Cabinet Office, for External Economic Policy since the Second World War. He has been a consultant for histories of the Hong Kong and Shanghai Banking Corporation and the British Bank of the Middle East and consultant to the City University's research project on the monetary history of Britain. He is the author of several books, contributions to books, articles and reviews on monetary and banking topics.

Hugh Rockoff is Professor of Economics at Rutgers University in New Brunswick, New Jersey. He is the author of *The Free Banking Era: A Re-examination, Drastic Measures: A History of Wage and Price Controls in the United States* and numerous articles in professional journals on the history of banking in the USA and Europe.

Kurt Schiltknecht is Director of the Economic Section of the Swiss National Bank and is Deputy Head of the Department I of the bank.

He lectures at the University of Basle and is a member of the National Research Council of the Swiss National Science Foundation. From 1967 to 1969 and 1970 to 1972 he was researcher at the Institute for Economic Research at the Swiss Institute of Technology in Zürich and from 1969 to 1970 and 1973 to 1974 he was visiting researcher at the Econometric Research Unit of the OECD in Paris and Economic Research Unit, University of Pennsylvania.

Anna J. Schwartz has been a member of the research staff at the National Bureau of Economic Research in New York for many years. She has collaborated with Milton Friedman on a series of studies including *A Monetary History of the United States 1867–1960* and *Monetary Trends in the United States and the United Kingdom: Their Relation to Income, Prices, and Interest Rates, 1867–1975*. She is co-editor of *A Retrospective on the Classical Gold Standard, 1821–1931*.

Teresa Seabourne is a M.Phil./Ph.D. research student at the Centre for Banking and International Finance at the City University. Her present area of research is the monetary history of the UK from 1870 to 1970.

Michael Wagner is a lecturer at the University of Vienna, and Senior Research Associate at the Institute for Advanced Studies in Vienna. He is author of *Ökonomische Modelltheorie*, co-author of *Wachstumskrisen in Osterreich*, *Umverteilung und Lohnstruktur* and *Bankiers und Beamte* and has written several other monographs and articles on financial and labour markets.

Geoffrey E. Wood is Reader in Banking and International Finance and Senior Tutor at the Centre for Banking and International Finance. A graduate of the Universities of Aberdeen and Essex, he has taught previously at the University of Warwick, been a member of the Economic Section of the Bank of England and Visiting Scholar at the Federal Reserve Bank of St Louis. His publications include research papers on the demand for money, inflation and the balance of payments; he is co-author of *The Financing Procedures of British Foreign Trade* and co-editor of *Monetary Targets* (with Brian Griffiths), *Exchange Rate Policy* (with Roy A. Batchelor) and *Monetarism in the United Kingdom* (with Brian Griffiths).

Introduction

A research project on British monetary history from 1870 to 1980 has been going forward at the Centre for Banking and International Finance at The City University since 1979, financed largely by the Social Science Research Council (now renamed Economic and Social Research Council). The purpose of the study has been to further understanding of monetary developments in the United Kingdom over that century, and of the impact these developments had on the real economy, prices, interest rates, and the exchange rate.

An essential preliminary to a study of the data was the improvement of the data. British monetary statistics before 1914 have been largely the product of heroic efforts by individuals – notably David Sheppard and Shizuya Nishimura drawing on contemporary work by *The Economist*. Our work has started from that point but much has been drawn from original sources – in particular, from bank archives. Much work had to be done in the construction of the monetary series, in evaluation of them as compared to existing sets of data, and in dealing with problems caused by, for example, the use of the pound sterling in Southern Ireland after it became independent. The results of this work, together with discussion of how the series were constructed and evaluated, appeared initially in a series of working papers and journal articles, and have now been published in *A Monetary History of the United Kingdom, 1870–1982: Data Sources and Methods*, by Forrest Capie and Alan Webber (Allen & Unwin, 1985).

The analytical framework within which these data are to be examined is that of the demand for and supply of money. Money demand and supply functions are constructed, and the impact of discrepancies between demand and supply on interest rates, exchange rates, output, and prices, examined.

The analysis is to be ordered chronologically. Attention will be paid also to the changing structure of the banking system and the increasing monetisation and financial sophistication of the economy, changes in the money supply process, and, of course, to the exchange rate regime and how that affected the causal relationship between money and prices. Even within such a chronological framework, however, certain episodes stand out as being of particular note, and deserving lengthier treatment.

Paramount of these episodes, both at the time they occurred and in their potential importance for affecting future policy and the future actions of private individuals, are financial crises or, if that description is rejected, episodes that can be regarded as extreme observations. It is to these episodes that the chapters in this volume are addressed.

THE AIMS OF THE CONFERENCE

The conference brought together six papers on financial episodes which were, or came close to being, or have been construed as, crises. They examine the analytical framework appropriate to the study of crises, individual episodes within or leading to the period 1870–1970, the international aspects of crises, and especially the role of the central bank in a crisis. This coverage enables us to maintain the international aspect, important to the study of monetary policy in an economy such as the United Kingdom which at the start of our period was the dominant international banker and the major international trader, and, although less important in these roles by our period's end, still very exposed to external influences. Further, the focus on the lender-of-last-resort role – the central bank's function in a crisis – is significant in learning how attitudes to that role have changed, and how that in turn affected the attitude of the Bank of England to developments in the banking system, and the behaviour of the banking system itself. In addition, the lender-of-last-resort role, either domestic or international, has in the past few years been of considerable topical interest. Historical study of how and, most important, why the role evolved cannot but improve understanding the present.

Having set the conference in its context it is now time to turn to the individual chapters.

THE CHAPTERS

Of the six chapters, the first was an overview of the crises and three dealt with particular episodes; these were taken in historical order, and were followed by a discussion of the lender-of-last-resort, and finally by examination of the international transmission of crises. The discussion below follows that order.

What is a Crisis?

In the first chapter, Dr Anna J. Schwartz distinguishes between real and pseudo crises. The distinction is best made by quotation from her chapter 'A financial crisis is fuelled by fears that means of payment will be unobtainable at any price and, in a fractional reserve banking system, leads to a scramble for high-powered money. It is precipitated by actions of the public that suddenly squeeze the reserves of the banking system . . . The essence of a financial crisis is that it is short-lived, ending with a slackening of the public's demand for additional currency.'

This is in contrast with a disinflation or deflation. 'A disinflation or deflation may be long drawn out. Nominal wealth may decline, real debts may rise, but these are not financial crises. No financial crisis has occurred in the United States since 1933, and none has occurred in the United Kingdom since 1866. All the phenomena of recent years that have been characterised as financial crises – a decline in asset prices of equity stock, real estate, commodities; depreciation of the exchange value of a national currency; financial distress of a large non-financial firm, a large municipality, a financial industry, or sovereign debtors – are pseudo-financial crises.'

In other words, loss of wealth causes distress, but is not of itself a financial crisis; a financial crisis is when the stability of the banking *system* is threatened. Only then does the use of money threaten to disappear, albeit temporarily, from a society, and only then is the financial structure threatened.

Using that distinction, the views of various other writers are appraised and various episodes briefly examined.

Having considered episodes when markets or institutions were under pressure, but the financial system not threatened – pseudo crises, therefore – Dr Schwartz considers when a real financial crisis occurred. As so often in this area, the analysis starts with Bagehot. (If Adam Smith is, in George Stigler's words, the Shakespeare of the economics profession in general, Bagehot is certainly the Shakespeare of the financial system.) It was in 1873 that Bagehot pointed out that financial crises were prevented from occurring in England when the Bank, however hesitantly, lent without stint in a crisis. And in 1873 the USA experienced a financial crisis because, in Dr Schwartz's words, 'no institutional framework was immediately available to deal with the surge of demand for high-powered money by the public and banks'. That, then, is the analytical framework for distinguishing real from pseudo crises, and how to deal with real crises when they occur. A summary of when financial crises did or did not occur can be found on page 17. The chapter then turns to an appraisal of the views of Kindleberger, a prolific writer on this subject, who identifies all 'manias' – in a more fashionable term (e.g. Flood and Garber, 1983), 'bubbles' – with crises. Despite this identification, and despite (as Dr Schwartz emphasises) his not distinguishing between crises that occurred from crises cut short by appropriate policy, Kindleberger does acknowledge that crises – on his definition – have been becoming less frequent. His concern now is an international crisis, and his recommendation an international lender-of-last-resort – rejected by Dr Schwartz because it confuses a run on a currency with a threat to the financial system.

In a brief concluding section, it is argued that the analysis leads one to the position that current concern about crises is really about a pseudo crisis, that the financial system is not threatened, and that banks should be allowed to fail. Bankruptcy has a useful role in economic life. This and other policy implications are drawn together in the final section of this introduction.

Crisis as Catastrophe

The second chapter, by Roy A. Batchelor, examines two episodes in the UK in the nineteenth century – the collapse of Overend, Gurney & Company in 1866, and the liquidation of Baring Bros in 1890.

The author considers why they arose, and why, despite the different treatment the institutions involved received from the Bank of England, the damage was so limited. A striking feature of the chapter, it should be remarked at the outset, is the use of the mathematical technique known as 'catastrophe theory'.

The chapter comprises two models, and traditional 'historical' discussion. The first model, the catastrophe theory one, is used to structure discussion of the approach to the crisis. The second is a model, specific to banking, of a run on a bank as 'a rational reaction on the part of depositors to news arriving in a situation where they are imperfectly informed about the relative state of affairs of individual banks'.

The models are used to structure the analysis rather than for quantification – inevitable given the data on the two crises. Even though thus limited they are useful: for they elucidate the basic similarities of the *commercial* problems which precipitated the financial difficulties of Overends and of Barings. They also help clarify the approaches open to the Bank in dealing with the institutions' problems. The Bank could increase information, so as to enable depositors to distinguish between sound and unsound institutions; or it could replenish, even overreplenish, the assets of the bank which was in difficulties. In Overend's case they chose the first course, in Barings', the second. Why? Basically, it is argued from the models, supplying information is the more likely to succeed – and the Bank was additionally led to this course by the cost of saving Overend. Why did they choose the second course for Barings? The author suggests that this, the less secure course, was followed because, as the public were well informed about the relative position of Barings and other institutions, a run was unlikely even had Barings failed. To this conclusion from the models he adds an argument of his own, and touches on one of others. He argues that Overend and the Bank were on bad terms because of the criticism by Overend of the Bank's operations, and indeed because of some of the actions of Overend in the markets. The Bank was on good terms with Barings, and had a Baring on the Court; it wanted 'to save the "name" of Barings'. The author also touches on, but rejects as based on misleading balance sheet data, the claim of Powell (1915) that Barings' problems were much smaller in scale. Discretion, not rules, seems to have guided the Bank's operations. That is clearly true; but there may be a stronger case than Batchelor concedes for the use of this discretion. Professor Ford points out in his comments that Barings' difficulties were temporary. The investments in which they were involved were not fundamentally unsound, and the cause of Barings' problems was a delay in the flow of remittances rather than a collapse of the investment. Clearly, with hindsight, the Bank's action can be defended. This highlights a problem with analysis of such episodes. Information becomes clear to the historian which may, or may not, have been known at the time. It seems impossible to establish whether or not the Bank could foresee the resumption of remittances from Argentina. It is certainly possible that they could.

But in turn, if they could, why could not the markets? And if so, why was there a problem? The answer may be that the market could see the prospect of an end to the problems but one so uncertain that they could not have helped Barings over the difficulty. This is surely an area for further work.

1914

The chapter on 1914 comprises the only paper of the conference to deal with an episode associated with the outbreak of war. The episode is a contentious one. Keynes accused the commercial banks of aggravating a difficult situation by taking action justifiable only on a very narrow definition of their own interest, and even on that basis, action which could be justified only by a very short time horizon. This charge was increased in severity by de Cecco, who accused the banks not of foolish short-sightedness but of active malevolence, of seizing the opportunity given by war to attack potential rivals. How is the episode reappraised in this paper?

The problems caused in London by the imminent European War had two aspects – plunging stock prices, and the failure of remittance of funds from overseas. A rush for liquidity began, and the banks called in loans from the stock exchange and the discount market, weakening the first and driving the second to the Bank of England. Fortunately, the crisis started just before a bank holiday – which was extended. By a series of measures the stock exchange problem was solved, and assistance provided over the next few weeks to the bill market. The crisis was solved without a collapse. Were the banks as culpable as de Cecco – or even Keynes – claimed? Could advance preparations have been better? Could the situation, when it struck, have been better handled?

The view of Keynes on possible preparations is accepted. War was always a possibility – it could never be ruled out of account – but it never seemed so likely, or so definite in prospective date, as to allow preparations to be made by the financial markets. (See pp. 125–9 of '1931' for a formal model of such a setting.) Once the crisis struck, there was some dispute on what to do – the Treasury and the Bank resisting the proposal of the commercial banks to pool gold holdings and issue emergency notes. But once this confusion was over, the situation was, as the outcome makes clear, handled well. It may, as one of the paper's discussants suggested, have been handled at the cost of an inflationary issue of currency – but that is for a future study. The episode is, by and large, an example of central bank policy in a crisis emerging with a good deal of credit, and the commercial banks being acquitted of the charges of Keynes, and, *a fortiori*, of de Cecco.

1931

The year 1931 saw the final breakdown of an order that had lasted, in its most developed form, for over half a century. Britain left the gold standard. Britain had been the central country in the operation of that standard during its prime (1870–1914), so Britain's leaving the gold standard surely signalled the beginning of its demise. Why did Britain leave gold? Various hypotheses have been advanced. The earliest, associated with Keynes, is that after the interruption of the war it went back at too high a parity in 1925. Others have blamed the banking crisis of continental Europe for precipitating a liquidity crisis, which Britain, with gold reserves low and advertised as being so in an official report, could not withstand. A third view, identified notably with Moggridge, has pointed to the rapid and substantial adverse swing in the invisibles account, resulting from the fall in interest rates and invisible earnings as the depression started.

This chapter seeks to discriminate between these hypotheses. It emerges that there was no banking crisis in the UK. Indeed, in so far as one can tell bank profits were hardly affected. Nor was there any other crisis – although there was indubitably weakness in the stock exchange. The problems of the sterling area did not seem to impinge on gold holdings in London.

The UK's budgetary position, although of concern at the time, was, when adjusted for the level of economic activity, close to balance, and possibly in surplus – there was no prospect of debt growth so rapid that monetisation would inevitably follow. After examining the time series of prices and interest rates, it concluded that overvaluation cannot explain Britain's action. The conclusion is that the gold standard was brought down in 1931 because 'central banks did not understand central banking' – they turned bank failures into a banking crisis on the Continent and in the subsequent scramble for gold, the major gold holders, France and the USA, did not lend freely to save the system, but hoarded in a short-sighted effort to save themselves. Collapse was the result.

Transmission

In the Great Depression one can see the transmission process at work following the failure of central banks to pursue appropriate policy. That may in some eyes be regarded as a reliable and predictable method for transmitting crisis; but are there others? In his chapter, Michael D. Bordo examines these. What are the possibilities? Bordo suggests three are of major importance – a monetary contraction following a banking panic (as the public's cash ratio rises); a fall in velocity; or direct effects on real output via bankruptcies in the real sector or banks reducing financial intermediation. Before proceeding to an examination of these hypotheses, Bordo summarises the extensive literature on the transmission of crises. He identifies two views about which work can be grouped. One approach, developed particularly by Minsky and Kindleberger on the basis of work by Fisher, sees financial crises as a 'normal' ingredient of the upper turning point of the business cycle. The other, called 'monetarist' by Bordo, sees crises as unusual events, aggravating deflations when they occur but in no respect a normal part of them. The first view sees crises as transmitted internationally by international bank lending, the second by sharp and unanticipated fluctuations in monetary flows. The empirical section surveys six countries for the years 1870–1933. The conclusions which emerge are three. First, a nationwide banking system, other things being equal, makes crises less likely, and less severe when they occur. Secondly stock market fluctuations can produce monetary contractions (by affecting the demand for cash) and can, through international currency flows, be transmitted internationally. Thirdly – and in part inevitably given the quality of the data (as Bordo observes), it is not possible to reject one of the transmission mechanisms as never having operated. The 'monetarist' seems to have been the more important; but it was not of exclusive importance. The data appear to let one go no further.

Bagehot

The name of Walter Bagehot arose in almost every discussion at the conference. It was he, after all, who codified how central banks should behave in a crisis. His *Lombard Street* is a classic, a definitive manual for central bankers. That, at any rate, is the conventional view. This view is challenged in Hugh Rockoff's subtle and provocative contribution. Rockoff's point is that there are two Bagehots. One tells the central bank to lend freely, at high rates; the other, to protect the reserve. And he does not, Rockoff claims, provide clear guidance on when a central bank should do one, and when the other. Indeed, Rockoff argues that the main problems in nineteenth-century banking in Britain were not occasioned by the Bank being *unwilling* to lend in time of crisis; rather, 'the problem was typically one of recognising the right moment for extreme actions'.

Just as there are two Bagehots, there are two interconnected discussions in Rockoff's paper. One is an examination of Bagehot's *Lombard Street* in the light of more recently available data, and placing it in the context of other, earlier, writings – something Bagehot, more the man of affairs than scholar, did not do. Secondly, Rockoff considers the applicability of Bagehot's concern to protect the reserve to present conditions, when we are no longer on the gold standard. He argues that the modern counterpart of that concern is a desire to control the trend growth of money. When should a central bank depart from that rule? How can it be sure that by its actions designed to prevent crisis it will not turn apprehension into the crisis it seeks to avoid?

These issues are taken up by Rockoff's discussants, both (at the time of the conference) practising central bankers.

This chapter is a stimulating and fascinating blend of historical scholarship, economic analysis, and consideration of policy.

AN OVERVIEW

In concluding this introduction, three questions should be answered. What are the main findings of the discussion? What are the main areas of agreement in the chapters? And what, if any, are the implications for policy?

(In the last, we draw on a round table discussion which took place at the end of the conference. That focused on some of the central themes.)

Three chapters on particular issues – Batchelor, Seabourne, and Capie *et al.*, draw attention to the importance of preannounced rules for crisis management. If these are in existence, widely known and widely agreed, crisis seem unlikely to emerge even from the most difficult and unexpected situations. Seabourne shows the positive side of this; Capie *et al.* show the consequences of not having such rules.

But there are problems. Rockoff shows that rules, however well constructed, do not necessarily give guidance on how to apply them. Bordo shows how not applying them – for good or bad reasons – can spread a crisis. Schwartz' chapter aims at providing an overview, and it can indeed provide a useful summary also of the main findings of the conference, and the main conclusions for policy. These are as follows.

Policy should be minimal and declared; bank failures can and should be tolerated when they derive from poor management or unsound banking practice; and the lender-of-last-resort function is important but not without serious difficulties in applying. In a round table discussion after the papers these issues were pursued in relation to the world debt problems of 1983–4. Some strong differences still exist. The conventional view can be seen, in the words of Professor J. R. Sargent (then Group Economic Adviser to the Midland Bank), as rescheduling, retrenchment and recovery. The rescheduling postpones repayment dates (and sometimes includes fresh loans to allow the payment of interest); the retrenchment has to be done by the debtors along lines laid down by the IMF. The hope is that recovery in western industrial countries will allow the debtors to increase export earnings and ease repayment of loans. Those opposed to this believe that many of the loans are never going to be repaid and that reality must be faced – bankers must write down the value of their loans. A debt write-off would, of course, destroy the net worth of some individual banks. But the conclusion of this volume would be that world financial stability would not necessarily be threatened because of individual bank failures; banks in trouble would be taken over at a price by other banks, who would accept a proportion of their liabilities. The maintenance of stability while this is going on requires central banks to act as lender-of-last-resort.

1 Real and Pseudo-Financial Crises

ANNA J. SCHWARTZ

A widely held belief in the United States and the world financial community is that the default of major debtors – whether companies or municipalities or sovereign countries – could lead to bank failures that would precipitate a financial crisis. The remedy proposed by those propagating this view is that major debtors therefore must be rescued from the threat of bankruptcy to avert the projected dire consequences for banks and for the stability of the financial system. I shall argue that (a) a debtor whose affairs have been mismanaged should be liquidated or reorganised under new management; (b) default by major debtors need not result in bank failures; (c) if defaults do result in bank failures, so long as the security of the private sector's deposits is assured, no financial crisis will ensue. The bugaboo of financial crisis has been created to divert attention from the true remedies that the present financial situation demands.

A financial crisis is fuelled by fears that means of payment will be unobtainable at any price and, in a fractional-reserve banking system, leads to a scramble for high-powered money. It is precipitated by actions of the public that suddenly squeeze the reserves of the banking system. In a futile attempt to restore reserves, the banks may call loans, refuse to roll over existing loans, or resort to selling assets. Such a sequence of events is to be distinguished from what happens during a disinflation or a deflation. A deflation or a disinflation is a consequence of restricted growth of bank reserves but it is not precipitated by the public's behaviour. The essence of a financial crisis is that it is short-lived, ending with a slackening of the public's demand for additional currency. A disinflation or a deflation may be long drawn out. Nominal wealth may decline, real debts may rise, but these are not financial crises.[1]

No financial crisis has occurred in the United States since 1933, and none has occurred in the United Kingdom since 1866. All the phenomena of recent years that have been characterised as financial crisis – a decline in asset prices of equity stocks, real estate, commodities; depreciation of the exchange value of a national currency; financial distress of a large non-financial firm, a large municipality, a financial industry, or sovereign debtors – are pseudo-financial crises.[2]

A real financial crisis occurs only when institutions do not exist, when authorities are unschooled in the practices that preclude such a development, and when the private sector has reason to doubt the dependability of preventive arrangements. Institutional changes introduced since 1933 in the United States and since 1866 in the United Kingdom and the private sector's familiarity with and confidence in the responses of institutions and authorities assure that concern with financial crises is misplaced. What should be the object of concern with respect to the proposals to deal with pseudo-financial crises is the perpetuation of policies that promote inflation and waste of economic resources.

The first section reviews the last real financial crisis in England and notes developments at later dates when a financial crisis did not occur in England but did in the United States. The second section tries to account for the record in the two countries. The third section examines the link that Kindleberger (1978) attempts to establish between manias and financial crises from 1720 to 1975. Finally, the fourth section questions the emphasis currently given to financial distress as the trigger for financial crises and shows that it is based on a misinterpretation of the development of past real financial crises. It is not financial distress that triggers a crisis. The failure of authorities or institutions to respond in a predictable way to ward off a crisis and the private sector's uncertainty about the response are the triggers of a real financial crisis.

ENGLAND'S LAST REAL FINANCIAL CRISIS IN 1866 AND LATER DATES WHEN NONE OCCURRED THERE BUT DID OCCUR IN THE UNITED STATES

I begin by reviewing the circumstances that led to a financial crisis in England in 1866 and then turn to developments in 1873, 1890, 1907, 1914, and 1931 – dates when real financial crises might have but did not occur in England. I also refer to the experience of the United States at these dates leaving for the next section reference to its experience in 1884, when a financial crisis was averted and in 1893, when it was not. In that section, I try to show why the record changed after 1866 in England, and why it was variable in the United States.

1866

The onset of the financial crisis in 1866 may be traced to the collapse in January of a firm of contractors, Watson, Overend & Company, and two other companies, the Contract Corporation and the Joint Stock Discount Company, with which the first had ties. These three drew on paper issued to one another and discounted with Overend, Gurney & Company, among others. Overend, Gurney in earlier years had been a solid conservative partnership, one of the pillars of the City. About 1860, a younger generation then in charge of the business became less circumspect in its lending operations, accepting equity interests for unrepayable loans extended to ironworks and shipping companies. Losses led to a decision to incorporate with the possibility of turning over a new leaf. The new company was launched in 1865 just after the conclusion of the US Civil War, when there was every reason to anticipate a strong revival of demand for British exports, but the new company did not live long enough to benefit from it. The failures noted above in January 1866 were followed by additional ones in March and April, but again those were firms of marginal significance. However, when on 10 May Overend, Gurney shut down, the market was shaken. The next day panic broke loose.

1873

Twice during the year financial crises were said to have occurred but only the second time was the characterisation accurate. The first occasion, centred on the Continent, began on 9 May with a sharp decline in prices on the Vienna Stock Exchange. The price decline spread to Germany, Switzerland, and Italy, affecting assets like real estate, building, railways, and iron and steel ventures that had been in great favour. Contraction and liquidation followed but no disruption of payments. In England, the only reflection of events abroad was a series of increases in the Bank rate over a four-week period, followed by stepwise reductions over the succeeding ten weeks.

The real financial crisis, centred on the United States, had its beginnings on 8 September when the New York Warehouse & Security Company, organised to lend on grain and produce but involved in railway loans, failed. Five days later, Kenyon, Cox & Company, a stock brokerage firm that had endorsed the paper of another railroad, also failed. A depressed railroad bond market had led these railroads to obtain temporary financing; with the loans about to fall due, neither the lenders nor borrowers were prepared to pay up. The failures were marginal firms, but on 18 and 19 September two leading firms were suspended, Jay Cooke & Company (failure followed the suspension) and Fisk & Hatch (resumed but failed in 1884). At the same time runs began on two small banks, and on 20 September, on a larger New York bank. Panic selling on the New York Stock Exchange led to the closing of the market for ten days. Currency went to a premium as the New York and interior banks restricted payment in greenbacks. By 22 October, the currency was obtainable virtually at par.

Gold was exported to the United States on 25 September by the Bank of England, exports from other central banks as well continuing until the end of October. Bank rate rose. Since investors in England and Germany were holders of American securities, the stock market crash in New York had reverberations. A sharp sell-off on the London Stock Exchange on 6 November led to a rise in Bank rate to 9 per cent the next day, but the payment system was not impaired.

1890

Two monetary disturbances occurred, one in New York, the other in London. Prices on the New York Stock Exchange in November had been falling, partly due to selling by English investors, in order 'to carry the load of investments of a less desirable description' (Sprague, 1910, p. 132) in South America. On 11 November, the failure of Decker, Howell & Company was announced, involving the Bank of North America. The next day a stock brokerage firm failed and another bank closed. On 15 November, the failure of Baring Brothers in London was cabled to New York and stock prices fell. The following week several firms failed but panic did not develop.

In England, the imminence of failure by Baring Brothers, owing to imprudent investments in the Argentine, became known to the Bank of England on 8 November. In addition to underwriting South American securities, Barings had a large short-term banking business and considerable liabilities on deposit account. The actions undertaken by the

Bank of England and a syndicate of bankers, to be discussed in the following section, prevented a crisis.

1907

London was exposed to a series of disturbances from abroad in October, beginning with a stock market decline in New York. The London and Amsterdam stock markets registered sympathetic declines in the prices of American railway securities, but the main disturbance began during the week of 14 October when five banks that were members of the New York Clearing House and three outside banks required assistance from a group of Clearing House banks. These eight banks were controlled through stock ownership on margin by a few men of no great financial standing, who used the banks to further speculation in the stocks of copper-mining companies. A decline in the price of those stocks alarmed depositors who started runs. Order seemed to have been restored by Monday 21 October, when the Knickerbocker Trust Company, the third largest trust company in New York, began to experience unfavourable clearing balances because the president had connections with one of the men in control of the banks that were in difficulty. The former's resignation did not allay distrust. On 22 October a run on Knickerbocker forced it to suspend business. The next day, a run began on the second largest trust company, and the day following on still another trust company. Assistance was given to these two companies, but by that time alarm had spread to the rest of the country. Restriction of payments by the banks followed and currency went to a premium over deposits.

Despite the repercussions from abroad, no financial crisis developed in London. Three increases in Bank rate from 31 October to 7 November sufficed to replenish gold exported to New York during the crisis there. No bank failures occurred, although voluntary company liquidations were abnormally high in 1908, presumably because of the level interest rates reached in 1908 (Clapham, 1945, II, p. 393).

1914

The problems that arose with heightened war fears in Europe were not dissimilar to those that characterised earlier peacetime episodes of threats to the dependability of the credit and payments system. What was different was the range of financial markets – long-term capital, short-term credit, foreign exchange, and gold markets – affected in both England and the United States.

In the summer of 1914, New York, as usual, was in debt to London on short-term account, dependent for its supply of sterling exchange on the proceeds of commercial bills accepted in London and bought on a daily basis by the London discount market. The disruption of remittances from European clients of English accepting houses to cover maturing bills led, on 27 July, to a cessation in London of discounting of foreign bills. At the same time, heavy liquidation of foreign-held securities was in process on the London and New York stock markets, the proceeds of sales in New York, on London's instructions, to be remitted abroad. New York banks without sterling exchange could remit only in gold, draining reserves. Moreover, the New York banks could not count on the proceeds of the sales to provide bank accommodation for domestic purchasers of the securities. For the London clearing banks, their main liquid assets – bills, loans to the bill market, and loans to the Stock Exchange – ceased to be liquid. Both London and New York closed the stock markets on 31 July. A countrywide panic both in England and the United States threatened.[3]

1931

Britain's abandonment of the gold standard on 20 September has been described as a crisis, as have all the subsequent devaluations of the pound and more recently of the dollar. The overvaluation of sterling reflected in weakness in the current account in fact was corrected by the decision to stop selling gold at a fixed price. As Moggridge has noted (1982, pp. 181–2), the many repercussions of Britain's suspension of convertibility included the decision of others to follow in her wake; elsewhere the imposition of exchange controls, tariffs, and trade controls; a traditional tightening of monetary policy in the United States in response to an external drain of gold followed by a massive wave of bank failures; and further deflation not only in the United States but in all countries that remained on gold. The so-called crisis does not refer to the situation in other countries. Indeed, there was no crisis internally, except for Bank of England, Treasury, and other officials involved in negotiating credits for the Bank before the event and scheduling meetings on what to do next as reserves dwindled. As the text of the press notice announcing the decision stated, 'There will be no interruption of ordinary banking business. The banks will be open as usual for the convenience of their customers; and there is no reason why sterling transactions should be affected in any way' (Sayers, 1976, 264). Schumpeter commented, '[I]n England there was neither panic nor – precisely owing to the way in which the thing had been done or, if the reader prefer, had come about – loss of "confidence", but rather a sigh of relief' (Schumpeter, 1939, 956).

WHEN DID A REAL FINANCIAL CRISIS OCCUR?

I begin the answer to the question by citing Bagehot's analysis with respect to 1866, the last real financial crisis in England (Bagehot, 1873, repr. 1902, pp. 64–5):

> And though the Bank of England certainly do make great advances in time of panic, yet as they do not do so on any distinct principle, they naturally do it hesitatingly, reluctantly, and with misgiving. In 1847, even in 1866 – the latest panic, and the one in which on the whole the Bank acted the best – there was nevertheless an instant when it was believed the Bank would not advance on Consols, or at least hesitated to advance on them. The moment this was reported in the City and telegraphed to the country, it made the panic indefinitely worse. In fact, to make large advances in this faltering way is to incur the evil of making them without obtaining the advantage. What is wanted and what is necessary to stop a panic is to diffuse the impression, that though money may be dear, still money is to be had. If people could be really convinced that they could have money if they wait a day or two, and that utter ruin is not coming, most likely they would cease to run in such a mad way for money. Either shut the Bank at once, and say it will not lend more than it commonly lends, or lend freely, boldly, and so that the public may feel you mean to go on lending. To lend a great deal, and yet not give the public confidence that you will lend sufficiently and effectually, is the worst of all policies; but it is the policy now pursued.

Bagehot thus stressed the importance of predictable action by the monetary authority to prevent a panic; failing that, a bank holiday was the course to follow. In 1866, the Bank's actions were hesitant so the public was not convinced that there was no reason to panic. H. H. Gibbs, Governor of the Bank, 1875–7, referred to the 1866 crisis as 'its only real blunder in his experience', because, instead of lending freely at an appropriately high rate, as Bagehot advised, 'it erred in lending at too low a rate before the crisis turned into panic' (Presnell, 1968,

p. 188). Although in 1873, when Bagehot wrote he still regarded the Bank's behaviour in 1866 as undependable, Gibbs did not blame the then Governor since 'the matter was not as well understood as it is now', noting that the Bank had done the right thing in 1873, when the underlying situation was just as troublesome as in 1866.[4]

The United States, by contrast, experienced a real financial crisis in 1873 because no institutional framework was immediately available to deal with the surge of demand for high-powered money by the public and banks. Belatedly, the crisis was alleviated by the issue against collateral of clearing-house loan certificates for use in the settlement of clearing balances and by US Treasury redemption with greenbacks of outstanding government debt.[5]

During the next two decades both England and the United States were spared the experience of financial crisis in circumstances that might have been breeding grounds for it. The impact of the failure of the City of Glasgow Bank in 1878 was sufficiently great to suggest to some observers that suspension of the Act of 1844 was required (Presnell, 1968, p. 189), but it was not.[6]

In May 1884, the failure of a Wall Street brokerage firm involving a bank whose president was a partner in the brokerage firm was followed by the suspension of several other banks. However, a phenomenal rise in money market rates brought in an inflow of foreign capital and the supply of funds was further expanded by prompt issue of clearing-house loan certificates. The suspended banks were thereby enabled to resume. Sprague commented (1910, pp. 113–15):

> It will be seen that the steps taken to allay alarm were immediate and effective. . . . The success which crowned the efforts of the banks in dealing with the crisis affords convincing evidence that if clearing-house loan certificates are to be issued at all, they should be issued at the beginning of a disturbance. Local runs on the banks did not become severe, because announcement was made that assistance would be granted at the moment when the disasters which might have weakened general confidence became known to the public.[7]

The final episode of the two decades under consideration, when financial crisis did not occur either in England or the United States, was occasioned by the troubles of Baring Brothers in 1890. In the United States, Sprague noted (1910, p. 142) that it was 'the prompt action taken by the clearing-house authorities', by issuing loan certificates to meet the needs of particular banks experiencing runs, that prevented 'the spread of panic'. Sprague summarised (p. 144) 'one of two specifics for the proper treatment of a panic – the continuance of loans to solvent borrowers. A second equally important specific is the prompt payment by the banks of every demand by depositors for cash'. In England, the principal device the Bank of England adopted to prevent a crisis – it also borrowed gold from France and bought it from Russia – was to advance sums to meet Barings' immediate maturing liabilities, with the guarantee of a syndicate of bankers to make good any loss sustained by the Bank in liquidiating Barings over a period of years.[8] No loss was sustained by the Bank and no call on the guarantors was needed. Presnell concludes: 'The news of the guarantee allowed knowledge of Barings' troubles to spread beyond the inner circles without causing panic; indeed, anxiety lifted' (1968, p. 207).[9]

For two decades after 1873 clearing houses and the US Treasury took actions that neutralised monetary disturbances so that crisis conditions did not develop. Why did similar actions in 1893 and 1907 not have comparable effects? No simple explanation is at hand to account for the occurrence of financial crisis in the United States in 1893. It is easier to account for the crisis in 1907.

Two features of the situation in 1893 that differed from earlier experience may be noted: fears that silver advocates would succeed in forcing the country off gold first had to be put to rest, and only subsequently did the condition of the banks as a result of mercantile failures excite independent concern. At that point the clearing houses issued loan certificates. Sprague reports (1910, p. 173), 'Serious strain had been met boldly and successfully', but that was not to be the end of the episode. A second wave of distrust of banks spread over the west and south with consequent withdrawals of cash reserves from New York banks. Thereupon the Erie Railroad went into receivership and the stock market suffered the worst decline of the year. Bank suspensions followed in the east as well as in the south and west. Starting with banks in New York, banks throughout the country partly restricted cash payments, sending currency to a premium. The restriction, which lasted from 3 August to 2 September, came six weeks after the issue of clearing-house loan certificates and when gold was arriving from Europe.

Why did the issue of loan certificates not cut short the episode? One suggestion is that some banks did not avail themselves of the opportunity to obtain the certificates and therefore were unable to offset the shrinkage of their reserves (Noyes, 1894, p. 22). In addition, individual banks with the bulk of bankers' deposits had reserve deficiencies even though aggregate reserves of the banks were adequate. The suggestion that best conforms to the view I am presenting is that as early as July (Noyes, 1894, p. 25) rumours of refusal of banks to convert deposits into cash incited the financial crisis. A misinformed public can nullify the beneficial effects of actions designed to avert panic.

In 1907, the explanation for the occurrence of crisis appears straightforward. Assistance to troubled trust companies was granted slowly and without dramatic effect. The runs on the trust companies depleted the currency holdings of the New York Clearing House banks which were also shipping currency to interior banks and paying it out over their counters to their own frightened depositors. Although the Treasury helped by depositing currency with these banks, New York was threatened with panic, loans were obtainable only with great difficulty, and stock market prices collapsed. Sprague argued that at this point the clearing-house banks should have issued loan certificates to enable banks to extend loans more freely to borrowers and also to prevent the weakening of particular banks with unfavourable clearing-house balances. In his view, the banks did not do so due to their mistaken belief that an issue of clearing-house loan certificates would cause restriction (Sprague, pp. 257–8, 272–3). While local runs in New York subsided, alarm spread throughout the country. Loss of confidence was displayed less by the public than by country banks. They demanded currency for the funds on deposit or on call in New York. Belatedly, the New York Clearing House issued loan certificates and immediately restricted the convertibility of deposits into currency. Countrywide restriction followed. In 1907, the right actions were taken too late to be effective.[10]

The wartime features of the 1914 episode make it not wholly comparable to earlier cases of threatened crises that were averted. Yet to cope with the problems that rose in the summer of 1914, some of the methods relied on in peacetime episodes were applied. Foremost was the provision of emergency currency issues, in the United States, both clearing-house loan certificates and Aldrich – Vreeland currency (issued by groups of banks under the Act of 1908 establishing the National Monetary Commission), and in England, Treasury Currency Notes, which soon displaced gold coin. Initially, in the United States, concern was directed to limiting shipments of gold, but that became otiose: with the reopening of the sterling acceptance market in London, the belligerents' growing demand for exports, and the balance of trade turning strongly in favour of the United States. In England, initially Bank rate was lifted to 10 per cent, the level at which it had stood on the suspension of the Act of 1844 on three previous dates. This time no suspension was needed, and Bank rate was lowered to 5 per cent within the week to remain unchanged for the duration.

The additional measures taken to restore the channels of international and domestic financial activity were basically government subsidies (to the export trade in the United States in the form of war risk insurance) or government guarantees against loss (to the banking system in England). The guarantees in England led to the termination of an extended August Bank Holiday and of moratoria on the payment of bills making possible the renewal of availability of acceptance credits in London. A protracted closing of the stock markets in both New York and London was ultimately ended.

Britain's decision to suspend convertibility into gold in September 1931, as I noted earlier, does not qualify as a financial crisis. Real financial crises *par excellence* were experienced by the United States from 1930 to 1933. The lender-of-last-resort was responsible for a series of crises that intensified over time because it did not recognise the need to provide liquidity to the fractional reserve banking system that was confronted with surges of repeated runs. A multiple contraction of deposits was enforced by the inability of the banks to acquire adequate amounts of high-powered money. By March 1933 the entire financial system was prostrate.

The reasons may now be summarised, accounting for financial crises that did or did not occur in the past. In both cases the setting is one in which the financial distress of certain firms became known to market participants, raising alarm as creditors became concerned about the value of their claims not only on those firms but also firms previously in sound condition. Banks that were creditors of the firms in distress became targets of suspicion by their depositors. When monetary authorities failed to demonstrate readiness at the beginning of such a disturbance to meet all demands of sound debtors for loans and of depositors for cash, a financial crisis occurred. A financial crisis *per contra* could be averted by timely predictable signals to market participants of institutional readiness to make available an augmented supply of funds. The sources of the funds supplied might have been inflows from abroad – attracted by higher domestic than foreign interest rates – or emergency issues of domestic currency. The readiness was all. Knowledge of the availability of the supply was sufficient to allay alarm, so that the funds were never drawn on. In a few instances, orderly liquidation of the firms in distress, with a guarantee against loss by the liquidator, isolated the problem so that it did not spread to other firms and averted a financial crisis in this way.

A breakdown of the payments system has not occurred in the last century and more in England – ignoring the 1914 episode – and in the last half-century in the United States. The lesson has been learned that the financial distress of the few must not be permitted to become a financial crisis for all. Individual debtors fail but their difficulties do not become widespread and undermine creditors in general. Bad banks fail, or more likely are reorganised under new management or merged with a good bank, but if a run on a bank occurs – it is said to have occurred on the Banco Ambrosiano in the recent scandal in Italy – it is not permitted to cumulate into a banking panic. In the United States, federal deposit insurance attempts to remove the problem of a loss of confidence in the ability of banks to convert deposits into currency and thus to eliminate the reason for bank runs, but, as the experience of other countries proves, such insurance is not essential. Not only are authorities better educated. So also is the public. As its experience has grown with the institutional arrangements that prevent disruption of the payments system, its behaviour contributes to the dependability of the system.

MANIAS, PANICS, CRASHES

The preceding sections have focused on the relation between financial distress of firms with perceived significant market presence and the historical incidence of financial crises. In this section the focus shifts to the validity of the identification of manias with financial crises (Kindleberger, 1978).

For Kindleberger, manias, panics, and crashes are three phases of the same process. During manias, investors shift from money to real or financial assets. During panics, they try to shift from real or financial assets to money. Crashes are the denouement of the process, with the collapse of prices of whatever was eagerly acquired during the mania – 'commodities, houses, buildings, land, stocks, bonds' (1978, p. 5). He takes for granted that manias occur during cyclical expansions and the panic phases at peaks, while disclaiming that every business expansion leads 'inevitably to mania and panic. But the pattern occurs sufficiently frequently and with sufficient uniformity' (p. 5). Finally, he regards the manias, panics, and crashes that he discusses as financial crises per se.

In current economic analysis, the word 'bubble' has supplanted the pejorative 'mania'. In the definition proposed by Flood and Garber (1982, p. 275), 'The possibility of ... a price bubble exists when the expected rate of market price change is an important factor determining current market price.' No reference is made to cyclical conditions in the definition. In my view, bubbles may arise independently of the economy's cyclical stage, although business expansion may foster them. No one has systematically examined all the cases, so the ones associated with particular cycle movements have had the lion's share of attention. Kindleberger's assertion that, according to a monetarist view, 'mania and panic would both be avoided if only the supply of money were stabilized at some fixed quantity, or at a regular growing level' (pp. 5–6) does not accord with my monetarist view. Bubbles, like bankruptcies, would occur even if the money stock were free of destabilising cyclical swings. The Florida land boom of 1925–6 and the gold price bubble of 1979–80 were created by opportunities those markets appeared to offer rather than the pattern of monetary growth.

A basic fact concerning bubbles is that they leave eager investors in sure-fire, get-rich schemes at the take-off considerably poorer at the landing. The loss of wealth attendant on misguided, unprofitable, voluntary investment decisions is, of course, not confined to bubbles. Bankruptcy proceedings are a daily occurrence in economic life. Willingness to spend may be reduced and previously glowing expectations may be replaced by uncertainty. But loss of wealth is not synonymous with a financial crisis.

At the stock market peak in 1929, the total value of all shares listed on the New York Stock Exchange was about $200 billion. The decline in October is estimated at nearly $15 1/2 billion, so many investors undoubtedly were poorer. Yet no financial crisis occurred following the great crash. The reason is that prompt and effective action by the New York Federal Reserve Bank provided additional reserves to the New York banks through open market purchases. Kindleberger acknowledges that the crash did not 'lead to a money market panic . . . or to runs on banks, probably because of the effective action of the New York Federal Reserve in pumping funds into the market' (p. 113), but still classifies the crash as a financial crisis apparently because it 'spread liquidation to other asset markets, such as commodities, and seized up credit to strike a hard blow at output' (p. 113). Any deflation would thus qualify as a financial crisis.

In a perceptive comment on bubbles, Wood (1983) has noted that they concern markets 'where quantities traded have varied little, while there have been enormous variations in price. They are interesting, but the fate of nations seldom depends on them'.

Kindleberger provides a tabulation in an appendix to his book that lists some three dozen financial crisis during two and a half centuries, characterising each one by the subject of the mania, how it was financed, dates of the peak and crash, and a final entry identifying the lender-of-last-resort. It is the final entry that motivates Kindleberger's study. He argues the importance of a lender-of-last-resort 'who comes to the rescue and provides the public good of stability that the private market is unable to produce for itself' (p. 4).[11] Yet he does not discriminate between episodes in which successful action was taken to prevent the development of a crisis and episodes in which no action was taken or the action was unsuccessful.[12]

Despite his designation of all episodes as financial crises without differentiation of those where the 'rescue' provided stability, even Kindleberger notes that there has been a dwindling of the number and a lessening of the severity of domestic financial crises since 1866 in Britain and since 1929 in the United States and on the Continent. He considers three possible explanations: (i) the decline of usury laws, making it possible for interest rates to be raised sufficiently to limit manias; (ii) the shunning of manias by markets that had learned from experience; (iii) the calming of anxieties owing to the known existence of a lender-of-last-resort. He dismisses the first two out of hand, but his position on the third is ambiguous. Nor is it clear why at this point he cites Minsky's reference (1977) to 'near panics' in 1966, 1969–70, and 1974–5, and 'incipient crises' in 1974 (p. 218).

The record on domestic financial crises may thus be reassuring to Kindleberger, but his current concern is the greater frequency now than in the nineteenth century of foreign exchange crises. The solution he suggests is an international lender-of-last-resort.[13] The recent analytical literature on bubbles also encompasses runs on a currency that is fixed in price in terms of at least one other currency and runs under flexible exchange rates (Flood and Garber, 1982). The underlying assumption that a run on a currency is a crisis seems to me untenable. The market will sell off an overvalued currency under fixed or floating exchange rates and will shift to an undervalued currency. If authorities resist the market's evaluation, it may be costly for them, but the problem facing the currency is more fundamental: the economic policies that are responsible for the currency's plight are the heart of the matter. If there is a crisis, it resides in the failure to adjust those policies.

I conclude that manias, panics, and crashes reduce wealth. They are not *per se* financial crises unless the shift from tangible or financial assets to money leads to a run on banks. A lender-of-last-resort can forestall such a development, so I agree with Kindleberger that there is an important role for such an entity, although I do not subscribe to the notion that only a public authority has in the past filled or can at present fill that role.

FINANCIAL DISTRESS VERSUS FINANCIAL CRISES

In my lexicon, the events since the mid-1960s that have been termed 'financial crises' or 'threats of a financial crisis' have been pseudo-financial crises. Essentially the response to each of these events (to be noted in what follows) has been a form of bail-out, for which the justification was that the action averted a crisis. Since no financial crisis would in fact have been experienced had a bail-out not been undertaken, the events were pseudo-financial crises. Moreover, the policies adopted were economically inefficient or inflationary in effect.

The first event to be considered here was the failure of the Penn Central Railroad in June 1970. The Federal Reserve was concerned lest the company's default on its $200 million commercial paper borrowings would jeopardise that market. The Fed assumed that lenders would not discriminate between a troubled issuer and other perfectly sound issuers. The scenario envisaged by the Fed was that the latter would need to pay off their commercial paper because of generalised distrust of the instrument. Accordingly, the banks were informed that the discount window was 'wide open' (Maisel, 1973, p. 9) if they needed funds to make loans to customers unable to roll over commercial paper. In addition, to enable banks to bid freely for funds in the open market, the Fed suspended interest rate ceilings on 30 to 89-day large denomination certificates of deposit – an action that was desirable in its own right. Maisel concludes that the Fed's actions averted a panic (p. 4). However, if there were commercial paper issuers that faced difficulties, as Carron notes (1982, p. 398), it was not owing to the condition of the market as such but to 'conditions peculiar to those firms' (Chrysler Financial and Commercial Credit among others). The verdict of the 1971 *Economic Report of the President* (p. 69) was that no 'genuine liquidity crisis existed in mid-1970'.

Events in 1973–4 centred on bank failures in the United Kingdom, West Germany, the United States, and Switzerland that were thought to threaten the international financial order. Hirsch (1977, p. 248), who believes that co-operation to achieve 'collective intermediate goods' of bank stability is technically easier to organise 'in a small group of like minded individuals and institutions than in an open group' (p. 249) – a view reminiscent of de Cecco's – describes what happened in Britain when 'fringe banks', bank new-comers, experienced difficulties in December 1973. A deterioration of the market value of real estate investments of these banks led to deposit withdrawals and the switching of new deposits to established banks. To save depositors of the fringe banks from losses, the four-member oligopoly of deposit banks had to commit resources to that end. Hirsch interprets the action taken by the established banks as in their self-interest by removing a source of competition. Whatever the motivation of the established banks, their collective action bespeaks an understanding that the failure of individual banks must not be allowed to contract the aggregate money stock.

Two views have been presented with respect to the actions taken by the Federal Reserve when Franklin National Bank announced, in May 1974, that it had lost heavily in forward transactions in the foreign exchange market. The Federal Reserve initially announced that it would advance whatever funds Franklin needed, so long as it remained solvent, the loans ultimately reaching a maximum of $1.75 billion in early October. At that point the bank was merged with another institution and the FDIC assumed the Federal Reserve's loan.

One view (Carron, 1982, p.400) is that the preconditions of a genuine financial crisis existed, as evidenced by the fact that corporations paid premiums on their borrowings that reflected risks perceived in the banking system rather than in their own positions. The preconditions were, however, mitigated both because markets remained orderly with no lack of confidence on the part of investors and the central bank intervened effectively. An opposite view is that the immediate impact of Franklin's failure was erased by a Federal Reserve bail-out that led market participants to believe that no bank failures would be tolerated and that encouraged 'banks to become more reckless than ever' (Wojnilower, 1980, pp. 298–9). It was not only the losses in the foreign exchange market that the Franklin case revealed. The aftermath of its failure also disclosed the near-bankruptcy of real estate affiliates many banks owned. The affiliates had financed construction with short-term funds and invested in real estate and mortgages whose value declined when interest rates rose. Selling off real estate at distress prices further compromised the position of the affiliates, so that they experienced problems in selling their paper.

The perception of increased risk in lending to banks raised the cost of funds for them. Does this justify a bail-out or concern that a financial crisis was imminent?

Banking difficulties in Europe in 1974 that arose because of losses sustained in the foreign exchange market were apparently met without bail-outs. The Bundesbank announced the liquidation of Bankhaus I.D. Herstatt. Neither Westdeutsche Landesbank Girozentral of West Germany nor Union Bank of Switzerland was mortally wounded by its losses.

It was not banking difficulties but financial distress of two large real sector firms – Lockheed Corporation (1971) and Chrysler Corporation (1979) – and a municipality – New York City (1975) – that also provided occasions for a prognosis of a threat of financial crisis. In each case federal government legislation was enacted to guarantee private loans to these entities. The object was to avoid bankruptcy. Though Penn Central Railroad had filed for bankruptcy and subsequently restructured its operations to become an efficient firm, the view that has since come to prevail is that bankruptcy proceedings by themselves will create a financial crisis. The loan guarantees thus serve to mask the inefficient use of resources that had produced financial distress. It is true that some restructuring of claims on and operations of the entities was required as a condition of the guarantees, but it is not clear why reorganisation under bankruptcy proceedings would have precipitated a financial crisis. Again, the underlying assumptions seems to be that markets cannot discriminate between a firm or municipality in financial distress and others in sound condition. The inefficient are sustained in their misuse of resources because of the imagined hardship that would be imposed on the efficient.

Another class of events that is said to raise the prospect of domestic financial crisis is still impending – the impairment of the ability of many sovereign countries to make scheduled payments on their outstanding bank loans. Short-term loans extended to governments and to private borrowers abroad in some cases appear to be beyond their prospective capacity to repay. Acknowledgement of default on outstanding loans would require write-downs that would reduce capital of the banks involved and that would undoubtedly raise the cost to them of funds obtained in the open market. This course has been rejected on the ground that confidence in the stability of the banking system would be shaken. The alternative chosen has been the subterfuge that all the loans will be repaid, with the banks exhorted to provide an increase in lending sufficient to enable delinquent borrowers to maintain interest payments and to reschedule principal. In addition, the goal of stable non-inflationary monetary growth has been sacrificed as part of the effort to resolve the international debt problem. It is taken for granted that, if the policy of papering over the true economic prospects of the borrowing countries ultimately fails, standing in the wings will be the authorities ready to bail out the lenders. The costs of renewed inflation will then be dismissed as an unfortunate side effect.

Real financial crises need not occur because there is a well-understood solution to the problem: assure that deposits can be converted at will into currency whatever the difficulties banks encounter. The solution does not preclude failure of mismanaged banks. Recent discussion of moral hazard in relation to real financial crises would be more apt in relation to pseudo-financial crises. They provide the rationale for bail-outs and shoring up inefficiency. Pseudo-financial crises in recent years have generated expectations 'that no monetary authority will allow any key financial actor to fail' (Wojnilower, 1980, p. 299). Political authority seems well embarked in the direction of not allowing any key non-financial actor to fail, and of encouraging inflationary actions by domestic monetary authorities and international agencies in the cause of pseudo-financial crises.

NOTES

1. The example of the deflation in 1920–1 in the United States may be cited. Bank reserves declined from $2.8 billion in April 1920 to $2.4 billion in August 1921. Wholesale prices (on the base 1926) fell from a peak of 167 in May 1920 to a trough of 91 January 1922. An index of liabilities of business failures rose from a trough of 6.0 in January 1920 to a peak of 71.2 in February 1922. Although 506 banks suspended business in 1921, there was no financial crisis. The deposit-currency and the deposit-reserve ratios in August 1921 were higher than in April 1920.
2. Financial distress defines the condition of an individual, a non-financial firm or an individual bank, or an industry that has assets with realisable value in money that is less than the amount of its indebtedness.
3. De Cecco (1975) argues that no problem would have arisen, had not the joint stock banks arbitrarily begun a credit squeeze in the middle of July, recalling loans they had made to bill brokers, and refusing to finance foreign clients of the accepting houses who usually borrowed in London to meet their maturing bills that the London houses had accepted. Stock Exchange dealers who worked on loans from foreign banks dumped their stocks to be able to return borrowed money, compelling the joint stock banks to call for extra margin from customers with Lombard loans, since the value of the collateral had declined. De Cecco says that the banks assumed a crisis of confidence on the part of the public would occur but in fact it did not happen. Therefore the banks engineered a crisis of confidence by refusing to pay out gold to the public and themselves drawing on the Bank's gold. The motive for the banks' behaviour, according to de Cecco, was to 'substitute themselves in lucrative

international business' and 'exclude traditional intermediaries from their functions', though they wanted only 'to threaten them with the possibility of . . . death, in order to have them rescued *in extremis* and to paralyse their future action' (p. 149).

According to Sayers (I, p. 70), it was sales of internationally traded securities on European stock exchanges that initiated the credit squeeze in London. He also notes that the joint stock banks' refusal to pay out gold before the August Bank Holiday may be interpreted in a more favourable light than de Cecco presents (I, p. 72).

4. De Cecco (1975, pp. 80–2) dismisses Bagehot's analysis. According to de Cecco, the Bank deliberately sought the fall of Overend, Gurney because 'they were encroaching upon the very branch of business on which the Bank throve: the discounting of bills from all over the country. . . . So conflict between the two giants seemed inevitable, particularly as their business had become very similar in nature' (p. 80). 'The Bank watched its rival fall without making any attempt to come to its rescue; on the contrary, it implemented a six-month "dear money" policy specifically to make Gurney's fall inevitable. Only after its rival had gone under did the Bank go to the market's rescue by extending unlimited assistance to anybody needing it, to allay the panic induced by Gurney's failure (p. 82).

   If de Cecco is right, the Bank was culpable because it deliberately ignored 'what was well understood', but the evidence does not support de Cecco's opinion that by 1866 the Bank understood what needed to be done in a timely way to prevent a crisis.
5. In Austria, in 1873, the main response to the stock market decline which was followed by a large number of insolvencies and bankruptcies was the suspension of the Banking Act of 1862 to 'assist the mobilization of central bank funds in case a liquidity shortage should make itself felt' (März, 1982, p. 188). No shortage occurred. Six months later, a consortium of banking houses and the central bank rescued from collapse the Boden-credit–Anstalt, an issuer of mortgage bonds with credit standing abroad equal to that of Austrian treasury certificates. The firm had been involved in 'risky stock-exchange operations' (p. 189).
6. *The Economist*, 5 October 1878 (Gregory, 1929, II, pp. 289–90), commented on the bank's failure: 'There was no run, or any semblance of run; there was no local discredit. . . . The fact that the other Scottish banks are willing to take up the notes of the City of Glasgow Banks appears to support the belief that all the liabilities of the bank will be met in full. The danger of discrediting the circulation may, however, have had some influence on the other banks in determining their action in this matter.'
7. Pressnell (1982, p. 152) reports the actions taken in Ceylon, when the Oriental Banking Corporation, a major international bank with many branches in Southeast Asia and in Australia, collapsed in May 1884. The colony's governor guaranteed the bank's substantial note issues and the other banks imported silver rupees from India. A financial crisis was averted.
8. A similar device had apparently been used by the Bank of France in 1889. Pressnell (1968, p. 205) cites a French historian as crediting France with helping England in 'two ways in 1890: with gold and by her example'. The

example refers to the use of a collective guarantee by French banks in support of the Bank of France. A certain Comptoir d'Escompte, in 1889, experienced a run as the result of unwise loans it had made to a company that speculated in copper. The Bank provided the Comptoir with funds to reimburse its depositors and creditors and then liquidated it.

9. According to de Cecco (1975, p. 92), because of the Bank of England's rivalry with the joint stock banks, only merchant bankers were first asked to underwrite the guarantee, and the joint stock banks only later. He concludes that the Baring crisis 'proved to be the swan song of the power of the Bank of England and of the merchant banks. Barings were prevented from going down and taking other houses with them; but this was made possible only by a series of expedients – all traditional instruments of policy had been abandoned' (p. 95).

   Pressnell deplores the device of the guarantee as 'not central banking', as well as loss of the opportunity the Barings' situation created to advance reform of the Act of 1844, and more particularly the need for larger banking and larger gold reserves.

10. Bonelli's article (1982, pp. 51–65) on the '1907 financial crisis in Italy' should be retitled 'the 1907 financial crisis that did not occur in Italy'. He defines the crisis as a prolonged decline in prices of shares that brought one of the largest mixed banks close to suspension. It did not happen because the Banca d'Italia, the largest of the three issuing banks, initiated and co-ordinated 'anticrisis measures' (p. 51). 'It began to provide liquidity in all directions by means of discounts and advances . . . it also announced that its reserves were increasing, that it could issue money without any difficulty, and that it could even count on the government's readiness to take any extraordinary measures that might become necessary (to wit, removal of the ceiling established by law as regards the volume of circulation not enjoying full metallic coverage)' (p. 58).

11. Kindleberger cites no evidence in support of the proposition that the private market is unable to serve as the lender-of-the-last-resort. The clearing houses at times undertook that function under the National Banking System in the United States.

12. An oddity is that the tabulation includes an entry for 1819 in England. The listing for that episode is 'none' under 'crisis', and 'none needed' under 'lender-of-last-resort'.

13. I share the view expressed by Griffiths (1983) that the proposal should be rejected. The grounds for rejection that he cites relate to the role of banks and international debt. They also apply to foreign exchange markets.

REFERENCES

Bagehot, W. (1873) *Lombard Street*. Repr. 1902 (New York: Scribner's).

Bonelli, F. (1982) 'The 1907 financial crisis in Italy: a peculiar case of the lender of last resort in action', in Kindleberger, C. P. (ed.) *Financial Crises: Theory, History, Policy* (Cambridge: Cambridge University Press).

Carron, A. S. (1982) 'Financial crises: recent experience in US and international markets', *Brookings Papers on Economic Activity* (2): 395–422.

Clapham, Sir. (1945) *The Bank of England: A History*. Vol. II, 1797–1914 (New York: Macmillan).

de Cecco, M. (1975) *Money and Empire: The International Gold Standard, 1890–1914* (Totowa, NJ: Rowman and Littlefield).

Economic Report of the President. (1971) (Washington, DC: US Government Printing Office).

Flood, R. P. and Garber, P. M. (1982) 'Bubbles, runs, and gold monetization', in Wachtel, P. (ed.) *Crises in the Economic and Financial Structure* (Lexington, Mass.: Heath).

Gregory, T. E. (ed.) (1929) *Select Statutes, Documents and Reports Relating to British Banking, 1832–1928*. Vol. II, 1847–1928 (London: Humphrey Milford).

Griffiths, B. (1983) 'Banking in crisis', *Policy Review* 25 (Summer): 28–35.

Hirsch, F. (1977) 'The Bagehot problem', *The Manchester School of Economic and Social Studies* 46 (September): 241–55.

Kindleberger, C. P. (1978) *Manias, Panics, and Crashes: A History of Financial Crises* (New York: Basic Books).

Maisel, S. J. (1973) *Managing the Dollar* (New York: Norton).

März, E. (1982) 'Comment', in Kindleberger, C. P. (ed.) *Financial Crises Theory, History, Policy* (Cambridge: Cambridge University Press).

Minsky, H. P. (1977) 'A theory of systematic fragility', in Altman, E. I. and Sametz, A. W. (eds) *Financial Crises: Institutions and Markets in a Fragile Financial Environment* (New York: Wiley).

Moggridge, D. E. (1982) 'Policy in the crises of 1920 and 1929', in Kindleberger, C. P. (ed.) *Financial Crises: Theory, History, Policy* (Cambridge: Cambridge University Press).

Noyes, A. D. (1894) 'The banks and the panic of 1893', *Political Science Quarterly* 9 (March): 12–30.

Pressnell, L. S. (1968) 'Gold reserves, banking reserves, and the Baring crisis of 1890', in Whittlesey, C. R. and Wilson, J. S. G. (eds) *Essays in Money and Banking in Honour of R. S. Sayers* (Oxford: Clarendon Press).

Pressnell, L. S. (1982) 'The sterling system and financial crises before 1914', in Kindleberger, C. P. (ed.) *Financial Crises: Theory, History, Policy* (Cambridge: Cambridge University Press).

Sayers, R. S. (1976) *The Bank of England, 1891–1944*, 3 vols. (Cambridge: Cambridge University Press).

Schumpeter, J. A. (1939) *Business Cycles*. 2 vols. (New York: McGraw-Hill).

Sprague, O. M. W. (1910) *History of Crises under the National Banking System*. National Monetary Commission (Washington, DC: US Government Printing Office).

Wojnilower, A. M. (1980) 'The central role of credit crunches in recent financial history', *Brookings Papers on Economic Activity* (2): 277–326.

Wood, G. E. (1983) Review of *Crises in the Economic and Financial Structure*, Wachtel, P. (ed.) *The Banker* (June): 266–7.

Comment on Real and Pseudo-financial Crises

ALLAN H. MELTZER

Anna Schwartz's chapter makes a useful distinction between actual and pseudo-financial crises. The distinction is a reaction against the tendency to dilute the language by using extreme terms to refer to ordinary problems. The tendency arises on one side from the understandable desire of the people with the problem to convince the public that the prevention of chaos or disaster depends on special assistance being rendered by government to them and, on the other, by the eagerness with which governments respond to such pleading when it is made by a large, vociferous group. In cases of financial distress, it is in the interest of creditors to palm off the debts of insolvent or illiquid borrowers on the taxpayers by arousing fears of a financial collapse and a return to the depressed conditions of the thirties.

Schwartz attacks this argument with her characteristic vigour, thoroughness and careful scholarship. I will restate her argument in two main propositions, expand the discussion of one, and briefly relate the two propositions to current financial distress. I agree with her conclusions and have no fault to find with her brief but succinct episodic history of past British and American financial distress. I have a few comments on her discussion of the lender-of-last-resort, so most of my attention is on that.

TWO PROPOSITIONS

Two propositions about crises summarise Schwartz's main conclusions. First, insolvency or illiquidity of a bank is neither a necessary nor a sufficient condition for a financial panic. Secondly, failure of the central bank to protect the money stock from a sudden, relatively large decline, unanticipated as to timing or magnitude, is a sufficient condition for a crisis. The precipitating cause of the monetary contraction may be a financial failure, but the widespread expectation of a series of failures serves just as well.

The first proposition reminds us that financial panics involve the system, not an individual institution. The task of the lender-of-last-resort is to protect the system from mistakes or misfortunes that affect some of its parts. Schwartz emphasises that the British banking system did not experience any panics after 1866. The reason is not that the world was calmer, more stable or more certain after 1866. Two changes occurred. The Bank of England recognised its responsibility to prevent a panic and always acted promptly when a financial crisis threatened. The public became convinced that the Bank had the power to prevent a crisis; soon after the Bank acted decisively, the panic ended and deposits (or notes) returned to the commercial banks. This is the legacy of Walter Bagehot, whose writings in *The Economist* and whose book, *Lombard Street*, show a clearer understanding of the problem than many of today's Cassandras.

Bagehot's book does not criticise the directors of the Bank of England for failing to act. On the contrary, he recounts in lively detail how they responded to the panics of 1824, 1866 and at other times. Bagehot's main criticism, in current terminology, is the lack of credibility and the absence of precommitment. According to Bagehot, the Bank acted, at times, as if it intended to protect its gold reserves by contracting loans and advances. Bagehot argued that this policy is mistaken; the way to protect the Bank's reserve is to expand, even if this requires temporary suspension of convertibility. Further, Bagehot insisted on the importance of precommitment. Panics occur because the public does not know how the Bank will respond. His main recommendation is that the Bank should announce in advance that, although it is privately owned, it accepts the responsibility of a bank of issue to protect the money stock.

Schwartz defines financial distress as a condition in which an individual or firm hold assets with (realisable) current market value below its outstanding liabilities. She shows that there were many ways for banks, non-financial firms or individuals to reach this position. There does not appear to be a uniform pattern or cause of distress that can be identified in advance. Sometimes the problem started abroad, sometimes at home. The initial cause could be a war or some peacetime event. Whatever the cause, when news of the distress spread through the market, Schwartz points out, fear of default by creditors of the firm (or individual) rises. A critical point is reached at which the solvency of secondary or tertiary firms – particularly the banks that are creditors of the insolvent firm and the insolvent firm's creditors – is in question.

In contrast to the diversity of causes, there is one dominant solution. Once the market is assured that the supply of base money will increase sufficiently to prevent the insolvency of otherwise solvent banks and non-financial firms, the demand for currency or specie declines, and a crisis is averted. Schwartz follows Bagehot by emphasising precommitment when she writes (p. 21): 'Knowledge of the availability of the supply was sufficient to allay alarm.'

Bagehot's summary brings out the excess burden imposed by uncertainty about policy.

> In common opinion, there is always great uncertainty as to the conduct of the Bank: the Bank has never laid down any clear and sound policy on the subject. . . . The public is never sure what policy will be adopted at the most important moment . . . And until we have on this point a clear understanding with the Bank of England, both our liability to crises and our terror at crises will always be greater than they would otherwise be.[1]

ROLE OF THE LENDER-OF-LAST-RESORT

Schwartz's distinction between real and pseudo-financial crises permits her to separate historical experience into periods of distress and panics. She notes that after the Bank of England accepted its responsibility as lender of last resort, in 1866 on her chronology, there were no financial panics or crises in the United Kingdom. Periods of financial distress, at times, required the suspension of specie payments, but distress did not degenerate into financial panic.

In the United States, uncertainty about the lender-of-last-resort function remained high until deposits were insured after 1933. The important institutional change in the United States was not achieved by having the Federal Reserve precommit to serve as lender-of-last-resort. Responsibility was divided by the 1930's legislation between the Federal Deposit Insurance Corporation, organised to insure commercial bank deposits up to a pre-set (but periodically adjusted) maximum, the Federal Savings and Loan Insurance Corporation, with comparable responsibilities for thrift institutions, and the Federal Reserve.

Later, other institutions were added to provide comparable services for brokerage houses.

None of the institutions that insures deposits has the power to create base money.[2] They can relieve financial distress in two ways. Either they sell some assets and distribute the proceeds to the depositors of the financial institution that is in distress or, by encouraging a merger or consolidation, get solvent financial institutions to accept the deposits and the (discounted) asset portfolio. In the latter case, the insurer assumes the portfolio loss.

If some unforeseen event causes financial distress at several banks or financial institutions simultaneously, deposit insurance is not capable of preventing a financial crisis. The Federal Reserve must act as lender-of-last-resort, supplying currency at a rate equal to the increased demand for currency, thereby preventing a sudden, sharp decline in the means of payment.[3]

It is not difficult currently to imagine the type of event that would exhaust the reserves of the deposit insurance agencies and that could not be resolved by merging financial institutions. Default by one or more of the Latin American governments in Mexico, Brazil and Argentina has the potential to produce severe financial distress. We cannot know whether such distress would be followed by a severe financial panic, by orderly liquidation of some insolvent institutions or by some action intermediate between the two. The reason that we cannot know what the governements' response would be is that central bankers and governments have not chosen to tell us. We are back in the position described by Bagehot, and quoted above, in which uncertainty is greater than it has to be.

Uncertainty could be reduced by a clear statement from the lenders-of-last-resort in each country. The statement should make clear the conditions under which central bank loans will be available and the assets which will be accepted as collateral. Bagehot's two main rules remain applicable.

The first rule determines the quantity of advances. The central bank should lend freely at a penalty rate. This rule makes clear that the only quantitative restriction on the volume of discounts is the penalty rate. When banks, and other financial institutions, can borrow in the market, they will not pay a premium for advances from the central bank. The penalty rate assures us that, in ordinary times, the central bank will not discount. The central bank will be active when (or if) there is a sudden scramble for liquidity – that is a panic.

Bagehot's second rule specifies that the assets on which the central bank lends during a panic should include 'everything which in common times is good "banking security"'.[4] He continued:

> The *amount* of the advance is the main consideration for the Bank of England, and not the nature of the security on which the advance is made, always assuming the security to be good. An idea prevails (as I believe) at the Bank of England that they ought not to advance during a panic on any kind of security on which they do not commonly advance. But if bankers for the most part do advance on such security in common times, and if that security is indisputably good, the ordinary practice of the Bank of England is immaterial. In ordinary times, the Bank is only one of many lenders, whereas in a panic it is the sole lender.[5]

A third rule is now required to recognise the fact that banking is now international in a way that differs from Bagehot's day. Branches of foreign banks typically do not have the same opportunity as domestic banks to discount at the central bank in the countries in which they are resident. Further, foreign banks have located in so-called 'offshore' centres that do not have central banks.

Schwartz points out that some economists have recommended the creation of an international lender-of-last-resort.[6] She does not agree with this recommendation, and I believe she is correct.

The unique ability of a lender-of-last-resort is the ability to produce base money on demand. If banks demand dollars, and are willing to pay a penalty rate to obtain them, the Federal Reserve can supply them without limit. (If there is a limit, it must be suspended as it was in Britain during several financial crises.) Only the Bundesbank can supply Deutsche marks in response to demands of this kind, etc. An international lender-of-last-resort would only have exclusive power to issue unlimited quantities of base money on demand, if it was a world monetary authority and there was a world money stock.

Under the current regime of fluctuating exchange rates, there is no role for a world monetary authority. And there is no role for an international lender-of-last-resort, since the authority to create base money remains with the individual countries.

There should be precommitment by the central banks to provide discounts, at a penalty rate, to all holders – foreign and domestic – of 'good banking securities' dominated in their currency. A statement of this kind would reduce uncertainty and, as Schwartz demonstrates, prevent a period of financial distress, or pseudo crisis, from becoming a real crisis.

NOTES

1. Walter Bagehot, *Lombard Street*. Reprinted from the Scribner, Armstrong edition of 1873. Homewood, Irwin, 1962, p. 101.
2. I first called attention to the ambiguity in the US lender-of-last-resort function in 'Major Issues in the Regulation of Financial Institutions', *Journal of Political Economy*, August 1967.
3. Some suggest that this action is inflationary, but it is not. The action prevents a fall in the price level but does not require an increase.
4. Bagehot, *Lombard Street*, p. 100.
5. Bagehot, *Lombard Street*, p. 101. Italics in the original.
6. She cites P. Kindleberger, *Manias, Panics and Crashes: A History of Financial Crisis*. New York: Basic Books, 1978.

Comment on Anna Schwartz's Chapter

D. E. MOGGRIDGE

Anna Schwartz always has something interesting to say. This time it is about real and pseudo-financial crises. In this case, after defining a real financial crisis as an occasion when the fears of the private sector over the one-to-one convertibility between bank deposits and high-powered money threaten to produce a sharp fall in the quantity of money, she is prepared to argue that such an event has not happened in Britain since 1866 and in the United States since 1933; that such an event is unlikely to occur if the authorities respond in a predictable way and secure private sector bank deposits; and that much of the current talk about financial crisis is a 'bugaboo . . . created to divert attention from the true remedies that the financial situation demands'. These true remedies are not bail-outs or subterfuges such as rescheduling but rather an acknowledgement of default where necessary, with all that this would entail, and the avoidance of misguided, i.e. inflationary, policies.

By putting her case so strongly, Anna Schwartz's chapter should help clarify the discussion, but I am rather doubtful that her presentation makes all the issues particularly clear. Indeed, I am not certain that her 'lessons from history' are as clear as she might like them to be.

For me, the problem arises from her definition of a financial crisis as a narrowly domestic event. It means that she ignores two important cases, neither of which she can call a full financial crisis, where problems were avoided in the country concerned not by the authorities responding in a 'predictable' manner but by them taking unprecedented, and therefore unpredictable, steps. As both of these cases have features which were perhaps more similar to the present situation than her other examples, I think we should look at them briefly.

The two occurrences are the 'crises' of 1914 and 1931. In both instances my concern is with their British manifestations.

In these two crises, British firms and financial institutions were unable to realise foreign assets. The problem was not that all the individual loans had gone bad, but that obstacles had been put in the way of repayments by debtors who might or might not ultimately prove to be solvent. In 1914, it was the closing of financial markets, the interruption of trading relations and the suspension of gold convertibility that did the trick; in 1931, it was exchange controls and standstill agreements that prevented individual borrowers from meeting their obligations. Whatever the means, the result was sovereign governments not only suspending payments on their own debts but also their suspending payments by their nationals whether they were solvent or not.

In neither case was there a serious run on the banks as such. Indeed, it was the absence of such an event, or its containment in 1914, that prevented either 1914 or 1931 from being on Anna Schwartz's list of 'real' crises. Yet in both instances, the suspension of payments by foreigners had substantial adverse effects on the balance sheets of British financial intermediaries, and it could be argued that there was a need to shore up the financial structure in conditions of considerable uncertainty so as to prevent a possible run. Moreover, this shoring up seems to have sometimes been more akin to bail-outs, reschedulings, or papering over the cracks than Dr Schwartz seems prepared to recognise. In 1931, for example, it involved bailing out one clearing bank, two overseas banks, an accepting house and one merchant bank in order that an already difficult situation would not be further complicated by institutions failing, even though in more than one case it was clear to the Bank of England that the institutions involved would ultimately fail – as they later did. Nor were such actions limited to the summer of 1931, for in the spring of 1932 two of the same institutions and another merchant bank also received assistance. Over and above this assistance to particular firms, there was also the matter of the standstill agreements whose consequences were not completely off the Bank's plate until thirty years later. Similarly in 1914, there was the run of moratoria to protect firms' balance sheets – moratoria which would not be cleared off until well after the end of the war. In both cases, the action of the authorities was to a considerable degree unprecedented – and, therefore, hardly predictable in the usual sense of the word.

Of course, one might try and argue that the authorities' actions in 1914 and 1931 bore a family resemblance to the handling of the Baring affair of 1890, when it could be said that the steps taken were really designed to preserve the 'reputation' of the London market, but this would, I think, be taking matters rather too far. I am therefore left wondering whether the presentation of the crisis problem in the case of crises arising from a disruption of international payments, resulting from the actions of sovereign states, is really adequately dealt with in the paper.

Also, I wonder whether Anna Schwartz's emphasis on preserving the security of all private sector deposits is not too all-embracing. It certainly goes beyond current practices of deposit insurance which, where it exists, does not extend to really large depositors. Perhaps such an extension may be necessary, as witnessed by the American practice of merging banks in difficulties partly to protect large, uninsured depositors. However, it does raise the problem of moral hazard which Dr Schwartz seems to believe is not a serious matter in 'real' financial crises and may push us closer to bail-outs than some may want to go.

Finally, I wonder whether by restricting herself in her definition of financial crises to the equivalent of bank runs and calling everything else financial distress or pseudo crises does not really beg other important questions. It seems clear, for example, that longish periods of financial distress do have knock-on effects which can be seriously disruptive to the real economy. Certainly this happened in 1931 and in the recent past the difficulties of individual borrowers has, through what the BIS calls the 'regionalisation syndrome', produced problems for others. Yet, I would gather from the chapter that all one need do in these cases is to get on with orderly liquidation and reorganisation, although who is to preserve order and how one is to prevent knock-on effects is unclear. This is particularly the case when the discussion extends from domestic firms to sovereign countries and their instrumentalities, for here, although the IMF may occasionally take on the guise of a reorganiser, the processes involved are rather different – not to say more difficult.

Thus, although, I find the chapter both interesting and stimulating, I am not certain that its focus was really broad enough to highlight fully the relevant issues of past or contemporary policy.

2 The Avoidance of Catastrophe: Two Nineteenth-century Banking Crises

ROY A. BATCHELOR

INTRODUCTION

This chapter tells the tale of the two most severe banking crises to trouble Victorian England. The collapse of Overend, Gurney & Co. Ltd in 1866, and the liquidation of Baring Bros in 1890, caused a degree of consternation in the financial community which was quite remarkable in an era when each passing year bought its crop of bank failures. Equally remarkable, however, is the fact that neither of these panics was translated into the sort of domino collapse of the whole banking system so characteristic of the economies at the periphery of the international trading system. Less than ten years before the Overend, Gurney crisis, several hundred banks in the eastern United States were brought down in a single run. The very year before the Baring crisis, and directly contributing to it, the entire financial system of the River Plate republics fell; and only three years later, the Australian banking system suffered a similar fate.

Our analysis of the two episodes must therefore address two issues. First, how did the crises arise? Secondly, how was crisis prevented from becoming catastrophe?

We start by describing the events surrounding the crises of 1866 and 1890. The histories contain many parallels. Both crises were the products of bad asset management. The two great houses concerned grossly overcommitted their funds to risky enterprises – finance bills for contracting companies, South American securities – which subsequently failed. Each crisis developed in two stages; the failure of bubble companies and utilities at home and abroad, and the succeeding loss of confidence in the financial system. The histories do, however, have very different outcomes. Gurneys failed, never to reappear. In the course of the crisis, interest rates were driven to record levels; and for years after, banks and discount houses held substantial reserves at the Bank of England, fearful that the episode would be repeated. Barings was reconstructed within weeks. Interest rates rose only slightly and briefly; and although the Bank of England subsequently took on a greater responsibility for bank solvency, the crisis made no permanent mark on bank behaviour.

To help sort out the analytical issues surrounding the crises, we develop two theoretical models. Both use in an informal way the language and concepts of 'catastrophe theory'. This is a branch of mathematics which seeks to describe systems which are well behaved under some sets of circumstances (some values of 'control variables'), but in other circumstances can exhibit sudden and irreversible changes. It is a natural vehicle for studying the mechanics of normally quiescent financial systems which periodically experience manic boom or bust phases, and some pioneering work in this area has already been undertaken (Zeeman, 1974; Schott, 1983). Our first model adapts this work to describe the external shocks initiating the Gurney and Baring collapses. Our second model is more novel. It uses catastrophe theory to describe how a subsequent bank run can arise, and to assess the relative contributions of policy and non-policy factors in starting and ending such episodes. The bank run is characterised as a rational reaction on the part of depositors to news arriving in a situation where they are imperfectly informed about the relative solvency of individual banks. The state of the banking system is determined by two control variables – the riskiness of bank assets, and the degree of information about individual bank balance sheets. Both can be affected by non-policy events – the state of the real economy, the track record of each bank – and by the last resort lending policies and balance sheet restrictions imposed by the central bank. The resulting model shares with standard catastrophe models the property of hysteresis, neither the security price collapse nor the sequence of bank failures being easily reversible. The model does of course generate runs, and does so without invoking irrational behaviour on the part of the public. However, as with earlier catastrophe theory models of financial crises, the model yields a genuine catastrophe situation only if some particular assumptions are made about precisely how confidence in individual banks is created and destroyed. Whether financial crises are true catastrophes will only be decided by empirical evidence on the validity of these assumptions. Fortunately, for our present purpose of understanding the Gurney and Baring episodes the general bank run model suffices.

This chapter therefore concludes by offering an interpretation of the two crises in terms of this theoretical framework. Why did the failure of Gurneys' cause such consternation; why did the failure of Barings pass off with such little disturbance? Why did neither trigger a collapse of the whole banking system? There are two competing explanations. One is that these outcomes were determined by the initial conditions. The crimes of the Gurneys were simply greater than those of the Barings. The financial community was too well informed about both to believe that other institutions were being equally irresponsible. The alternative hypothesis is that catastrophe was avoided in both cases only by prompt action of the Bank of England; and that Gurneys failed because assistance was provided only to the major London banks, while Barings survived because they were supported directly. Conventional wisdom attributes considerable responsibility to the Bank for maintaining the integrity of the system through these crises. Our assessment is that the two cases were somewhat different. In 1866 there was suspicion that many finance houses were little better than Gurneys, and consequently there was a genuine danger of a run. The Bank's actions, in temporarily expanding the supply of notes to banks with good security, was appropriate and helpful. In 1890, however, there was no such danger. Barings was known to be a special case; no other house was so heavily committed in Argentina and Uruguay. The actions of its directors in plunging into such securities was no less blameworthy than the actions of Gurneys directors thirty years earlier. The Bank's decision to launch a 'lifeboat' to save this particular bank, where other equally eminent names had earlier been refused, clearly requires some explanation. One possibility is that the Bank acted properly, but on the basis of an incorrect and exaggerated estimate of the probability of a run on London. It seems more probable that the Bank simply felt an obligation towards Barings. Gurneys had been long-standing rivals of the Bank, but the Barings were solid establishment figures, with representatives in Parliament and on the Board of Directors of the Bank itself. The decisions to save Barings but to let Gurneys go seem to have been motivated less by a consistent theory of monetary management than by the politics and personalities of the City.

GURNEYS' FRIDAY

Overend, Gurney & Company had their origins in the joint activities of the Gurney Bank of Norwich, and the London bill broking firm of Richardson, Overend & Company, towards the end of the eighteenth century. Both firms were run by Quaker families. Samuel Gurney, cousin of the head of the Norwich bank, Hudson Gurney, joined Richardsons in 1807. In the ensuing half-century, the firm – soon reconstructed as Overend, Gurney & Co. with Hudson at its head – grew enormously in stature and prosperity.

Both of the Gurneys took an active part in public debate on monetary policy. Their views were, significantly, often at variance with those of the Bank of England. Hudson, for example, found himself – along with Alexander Baring, but with few other allies – arguing in 1819 against the resumption of specie payment for notes at pre-war parity, a measure which had overwhelming official support. In an effort to persuade the Bank to act consistently with this policy, he subsequently (in 1826) threatened to send £$\frac{1}{2}$ million in notes to the Bank unless they restricted growth of new note issues. Twenty years later, this sort of discipline was formally imposed by the Bank Charter Act, which tied the note issue rigidly to the Bank reserve, and insulated the Bank's commercial banking activities from its responsibilities as the Chief bank of issue. The Gurneys were still not satisfied. Samuel Gurney supported his elder's opinions, and had at first been a strong advocate of Peel's Act. However, the crisis of 1847, in which a reserve shortage caused monetary contraction and deflation, necessitating the suspension of the Act, led him to the opinion that the Bank should not wholly divorce its banking operations from the needs of the rest of the banking systm. He, and the other managing partner in Gurneys, David Barclay Chapman, continued to argue the need for temporary last resort lending above the fiduciary limit, against the security of sound bills, in times of crises. When the Bank showed no signs of taking on such a responsibility, Chapman took the unusual step on one occasion, in October 1856, of going over its head to a Minister of State to seek assurances that such financial relief would be provided.

Apart from the good sense of their arguments in favour of a system which, much later, came to be accepted as the proper mode of operation of a central bank, Gurney and Chapman commanded respect for the huge commercial success of their company. Their business had started small and simple. They acted as agents for firms wishing to sell bills. The firms were carefully vetted for soundness. The buyers of the bills were generally country bankers, initially concentrated in East Anglia. By the 1820s, all the major London banks were also investing in Gurneys and other finance houses; by the 1830s the Bank of England itself was a regular investor, and on more than one occasion Gurneys bought back bills from the Bank to provide liquidity during a cash squeeze. Gurneys became a huge concern, by far the largest discount house, and one of the City's 'great houses'. By the 1850s, it was each year turning over bills to about half the value of the United Kingdom's National Debt; its profits were £200 000 a year. Its balance sheet was as large as that of the Bank of England; and its Directors clearly felt that this symbiotic relationship should be formally recognised.

In the mid 1850s, however, a change took place in the management of Gurneys which, in the short space of a single decade, reduced the firm to ruins. Samuel Gurney died in 1856; Barclay Chapman retired late in 1857. The new Board still contained Gurneys and Chapmans, but these men, while sharing their elders' ambitions, did not have their good sense. They also wanted an accommodation with the Bank; and they wanted to grow. But they tried to move too fast.

In 1860, they appealed to the Bank for relief after a sharp rise in the Bank rate. By this time, the Bank had a definite policy of *not* assisting the bill brokers in bad times, on the grounds that the brokers put little cash into the Bank during good times, and the request was refused. Gurneys' reply was to demonstrate its power, by organising a well-advertised mass note withdrawal by a group of Quaker-owned banks and brokers, perhaps inspired by Hudson's threatened gold raid of 1826. The Bank found its reserve falling by about £2 million (out of a total of £7 million) in the week of 4–11 April, and it received an anonymous letter claiming that Gurneys was quite capable of pulling out the remaining £5 million. The Bank did not relent. The notes were returned a week later (cut in two), and the bizarre demonstration served only to diminish Gurneys' weight in public affairs, and harden the Bank's heart against the discount houses.

The new management was equally cavalier in the conduct of its private business. High quality bill broking had never been the sole activity of the house, but from 1858 it started taking on extremely dubious bills, and lending on the flimsiest security. After the Act of 1861 authorising limited liability, a large number of speculative companies were floated, and many paid their contracting firms by means of 'finance securities'. The discount on these bills was, of course, considerable and Gurneys saw them as a source of quick profit. Of the precise nature of Gurneys other investments, only dark rumours survive. One story, retailed in *The Economist*, has Ward Chapman boasting that he 'lent money to certain parties "upon shells"' . . . at which 'All the country bankers in England began to ask, 'Is our money put out in shells or not?'[1] In spite of such episodes, Gurneys was held in high esteem in the country. Only among insiders in London were its affairs a continual source of concern.

In truth, the firm was slipping heavily into debt, and by 1865 the vast profits of the old firm had been turned into vast losses cumulating to £3–4 million. In a desperate attempt to attract more capital, Gurneys itself was floated as a limited company in July 1865. Ward Chapman was retired. The Gurneys remained, and several more responsible, if optimistic, new directors were appointed. On the strength of the Gurneys' name, an extravagant assessment of the value of partners property and goodwill, and a cosmetic presentation of the bill portfolio, the firm was sold. Outsiders regarded the transaction as a milestone in the advance of limited liability. Insiders were more cynical; *The Economist* suggested its chief virtue was that the firm would now have to publish regular accounts. Outside investors steadily drove Gurneys' shares to a substantial premium. City analysts were puzzled; by early 1866, the 'limited mania' had run its course, and a growing number of bubble companies and their associated contracting firms were failing. The supply of credit to surviving enterprises was curtailed, and interest rates had risen from 3 per cent at the time of Gurneys' flotation to 8 per cent by the year end (Table 2.1). This left the discount houses with heavy contingent liabilities on finance securities and capital losses on liquidated bills. The Joint Stock Discount Company and the Contract Corporation were forced to close, and shares of almost all the others were trading more than 50 per cent below par. It was later remarked of the buoyancy of Gurneys' shares that 'there was a halo about the commodity which made both buyers and sellers fancy it was excellent'.[2]

The public continued to trade Gurneys' shares. Wise depositors, mainly London based, began to withdraw their custom. There were rumours in January that the old partners were personally bankrupt, and that the firm had large liabilities arising from the failure of the eponymous – but actually unrelated – Liverpool railway contractors, Watson, Overend & Company, and Spanish merchants, Pinto, Perez & Co. By early May 1866, the deposits of the limited company had been drawn down from £14½ million to under £10 million. These rumours spread to the stock market, and Gurneys' shares were marked to a discount. The Bank rate itself rose again to 8 per cent. Finally, Gurneys

TABLE 2.1 INTEREST RATES AND SECURITY PRICES 1865–7

		Stock price (£)		
Date	*Bank rate* (%)	*Overend, Gurney*	*Discount Corporation*	*London and Westminster Bank*
1865 Dec	7	21½	12	95
1866 Jan	7	20⅛	10	95
Feb	7	19½	11⅛	96
Mar	6	15⅞	9	95¾
Apr	6	14½	9	96
May 2	6	14½	7	96¾
9	9	failed	7	90
16	10		7	90
23	10		7	91
30	10		7	91
Jun	10		7	91
Jul	10		7	94½
Dec	3½		9	97
1867 Dec	2		n.a.	98

Source: *Bankers' Magazine* 1865–7

admitted that they could no longer meet their obligations. On Thursday 10 May they sought assistance of £400 000 from the Bank. The Bank was in general not inclined to acquiesce in such arrangements, and in particular had no wish to aid its old, now disreputable, rival. The Gurneys' security was deemed inadequate, and that afternoon they were declared insolvent.

The sheer panic that broke in the City on 'Black Friday', 11 May 1866, is graphically described in the accounts of the time. The *Bankers' Magazine* records a 'terror and anxiety which took possession of men's minds for the remainder of that and the whole of the succeeding day'; 'a mob formed in the neighbourhood of Lombard St, Cornhill, Lothbury and Bartholomew Lane'.[3] *The Economist* was more perceptive, 'the country world, which always trusts the London world largely, became frightened. It was disconcerted beyond example and did not know what to do'. In consequence, 'no-one knew who was sound, and who was unsound. The evil was an overexpenditure of capital . . . not a drain of bullion . . . but a failure of credit from intrinsic defect'.[4]

In fact, the Gurney collapse set in train two processes. The first was the progressive failure of a number of country banks and firms with which it was directly associated. The English Joint Stock Bank, for example, immediately suspended payments. The second, and by far the more serious, was a run on London banks and finance houses by the country banks. This quickly became translated into a run on the Bank of England itself. The failure of the 'great house' of Gurneys led the country to fear that other houses might be in trouble. They liquidated their deposits and demanded Bank of England notes. This action had fatal results for a number of finance houses and banks which were genuinely bad risks. The Imperial Credit Association, the Commercial Bank of India and the East, the European Bank all suspended trading in the course of the next week. A number of basically solvent banks also failed, including Hallett Ommanney and Co. Ltd and the Bank of London, later to be taken over by competitors. The immediate crisis was, however, centred on the Bank of England. The massive demand for notes meant that the Bank lost over £3 million from its already depleted note reserve of £5 million (Table 2.2) in a single day, as it swapped these for the securities of frightened country bankers. Under the Bank Charter Act the Issue Department had no authority to

TABLE 2.2 THE BANK OF ENGLAND, 1865–7 (£ million)

	Liabilities			*Assets*			
Date	*Notes*	*Government deposits*	*Other deposits*	*Notes*	*Bullion*	*Government securities*	*Other securities*
1865 Dec	20.9	8.5	13.2	7.6	13.4	9.9	22.5
1866 Mar	22.0	8.4	13.2	7.7	14.4	10.9	21.9
Apr	22.6	4.4	13.3	5.8	13.9	10.7	18.5
May 2	23.3	4.9	13.6	4.8	13.5	10.7	20.4
9	22.8	5.8	13.5	5.0	13.2	10.9	20.8
16	26.7	5.9	18.6	0.7	12.3	10.8	30.9
23	26.0	6.0	18.8	1.4	11.6	10.8	31.1
30	26.7	6.1	20.4	0.9	11.9	10.9	33.4
Jun	25.7	7.3	21.2	4.7	14.9	11.1	31.2
Jul	25.9	2.5	18.5	3.5	13.9	9.8	26.7
Dec	22.4	8.7	18.6	12.3	19.2	13.0	20.2
1867 Dec	23.9	7.2	18.8	13.6	18.3	14.1	17.5

augment the note supply. There was a clear danger that a point would be reached at which the Bank would refuse to lend even on good security. The Bank itself was unwilling to press for a relaxation of the Act, since it would make nonsense of its philosophy of operating the Banking Department as a profit-motivated enterprise rather than an arm of monetary control. Indeed, the Bank added to the panic by hesitating over its normal purchases of the best security of all, new issues of government debt. The Chancellor, Gladstone, was, however, besieged by private deputations of bankers and merchants demanding the suspension of the Bank Charter Act, and this measure was announced late on Friday night. Bank rate, already 9 per cent, went to 10 per cent on Saturday. The suspension provided the necessary assurance of Bank support to the country bankers, and although a small drain on notes continued through the following week the fiduciary limit was never in fact broken. The panic gradually subsided.

Gurneys itself was liquidated, and one of the great names of British banking disappeared in a tangle of litigation brought by furious shareholders who felt that the 1865 prospectus had been fraudulent. With hindsight the company might have been saved, but by the time of its liquidation the loss of confidence in the value of the company's assets was so great that the possibility was never entertained. The discount market as a whole suffered permanent damage. It lost a large part of its country banking clientele to the Bank of England, and these depositors did not return even when the credit market became more settled. Bankers deposits at the Bank of England rose permanently from around 30 per cent to 40 per cent of its total liabilities (Table 2.2). The Bank's status also changed. Apart from this growth in its role as the bankers bank, it had in the course of the crisis taken on the lender of last resort role which had been urged upon it by Samuel Gurney a decade before. Although no formal amendment to the Bank Charter Act was made, and although the Bank had no occasion to intervene on such a grand scale for many years, it was henceforth understood that it would support the rest of the financial community at such times of extreme distress.

THE BARING CRISIS

Baring Bros & Co., the large international merchant bank which failed in 1890, also had its origins in the eighteenth century, in the bank founded in 1763 by John and Francis Baring to exploit their European connections in the financing of the textile trade. The family bank grew rapidly, and the standing of the family itself grew apace. Francis was ennobled in 1793.

The bank continued to grow in the next generation. The world had changed after the Napoleonic Wars, however, and Barings business adapted to exploit the new opportunities for profit which arose. One change was the lifting of restrictions on international flows of gold and short term money. Barings quickly became a broker in this market, with its clients concentrated in Europe, in Paris and St Petersburg. Another change was the growing need for finance for public development projects. Barings, together with Rothschilds and a few other London-based merchant banks, became specialised in long-term sterling lending to foreign governments and public bodies. Initially, these loans were also concentrated in Europe and – to a lesser degree – in North America. But in 1821–2 the boom in these loans spread to Mexico and Latin America, with large commitments made to Chile, Colombia, and Brazil.

In this lending there were, of course, new risks. Barings' European loans were generally well judged, and became a staple part of their business. Their North America lending was a little less secure. In 1836, together with a group of other merchant banks, they were called to account for the quality of their American assets. By this time, however, they had opened a New York office, and could mount a display of some expertise which induced the Bank to support them; in truth they may have been close to insolvency by the end of the decade. Their early lending in Latin America was certainly unprofitable. None of the loans made in 1821–2 was yielding income five years later. The extent of these losses was small, however, and it was shared with many other reputable institutions. It is no way tarnished Barings reputation as the pre-eminent merchant bank in London.

Barings business was not, of course, competitive with the Bank of England. On the contrary, Barings provided many services to the Bank. At a time when the Bank could not engage in direct swaps and borrowings with other central banks in continental Europe, Barings acted as an intermediary for these operations. The Duc de Richelieu quipped, in 1819, 'There are in Europe six great powers – England, France, Russia, Austria, Prussia and Baring Brothers.'[5] Almost continuously through the nineteenth century there were Barings on the Bank's Board of Directors. These men were generally also Parliamentarians, and were active in public debate over monetary issues, particularly touching on the conduct of the foreign exchanges. Although, as we have seen, Alexander Baring was, with Hudson Gurney, an opponent of Resumption, the Barings by and large took the Bank's part in such debates. Francis, for example, argued strongly for an extension of the Banks powers to intervene in the exchanges, following the suspension of the Bank Charter Act during the reserve drain of 1848.

As with Gurneys the middle the century brought a turn in Barings fortunes. The change was not marked by any wild behaviour or dramatic collapse, but its effects were nonetheless appreciable. Barings slowly lost market share to their more energetic rivals, the Rothschilds. As with Gurneys the decline seems to have been a matter of personalities. The dominant figures at the bank in the late nineteenth century – Thomas Charles Baring, Edward Charles Baring (Lord Revelstoke) – put themselves about much less than their predecessors. They were irregular contributors to Parliamentary debate, and – as the Bank had less need of Barings' services – poor attenders at the Bank's Court. Their authority within the bank was considerable, but their judgement of risks was poor. Their most notable acts seem to have been the improvement of their estates and the endowment of numerous (Anglican) churches. It is, all in all, hard to resist the impression that they lived off the social and financial capital of the previous two generations. This was, however, regarded as no bad thing. Of Lord Revelstoke, who led the bank into disaster, it was reported in the *Bankers' Magazine* that

> no dishonourable act has ever been recorded. That he was imprudent; that he neglected the hints of good advisers; that he relied too much upon his own judgement, and was altogether too impetuous and autocratic is probably true; but his uprightness has never been in question. The firm was an honourable firm, conducted by an honourable family.[6]

Almost in spite of the management, the name of Barings continued to be a byword for the quality of bills. As late as 1877, Bagehot welcomed the introduction of Treasury Bills by remarking that they were 'as good as Barings'.

The 'imprudence' which led to the collapse of the bank was a policy of specialising in the promotion and finance of South American public development projects. By the 1880s, the new frontier in South America had shifted to the southern states of Argentina and Uruguay, where the construction of railways promised a boom in urban development and trade with the interior. Between 1880 and 1890 over £100 million of sterling loans were made to the national and provincial governments and associated utilities of the River Plate republics. Undeterred by their earlier misadventures in South America, Barings took the lead in over £30 million of this lending, occasionally in partnership with J. P. Morgan. This was by far the largest involvement of any individual bank. Between 1888 and 1890, for example, they sponsored £13.6 million in Argentine loans; the next most active bank, C. de Murietta & Co. took on £4.5 million, and Antony Gibb & Son £1.5 million. These loans soon crowded out more staple items in the Barings asset portfolio. To some extent, this was involuntary. Much of the South American paper proved barely marketable. To a large extent it reflected a conscious policy decision to ride on the investment boom. British and European interest rates were low, Bank rate never rising above 4 per cent after 1883. The productivity of European investments seemed low by comparison with opportunities in the Americas. Barings itself took a large equity stake in the Buenos Ayres Water and Drainage Company. By late 1890, Argentine and Uruguayan loans counted for well over three-quarters of the bank's total portfolio; European loans amounted to less than 10 per cent.

As with the 'limited mania' which brought down Gurneys, so Barings collapse was preceded by the bursting of the bubble in River Plate financing. The Argentine national government ran into difficulties over interest payments as early as April 1890, and only the sale of the Western Railway at well above any objective market value to a not disinterested consortium of European financiers enabled payments to continue. Inside the country, the National Bank, which had been heavily involved in speculation on land prices, could pay no dividend when the property boom ended (land prices fell 50 per cent from 1889 to 1890), and the result was a run on the whole banking system. In Montevideo, the National Bank of Uruguay faced similar problems as a result of its own speculations on public works, and was forced to suspend payments. Both Argentina and Uruguay hurriedly negotiated short term loans with London (for £10 million and £2 million respectively). The run on the Argentine banks, however, precipitated revolution in Buenos Aires on 26 July, and in August the directors of the National Bank were dismissed. A representative of the national government, Dr Plaza, was dispatched to London to discuss the reconstruction or River Plate finances.

These events had put Barings under increasing pressure. The value of their Argentine securities fell by a third, the flow of income from South America began to dry up, and they had a further large liability arising out of the failure of the Water Company. Barings initially reacted by borrowing heavily from their London bankers, but by November –

with the arrival of the Argentine negotiator – the reality of their position became plain to the management. Plaza offered to write off the Water Company liability if Barings could raise additional credit to help the Argentine maintain interest payments on its other debts. Barings refused this, as they had refused a similar, less blunt, request from Uruguay, and on Saturday 8 November – through an intermediary – Revelstoke informed the Governor of the Bank of England, William Lidderdale, of the crisis within his bank.

The Bank and the Government were appalled. Both feared a massive drain of foreign capital if it were learned that the still-revered name of Barings was no longer a guarantee of the quality of a London bill. Both agreed that the position of Barings should be kept secret until this threat could be dealt with. They differed only over what should happen to Barings itself. To avert the drain, Lidderdale and Goschen induced Rothschilds to import £3 million in gold from France, and the Bank itself secured a further £1½ million from Russia. The Bank rate, which had been rising in anticipation of trouble in London since the summer, was raised further to 6 per cent. Goschen offered to suspend the Bank Charter Act, but Lidderdale refused. Goschen was reluctant to support Barings in the event that they were insolvent (and this was the opinion of Rothschilds); Lidderdale felt his reserve was sufficient, and in any case had different plans for Barings. He had before him the example of the Bank of France, which the previous year had organised a consortium to rescue a leading Parisian house which ran into liquidity problems after injudicious speculation in copper. He accordingly set to work one of Barings creditors (B. W. Currie, from Glyn, Mills, Currie & Co) and his own man (Buck Greene) – both close friends of Lord Revelstoke – to establish the true position of the bank. By the next Friday, he received an encouraging report that Barings was fundamentally sound, but needed some £10 million to finance current interest obligations. That same day, Lidderdale invited subscriptions to a fund to guarantee Barings' liabilities for a three-year period. The Bank itself, Rothschilds, and other leading merchant banks built the fund up to £3 million by the end of the day. On Saturday, the fund reached £10 million, with cash pressed from the largest domestic joint stock banks and discount houses. On Sunday it reached £17 million. By this time the 'secret' of Barings' illiquidity was out. Although there was a spasm of activity as country banks switched into cash, and the Bank's holdings of their bills rose temporarily by about 20 per cent, no mobs formed, no capital drain ensued, and the authorities felt well content that they had anticipated any flight from London bills.

Barings itself was put into liquidation. However, a committee had been set up under Lord Rothschild to address the problem of maintaining the flow of Argentine finances. The committee's report resulted in a favourable valuation of Barings, with the Buenos Ayres Water and Drainage Co. debt written off completely. The way was open for Barings to be refloated as a limited liability company a week later, the capital of the new firm, Messrs Baring & Co. Ltd, being provided by the Baring family and friends. Revelstoke retired to his society pursuits, but an equally testy figure from the bank's past, Thomas Charles Baring, became chairman.

Although the Baring crisis caused a flurry of activity at the Bank and the Treasury, its impact on financial markets was small. No other bank fell in its wake. Interest rates fell sharply in December and again in January, and by the summer of 1891 Bank rate was below 3 per cent, a measure of the extent of overkill in the Bank's accumulation of reserves. Lidderdale's reputation was made by the crisis, and he was elected a Privy Councillor. Two years later, however, when he again tried to engineer direct support for the other major Argentinian lender, Muriettas, he found that the City had reappraised the policy of selective support, and neither he nor his policies (nor Muriettas) survived another term in office.

CATASTROPHES AND RUNS

How best can we analyse the mechanics of crises such as those described above? Conventional economic theory is of limited use. The familiar models of economics are designed for a world which satisfies Marshall's observation that 'natura non facit saltum' – things do not change in jumps. Most of the time, most markets do indeed seem well behaved. As demand rises and falls, prices respond in a smooth and symmetric fashion. Moreover, supply elasticities are generally higher than demand elasticities, and markets dominated by rational and profit-seeking reactions to price signals are consequently stable. Some of the time, however, these laws of demand and supply seem to be suspended. The most obvious instances arise in individual asset markets – for commodities, currencies, shares – when rising prices increase rather than decrease demand, thus raising the level of prices further; and falling prices lead to a cumulative, rapid collapse of the whole market. The 'bubbles' in finance securities and Argentinian bonds described above are prime examples. Some less obvious instances arise at the macroeconomic level when income, rather than price, plays an equilibrating role. A system in which economies gravitate to equilibria at either very low or very high income levels, separated by an unstable region, can arise naturally from the rapid population increase and low savings propensities which attend rising incomes in poor countries. A common feature of all these bubbles, in prices and incomes, is that it is hard to return to normality. Although a large boom or crash may have been initiated by a small change in one variable – a rise in price, a fall in income – an equal and opposite change will not have an offsetting effect. Once a market has collapsed, it takes a long time for confidence to be restored. Once a country has lapsed into poverty it takes a 'big push' to beat the low-level equilibrium trap and return to sustained growth at a high income level.

Frequently, the behaviour of economic systems under normal conditions, and their behaviour under crisis conditions, are treated on different levels. The crisis phase is either described by a special model, or by a special case of the conventional model which arises when market participants become irrational. The attraction of catastrophe theory is that this dichotomy is avoided. It suggests that the two conditions described above, one involving gradual symmetric change and a set of stable equilibria, the other involving irreversible step changes and unstable equilibria, are not distinct phenomena, but simply different states of the same system. Catastrophe theory models can function as descriptions of the smooth continuous processes seen in normal times. On the other hand, they do permit the economy to stray into regions where the discontinuities and hysteresis effects so characteristic of manias and panics can occur. Catastrophe theory itself, in the form proposed by Thom (1972), has much larger claims that this, of course, and its mathematics have stretched the boundaries of traditional topological theory. Fortunately, largely through the efforts of Zeeman (1977), the language of the theory has been reduced to an accessible form, for use in theoretical – and hopefully empirical – work in describing discrete events in physical and social systems. A number of popular introductions to the subject are now available (Woodcock and Davis, 1978; Saunders, 1980), and the wide range of applications is displayed in Poston and Stewart (1978).

In economics, several attempts have been made to understand speculative markets through the medium of catastrophe theory, starting with Zeemans own (1974) analysis of stock markets, and including most recently an account of the mid-1970s UK property boom and collapse by Kerry Schott (1983), and a conjecture about the sources of exchange rate overshooting by de Grauwe (1981). Pertinent to our present paper, Ho and Saunders (1980) present a catastrophe model of bank failure based on inappropriate central bank responses to crisis conditions. Several attempts have also been made to analyse macroeconomic fluctuations in this framework. Varian (1979) and George (1981) adapt Kaldor's growth model to generate catastrophic switches between boom and recession; and the connection between multiple equilibria and catastrophe conditions in a neoclassical general equilibrium model is formally demonstrated by Balasko (1978).

In this section, we explore two catastrophe theory models which are potentially helpful in understanding the Gurney and Baring crisis. One is a model of financial crisis. It is applicable to the bubbles in finance securities and Argentine bonds which preceded the two banking crises. The second is a model of a bank run itself.

A Catastrophe Theory Model of Financial Crisis

The first model revolves around the reactions of a 'fast' variable, the price of a speculative asset (common stocks, property, finance securities, Argentinian bonds), to slowly rising and falling demand. In normal conditions, defined to be those when the asset is traded for its intrinsic usefulness (or 'fundamental' or 'hedge' purposes) a negative excess demand will induce a falling price, a positive demand a rising price. These cases are illustrated as points *a* and *b* in the left panel of Figure 2.1. The conventional law of supply and demand operates, and prices move smoothly along the continuous locus shown. In speculative conditions, defined to be those arising when assets are held for capital gain, the rate of change of price as well as the level of price affects demand. Positive hedge demand will cause prices to rise; the price rise will induce a further speculative pressure and prices will rise still further. On the other hand, falling prices will cause disinvestment, and prices will fall faster than in normal times in response to a given negative demand shock. The result is a bifurcation into a bull market and a bear market, as illustrated in the right panel of Figure 2.1. The greater the speculative interest in a market relative to the hedge interest, the more pronounced will be the separation of the two surfaces be, for a given initial shock.

The speculative scenario admits the possibility of a sharp price fall and hence bankruptcy of the many investors in the market. As soon as a certain number of speculators ('insiders') sell out, and excess demand becomes sufficiently negative, all remaining investors will recognise the

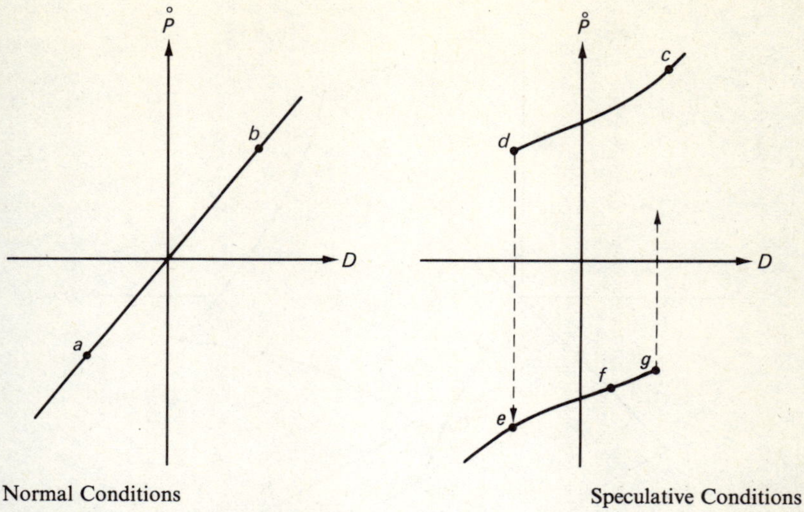

Key: P = asset price inflation
D = excess demand for asset

FIG 2.1 Asset Price Inflation and Excess Demand

probability of price falls, and attempt to sell out. Prices will fall immediately this process starts and the system will jump from the end of the bull market (point *d*) to the start of the bear market (point *e*). The greater the speculative interest in the market, the greater must be the reversal necessary to cause such a market collapse.

Note that a recovery in demand would not necessarily restore bull market conditions. Prices would continue to fall, but at a slower rate (point *f*). Only if some critical excess demand level is reached would confidence be restored and the economy jump from point *g*, say, to point *c*.

The process is an example of a 'cusp catastrophe'. When drawn in three dimensions, the normal and catastrophe situations of Figure 2.1 appear as sections of a continuous three-dimensional surface, taken at increasing values of a splitting variable (in this case, the share of speculators in the market). In Zeeman's stock market model, the splitting variable is the number of 'chartists' trading on price extrapolations, relative to 'fundamentalists'; in Schott's property market model it is the level of borrowing undertaken by investors with no natural position in the property market. The full set-up is shown in Figure 2.2.

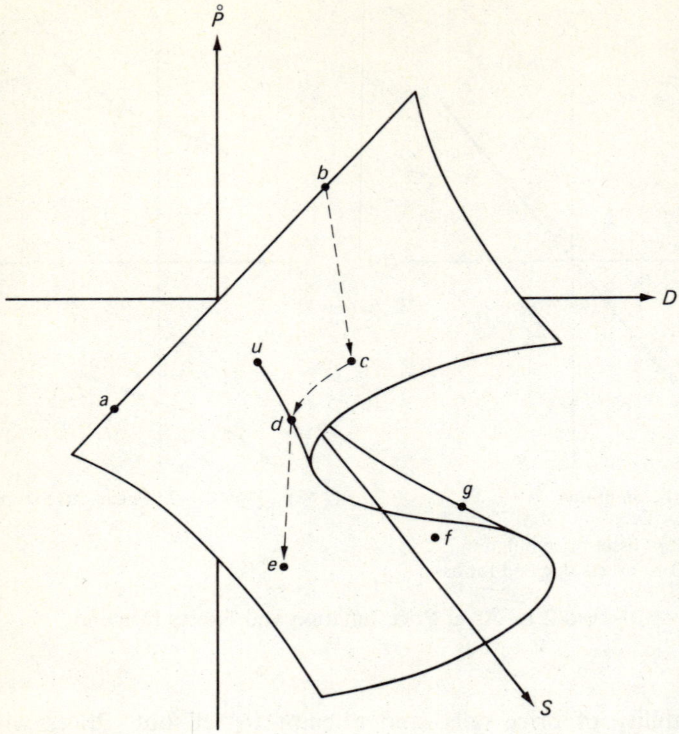

Key: $\mathring{P}$ = asset price inflation
D = excess demand
S = degree of speculative interest

FIG. 2.2 Asset Prices – A Cusp Catastrophe

The surface describes all equilibria of a single 'state variable', price change, corresponding to two 'control variables', excess demand and speculative interest. The boom, bust and recovery phases of a crisis can be described as a trajectory on this surface. A positive demand shock will move the economy to point *b*; rising prices attract speculators and the system moves towards point *c*; as the underlying demand vanishes, a few investors start to sell out, pushing prices down further, so that point *d* is reached; at this point, the catastrophic price fall to *e* occurs, as all remaining speculators try to sell out. This sort of catastrophic fall was a possibility from the moment that the speculative interest exceeded the splitting factor *u*, where the surface became folded. So long as $S<u$, the system would behave normally, with prices rising when demand is positive, and falling when it is negative. Recovery could be stimulated by some externally generated 'big push' in demand sufficient to move the system to point g; but since $S>u$ still, the possibility of catastrophe remains. The safer road to recovery involves reducing the other control variable S, reducing the speculative interest and moving from e towards a.

This model has a number of nice properties. It has obvious application to the 'limited mania' of the 1860s, and the South American bond speculation of the 1880s. In both instances, the pay-off to the underlying commercial activity was known to be of an uncertain and long-term nature; but the assets were valued for their potential for short-term price movements. The model allows a normal trading situation to degenerate smoothly into a potentially catastrophic situation. It allows small changes in the environment to precipitate sudden large changes in price. This catastrophe, once it occurs, is not simply reversible.

Such models have, however, come in for considerable criticism. Most fundamentally, Sussman and Zahler (1978) argue that the functional form of the cusp catastrophe is not logically implied by the axioms of economic theory. It is a pure self standing assumption and not a testable proposition. Economics is rarely so fussy in its choice of tools. Linear and loglinear functions are used throughout the discipline for their great didactic value, and the catastrophe surface seems no more objectionable than these elementary forms. We should make it clear that in all applications of catastrophe theory in economics, model builders have been obliged to make arbitrary assumptions in order to force the system into a catastrophe. This is true of the model sketched here. The act of trading on extrapolations of prices is not itself irrational, in spite of the arguments of Weintraub (1983); Blanchard and Watson (1982) provide several counter-examples. What is inexplicable in such a model is why a fold rather than, say, a simple discontinuity appears in the surface as this sort of trading grows. Other catastrophe models contain more explicitly irrational elements. De Grauwe (1983) for example, assumes a particular regressive exchange rate expectations scheme. Ho and Saunders (1980), in their bank failure model, assume arbitrary and inappropriate intervention by the banking authority; Flood and Garber (1981), while not working within a catastrophe theory framework, also characterise bank 'runs' as the consequence of unrealistic pegging of a price or exchange rate by the monetary authority.

The remainder of this section is addressed to the problem of constructing a model of a banking run. As we have seen, this may or may not follow from a financial collapse. It proves possible to characterise these possibilities as the stable and unstable facets of a catastrophe model; but a certain element of arbitrariness (though not irrationality) must be imputed to investors if this interpretation is to stand.

An Uncertainty Model of a Bank Run

We start by outlining the operations of a single financial intermediary ('bank'). Such an institution attracts deposit and capital liabilities (D and K), and invests these in a portfolio consisting of riskless reserves (R) and risky loans (A). The detail of the actual balance sheets of institutions as different as Gurneys (bill brokers) and Barings (merchant bankers) would, of course, reveal very different items within these broad classes of liabilities and assets. Gurneys' deposits consisted mainly of surplus short-term funds placed in the money market by domestic banks; Barings took the funds of non-bank and individual investors. Barings was a family concern until just after the 1890 crisis, and its capital represented the private wealth of the partners; Gurneys became a public company just before the 1866 crisis, and part of its capital was attracted from outside shareholders. The advances made by Gurneys were largely to English industrial and commercial enterprises, on security of their customers' short-term bills. Barings, on the other hand, provided medium-term bond financing, often to public utilities and governments, throughout the industrialising world – Russia, Europe and the Americas. In spite of these differences, the management problems of both types of institution are essentially the same – to maximise profits from the asset portfolio subject to being able to meet deposit withdrawals with a high probability; and to minimise the cost of raising liabilities subject to the need to reduce the probability of insolvency to some low level.

The risks which make it necessary for such banks to hold low-yielding reserve assets and to raise expensive capital liabilities come from random fluctuations in deposit inflows and the value of the stock of advances. The bank will face a liquidity crisis if its reserves are insufficient to cover a deposit withdrawal ($\Delta D > R$). It will actually be insolvent if its capital and income from assets is insufficient to cover interest payments to depositors. Suppose that in some period liabilities to depositors increase by ΔD, and assets' values change by ΔA. Then the bank is insolvent if

$$A + R + \Delta A < D + \Delta D \tag{1}$$

or $(\Delta D - \Delta A) - (A + R - D) > 0$

$$(\Delta D - \Delta A) - K > 0$$

Normalising for size by dividing through by the level of deposits D, and writing $\Delta D/D$ as Δd, $\Delta A/D$ as Δa and K/D as k, this condition becomes

$$\Delta d - \Delta a - k > 0 \tag{2}$$

or $z < 0$

where we define z as the 'safety level' of the bank, where

$$z = k - \Delta d + \Delta a \tag{3}$$

The probability of bankruptcy thus depends on two stochastic factors, the probability distribution of deposit flows and the probability distribution of asset values, and two factors – the reserve and capital ratios – which are decision variables for the bank. For convenience, we assume that d and a have zero mean, so that only their variances enter this calculation. We also assume that banks follow optimal policies with respect to the selection of r and k. This means that reserve and capital ratios depend on deposit and loan variances, and on the costs of emergency borrowing and insolvency (Baltensperger, 1980). Since these costs can be taken to be the same for all banks, differences in the probability of insolvency between banks will be (increasing) functions of the deposit and loan variances only.

Consider now a system of n such banks, ranked from 1 to n in decreasing order of riskiness, so that bank 1 is the riskiest (in terms of its z-value) and bank n the least risky. For simplicity, we also assume that the z values increase uniformly, so that if z_1 is the safety level of the riskiest bank, then the j-th bank will have $z_j = jz_1$. Without loss of generality, we can measure risk in terms of units of size z_1. Consequently, a fall in all asset values of j units will send banks $1, 2 \ldots j$ into insolvency, but banks $j + 1, \ldots n$ will be safe.

Depositors can hold their (liquid) wealth in two forms – as 'riskless' cash, or as deposits in these risky banks. The distribution of this portfolio will depend on depositors *perceptions* of the risks of each bank. An increase in the perceived risk of a single bank will cause deposits to flow out of that bank, an increase in the perceived risk in the whole banking system will cause a general switch from bank deposits into cash. If a bank is perceived to be insolvent *all* deposits will be withdrawn.

A key element of our model is that depositors may have less than complete information on the balance sheets of individual banks. Typically, depositors in banks are numerous, and do not possess even shareholders rights to information; on the other hand, the bank portfolio is often large and complex. Moreover, Leland and Pyle (1977) have suggested that a degree of confidentiality *must* surround bank portfolios, or outsiders could capture the returns to the asset manager's efforts by duplicating his investments. This assumption, of less than complete information, changes radically the impact of a shock to asset values on the banking system.

Consider first the case of complete information. A fall in asset values sufficient to render bank 1 insolvent will have no impact whatsoever on deposits as other banks, irrespective of the size of the shock to bank 1. Conversely, a specific increase in the asset values of a single bank will not cause investors to reappraise the risks of other banks, nor give rise to an expansion of the banking industry through new entry ('negative insolvency'). The relation between the change in the degree of insolvency of bank 1 (z_1) and the degree of insolvency in the system ($z.$) is simply a 45° line, as shown on in the left panel of Figure 2.3.

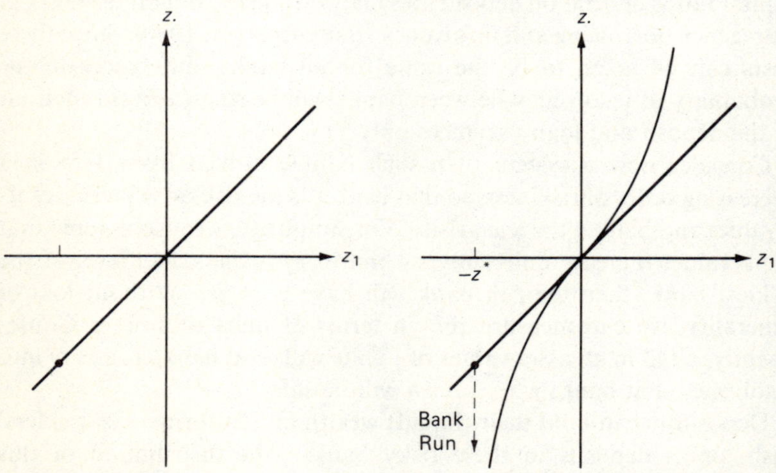

Full Information ($\Theta = 1$) Imperfect Information ($\Theta < 1$)

Key: z_l = *solvency level of bank 1*
$z.$ = solvency levelof banking system

FIG. 2.3 Effect of Bank 1 Insolvency on System Solvency

Consider now a situation where investors are less than fully informed about the individual banks balance sheets for the current year. The depositor can form some estimate of the z-value of each bank on the basis of the limited information which is available about the state of the balance sheet, say $\hat{z}_j = \hat{z}\ (\Omega_j)$. But it will be optimal to use other available information as well. In particular, the z_j estimate can be improved by using information on

– the z-scores of other banks

– the z-scores of other years

We look at the optimal use of each type of information in turn.

If differences in z-scores between neighbouring banks are normal random variates, with equal variances, the optimal estimate of the safety level of bank j will take the form of a weighted average of estimates of safety levels of all other banks in the system, with the weights decreasing exponentially according to how distant the bank is from bank j in the safety rank order. So we might say

$$\hat{z}_j = \lambda_j \sum_{i=1}^{n} (1-\theta)^{|i-j|} . (j/i) \hat{z}_i \quad (4)$$

where λ_j is simply a factor scaling the weights $(1-\theta)^{|i-j|}$ to sum to unity, and the estimated value of each bank i must be multiplied by (j/i) to form an estimate of z_j because of our assumption of uniform differences in risk. The crucial parameter is the discount factor θ. This can take values between 0 and 1, and *serves as an index of the amount of information on the relative safety of banks*. If θ is high, weights decrease quickly as we move away from bank j; because so much is known about individual banks, only the information on banks very similar to bank j are used in assessing its safety. If θ is low, the weights do not fall off so rapidly. Depositors' ignorance of bank performance is so great that even data on banks quite dissimilar from bank j is gratefully seized upon and used in assessing the risk of the bank.

The limiting cases $\theta = 1$ and $\theta = 0$ are of particular interest. When information on the relative standing of banks is complete, $\theta = 1$ and the weights on all z-scores in formula (4) go to zero except that on bank j, which tends to 1. When information on the relative standing of banks is wholly absent, $\theta = 0$ and the weights on all z-scores in formula (4) become the same. As a result the solution of the system of equations (4) will produce identical values of z_j for all values of j; each bank is assumed no better or worse than its neighbour.

The assumption of limited information about relative riskiness is sufficient to induce banking 'runs' in the sense that a given shock to asset values will induce a disproportionate number of bankruptcies. Suppose asset values at bank 1 fall by z^* units. Depositors in all other banks will revise downwards their estimates of the safety of these banks, bank 2 being the worst affected, and bank *n* the least. There will be a general switch from deposits into cash. This may be sufficient to break a number of banks 2, 3, ... *m* which are objectively solvent. A rise in asset values and entry of new banks would, conversely, spread optimism through the system. As a result, the relation between asset shocks and insolvencies and entries under conditions of incomplete information will be more highly geared than in the case of complete information, and will take the form shown in the right panel of Figure 2.3. In the degenerate case of no information on relative bank status ($\theta = 0$), the locus becomes vertical, the failure of bank 1 triggering the failure of *all* banks (which must be assumed to be identical to the failed bank), the survival of bank 1 triggering a flood of new entries. This extreme case of quality uncertainty is the 'lemons' problem discussed in Akerlof (1970),

So far, we have discussed only the contribution of the estimated *z*-scores of other banks to the assessment of the *z*-score of an individual bank. We now consider the contribution of current and past information on the balance sheet of the bank itself. If the *z*-score of a bank follows a random walk around a stochastic 'trend', the optimal forecast of *z* at time *t* is known to be an exponentially weighted average of past values of the variable: thus

$$\hat{z}_t = \varphi \sum_{t=0}^{\infty} (1-\varphi)^t z_{-t}$$

The discount factor in (5) can be shown to depend on the ratio of the variance of the random walk process to the variance of the underlying trend (Muth, 1960). The less unpredictable is the time series, the lower will be φ, and values of *z* from the distant past will be given a substantial weight in the calculation. In the limit, as $\varphi \to 0$, *all* past information, however distant, is given equal weight. The greater is the 'noise' in the series, the higher will be the optimal value of φ, and the less information is there in past values of *z*; only recent safety levels are used to gauge the solvency of the bank. In the limit, as $\varphi \to 1$, only current period information is used, and no regard is paid even to recent safety levels.

The value of φ determines the reaction of *z* to shocks to asset values. Suppose *z* has varied randomly around a constant rate $\bar{z}$ for a long period, so that $\hat{z} = \bar{z}$, but at *t* there are rumours that the bank is slipping into serious insolvency. Clearly $\hat{z}$ will fall, and the extent of the fall will depend on the weight given to recent information. If φ is large, the insolvency will be instantly recognised, and deposits withdrawn. If φ is low, insolvency may not be recognised, and depositors will continue to invest in the bank, though at lower levels. They will be impressed by the bank's 'reputation'. As the insolvency persists, so the perceived safety level of the bank will approach its true, negative value. A recovery in the fortunes of the bank will not necessarily be accompanied by a return of deposits in such circumstances. The longer the period of insolvency and the lower the value of φ, the greater must be the assurances given to depositors before their rating of the bank rises to a positive level.

These persistence effects introduce an asymmetry into the reactions of the banking system as a whole to rising and falling asset values. Imagine that asset values in bank 1 fall in a situation of incomplete information described by a non-zero parameter θ. A number (m) of additional banks will fail. Imagine now that the initiating change in asset values is reversed. The rating of bank 1 will not immediately improve to a solvency level, since its failure has a non-zero weight in perceptions of its current value. This undervaluation of bank 1 will also keep other banks undervalued. Recovery of the whole system can come about only in two ways. One is through the passage of time. Eventually, memories of the bank 1 insolvency will be forgotten, and one by one its neighbouring banks will be reconstituted starting with bank m. Alternatively, bank 1 can be given a positive endowment of assets. For each level of uncertainty θ and each discount factor φ there will be a corresponding change in asset values which will return the whole system to solvency. This endowment must be larger, the larger is θ and the larger is the initial deficit of bank 1. The endowment must also be larger, the smaller is the discount factor φ; if memories are long, it will take a large boost to a bank's assets to restore the confidence of investors.

A similar argument can be made for the case of a rise in the assets of bank 1. This will induce a general revaluation upwards in assessments of bank safety, and induce a number of new entrants to the industry. This boom will continue even if the change in the solvency position of bank 1 is immediately reversed; and it will take time, or a collapse of bank 1, to reduce the system to its original size. These pessimistic and optimistic phases of the system are illustrated in the left and right panels of Figure 2.4, for high discount and low discount cases respectively. The return loci show the system z-scores, and implicitly the

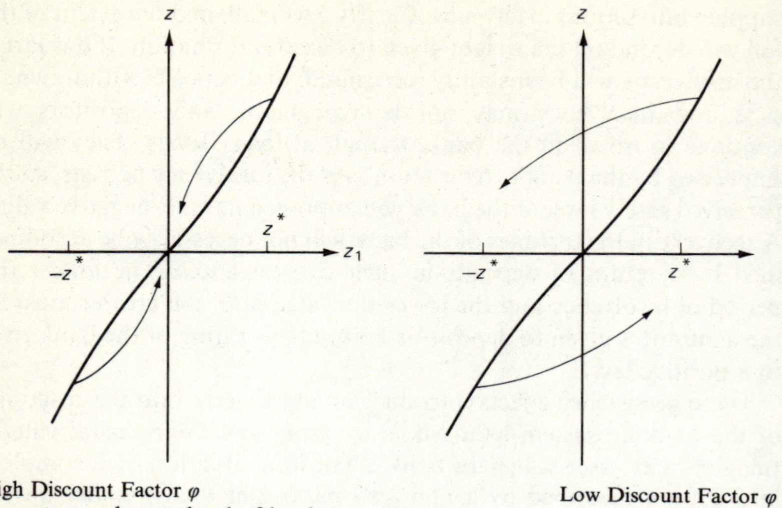

Key: z_1 = solvency level of bank 1
$z.$ = solvency level of banking system

FIG. 2.4 Banking System Insolvency: Alternative Recovery Paths

number of new/failed banks in the system, at various solvency levels of bank 1, in period $t + 1$, following a shock of size z^* to the asset values of bank 1 in period t.

There is an asymmetry in the system, but no genuine catastrophe. No point is reached where the mood of optimism or pessimism is completely broken by the reversal in bank 1's asset position.

In order to generate a catastrophe similar to that of Figure 2.2, we should have to assume that the confidence factor φ was itself a systematic variable. Specifically, for any given disturbance z^* there must be some endowment $k(\theta) z^*$, with $k < 0$ and $k' < 0$, which is sufficient to persuade depositors to forget the track record of the bank. As $z \rightarrow k(\theta) z^*$, then $\varphi \rightarrow 1$; if z exceeds $k(\theta) z^*$ the endowment is treated as a 'new' shock and not only will bank 1 recover but the system will expand through the recovery of confidence in neighbouring banks. The feasible states of the system, $z.$, following a shock z^* to bank 1, may then conceivably be described for all values of the splitting parameter θ by the cusp surface shown on Figure 2.5. The implications of this set-up are spelt out in the next section's discussion of the policy options

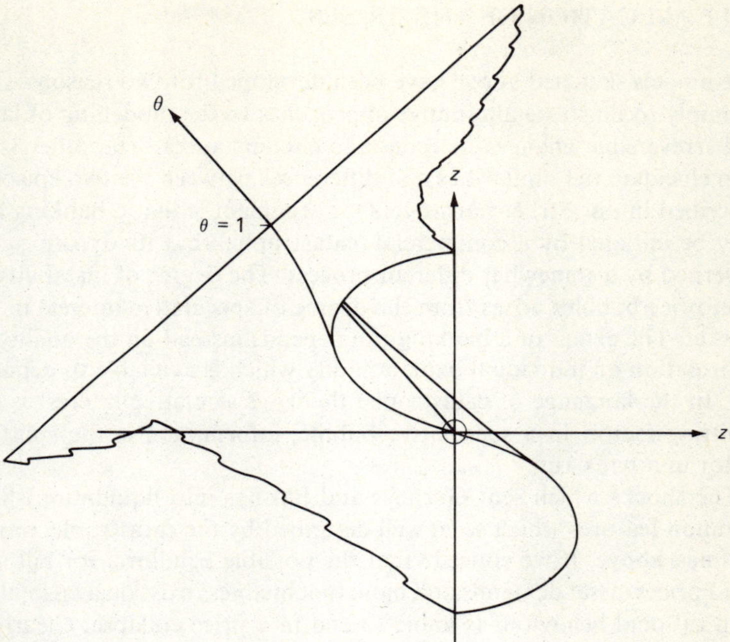

Key: z_1 = solvency level of bank 1
$z.$ = solvency level of banking system
Θ = information parameter

FIG. 2.5 Banking System Recovery Paths: A Catastrophe Representation

considered by the authorities after the Gurney and Baring crises. Before leaving the theory, however, it is worth noting that this catastrophe framework, rather like the catastrophe model of financial crisis described earlier, is the product of two steps. One is an argument based on a rational, optimising behaviour in the face of limited information; this yielded the prediction of a bank run. The other is a somewhat arbitrary argument based on the assertion that there is some shock to the system which will cause it to switch from one state to another, and that the size of this shock depends on the value of the initiating shock, and the information parameter. This may yield the cusp catastrophe. Whether such behaviour occurs in practice is an empirical issue rather than a consequence of *a priori* theorising.

AN EVALUATION OF THE CRISES

The models sketched above have been developed for two reasons. One is simply to illustrate alternative approaches to the modelling of large and irreversible changes in economic circumstances. The other is to help elucidate the similarities and differences between the two episodes described in our earlier narrative. Our argument is that a banking run may be initiated by a commercial 'catastrophe'; but its dynamics are governed by a somewhat different process. The degree of instability in asset price bubbles arises from the degree of speculative interest in the market. The extent of a banking run depends instead on the quality of information on individual bank liquidity which is available to depositors. In the language of catastrophe theory, speculative interest is the 'splitting factor' in a speculative bubble, information is the splitting factor in a bank run.

The shocks which sent Gurneys and Barings into liquidation share common features which seem well described by the catastrophe model outlined above. If we concede that the possible equilibria for bill and bond prices, asset demands and bank indebtedness exist on a cusp, then even rational behaviour is liable to end in a price collapse. Clearly it was rash of the early investors in bubble companies and Argentine mortgages to subscribe to these ventures. Their expectations were over-optimistic. But as long as there is a probability that such expectations are correct, it is rational for other investors to follow. Only after the expectation has been falsified will it cease to make sense, and all investors will sell out; but by this time many quite reputable banks may be involved.

The outcomes of the Gurney and Baring crises differed greatly, and we would argue that these differences can be equally well described in terms of the bank run model described above. The crucial difference between the two crises lay in the amount of information available to the public at large about the relative state of affairs at the respective banks.

Country bankers had no reason to suppose that Gurneys was any better or any worse than any other discount house. Their track record was long and secure. If anything, current rumour made them look better than many other houses in 1865, and their share price reflected this opinion. Only a few insiders in London were privy to the risks run by Gurneys, and these investors withdrew early in the year, and held their tongues for fear of causing mischief until the collapse had occurred. The upshot of this was that when Overend, Gurney failed, country banks had no means of telling whether the problem was specific to Gurneys or widespread through the money market. Their rational reaction was to assume the worst, and withdraw deposits from the whole system, hitting first those which looked – like Gurneys – overexposed in finance security lending. In terms of our model, the value of θ was low, and the size of the run consequently high.

The case of Barings was quite different. The extent of Barings involvement in the Argentine was well known. Summaries of bond issues and the sponsoring banks were published as regularly in *The Economist* through the 1880s as are new international bond issues today. The value of the information parameter θ was high. Only its long history of financial probity, its 'name', prevented its depositors from withdrawing as these assets were accumulated. Because the special position of Barings was well known, there was no mass withdrawal of deposits from private banks when the crisis came. Instead, only those banks known to be most similar to Barings were hit. Muriettas, in particular, suffered badly and finally closed in 1893. Banks with better diversified assets in Europe, North America and North Africa such as Rothschilds, gained rather than lost deposits.

If we regard these events as occurring on a catastrophe surface, we can see from Figure 2.6 that a number of options exist to prevent catastrophe or ameliorate its consequences. Suppose the system is poised on the upper fold of the cusp, at a point such as *a*, where the least suspicion of a fall in bank 1 (= Gurneys' or Barings') assets will cause a run on other banks and a fall to a point such as *b*. The authorities have two options. They can permit the catastrophe to occur, or they can try to maintain confidence in the system. If the first course is followed the extent of losses in the banking system can be reduced by either increasing information about the true (solvent) condition of most banks, or by giving bank 1 an endowment of assets sufficient to restore confidence. These two policies will move the system in the direction shown by the arrows *B*1 and *B*2. If the second course is followed, the authorities must either *decrease* the amount of information in the system (so that less weight is given to adverse rumours about bank 1), or provide direct assistance to bank 1. These policies shift the system in the directions *A*1 and *A*2.

In the Gurney case, the Bank took the first course *B*1. Its willingness to buy the bills of other leading banks and discount houses was a signal to the country banks that, in the Bank's opinion at least, these institutions were fundamentally sound. This is the sense of 'last resort' lending. In principle, the run could have been avoided by making good Gurneys' losses (policy *A*2), and increasing its solvency by an amount

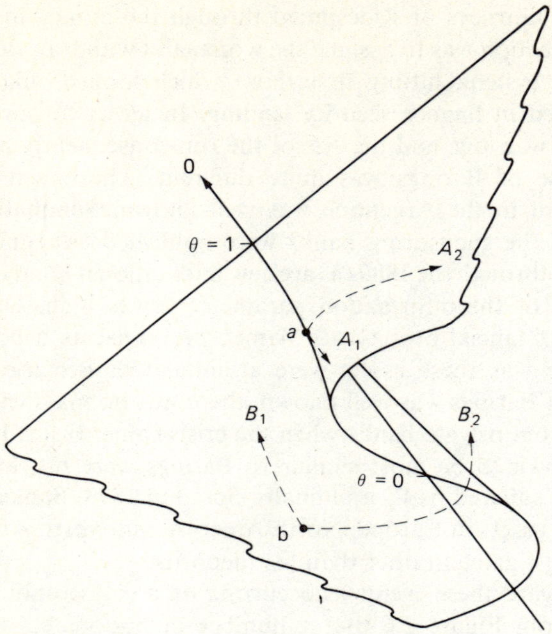

Key: Θ = information parameter
a = pre-catastrophe state
b = post-catastrophe state

FIG. 2.6 The Avoidance of Catstrophe: Policy Alternatives

sufficient to offset the loss in credibility which would follow the disclosure of a decade of reckless management. But this would have been expensive; there would have been no guarantee that the threat of a run would not reappear in the next decade; and the strained relationship between the Bank and Gurneys made such an action in any case unlikely. A third possibility, later pondered by Bagehot, would have been to cover up the Gurney bank's affairs totally, until the new management could recover the losses – in effect, our policy *A*1; but when the bank became public in 1865 that (dubious) option – and the reconstruction option B2 – was renounced.

The Bank's intervention in the Barings crisis is much more enigmatic. Superficially, the granting of an excessively large and long-lived guarantee on the assets of an ailing bank is consistent with the second route out of catastrophe described above (*A*2). On further inspection, it is unclear whether catastrophe was threatened at all. Many early historians of the period (for example, Powell, 1915) emphasise that Barings deficit was much less than that of Gurneys, and amounted to a liquidity crisis rather than genuine insolvency. Although there is something in this argument, it seems to be based on a comparison of the assets of the two banks at liquidation. It must be remembered that for this purpose Barings was allowed to write off a large capital loss, and was given a very favourable value for its surviving Argentine bonds. If true, of course, this argument vitiates the case for any *long-term* support at all for the bank, and puts into doubt the need for the monetary authority to organise further lending. Let us, however, grant that there was a potential insolvency at Barings; would this have triggered a banking run? Our reading of public reaction to the crisis is that catastrophe probably did not threaten, since the system was well informed about the relative risks being run by the major merchant banks. In terms of our catastrophe model the value of θ was high. This, of course, would vitiate *any* case for a large-scale support operation for the weakest bank.

The actions of the Bank of England in the Baring crises seem instead to have been motivated less by a desire to make the banking system secure than by a desire to save the 'name' of Barings itself. This is the only explanation for the scale and time span of the assistance given, for the appointment of auditors for Barings who were bound to produce a favourable report, and for the haste which was made in the Rothschild committee to roll over the whole Argentinian debt. There may have seemed good reasons for helping Barings' name survive. But the name of Barings was no more nor less reputable in the country than that of Gurneys before their collapse, and it is hard to resist the conclusion that it was the difference in political and personal relations between these institutions and the officials of the Bank of England which determined who should sink and who should swim.

NOTES

1. *The Economist*, 15 July 1865, p. 845.
2. *The Economist*, 19 May 1866, p. 1516.
3. *Bankers' Magazine*, June 1866, pp. 45–6.
4. *The Economist*, 19 May 1866, p. 1516.
5. Cited in Powell (1915), p. 340.
6. *Bankers' Magazine*, March 1981, p. 619.

REFERENCES

Akerlof, G. A. (1970) 'The market for "lemons"; quality uncertainty and the market mechanism', *Quarterly Journal of Economics* 89: 488–500.

Balasko, Y. (1978) 'The behaviour of economic equilibria: a catastrophe theory approach', *Behavioural Science* 23: 375–82.

Baltensperger, E. (1980) 'Alternative approaches to the theory of the banking firm', *Journal of Monetary Economics* 6: 1–37.

Blanchard, O. J. and Watson, M. W. (1982) 'Bubbles, rational expectations and financial markets', in P. Wachtel (ed.) *Crises in the Economic and Financial Structure* (New York: Lexington Books).

Fisher, I. (1933) 'The debt-deflation theory of great depressions', *Econometrica* 1: 337–57.

Flood, R. P. and Garber, P. (1981), 'A systematic banking collapse in a perfect foresight world', NBER Working Paper 691.

de Grauwe, P. A. (1983) 'Exchange rate oscillations and catastrophe theory', in E. Claasen and Salin, P. (eds) *Recent Issues in the Theory of Flexible Exchange Rates* (Amsterdam: North-Holland).

George, P. (1981) 'Equilibrium and catastrophes in economics', *Scottish Journal of Political Economy*, 28, 1: 43–61.

Ho, T. and Saunders, A. (1980), 'A catastrophe model of bank failure', *Journal of Finance*, 35, 5, December: 1189–1207.

Kindleberger, C. P. (1978) *Manias, Panics and Crashes: A History of Financial Crises* (London: Macmillan).

Leland, H. and Pyle, D. (1977) 'Information asymmetries, financial structure and financial intermediation', *Journal of Finance* 32: 321–86.

Minsky, H. P. (1977) 'A theory of systematic fragility', in E. I. Altman and A. W. Sametz (eds), *Financial Crises* (New York: Wiley).

Muth, J. F. (1960) 'Optimal properties of exponentially weighted forecasts', *Journal of the American Statistical Association* 55.

Poston, T. and Stewart, I. (1978) *Catastrophe Theory and its Applications* (London: Pitman).

Powell, E. T. (1915) *The Evolution of the Money Market 1385–1915* (London: Frank Cass, 1966, 3rd impression).

Saunders, P. T. (1980) *An Introduction to Catastrophe Theory* (Cambridge: Cambridge University Press).

Schott, K. (1983) 'The British financial crisis in 1974–5: a catastrophe theory approach', *Oxford Economic Papers*.

Sussman, H. J. and Zahler, R. S. (1978) 'A critique of applied catastrophe theory in the behavioural sciences', *Behavioural Science* 23: 383–9.

Thom, R. (1972) *Structural Stability and Morphogenesis* (New York: Benjamin; translated version, 1975).

Varian H. R. (1979) 'Catastrophe theory and the business cycle', *Economic Inquiry* 17: 14–28.

Weintraub, E. R. (1983) 'Zeeman's unstable stock exchange'. *Behavioural Science* 28: 39–83.

Woodcock, A. and Davis, M. (1978) *Catastrophe Theory* (Harmondsworth: Pelican Books).

Zeeman, E. C. (1974) 'On the unstable behaviour of stock exchanges', *Journal of Mathematical Economics* 1: 39–49.

Zeeman, E. C. (1977) *Catastrophe Theory: Selected Papers 1972–1977.* (Reading, Mass.: Addison-Wesley).

In addition to the above journal references, the histories of Overend, Gurney & Co. and Baring Bros & Co. have been pieced together from contemporary accounts in *The Economist* and the *Bankers Magazine*. Additional material on the history and performance of Gurneys came from the summing up of Sir Richard Malins *In re Overend, Gurney and Co. ex parte Oakes and Parke*, Law Reports (Chancery) Vol. III 1866–7; and from Sir John Clapham (1970) *The Bank of England: A History* vol. 2 (Cambridge University Press) and F. W. Fetter (1965) *Development of British Monetary Orthodoxy* (Harvard UP) On Barings, Clapham (1970) and L. S. Presnell (1968) 'Gold flows, banking reserves and the Baring crisis of 1890', in Whittlesley, C. R. and Wilson, J. S. G. (eds) *Essays in Money and Banking in honour of R. S. Sayers* (Oxford University Press) were also helpful.

The Avoidance of Catastrophe: Two Nineteen-century Crises – Comment

L. S. PRESSNELL

It was a splendid inspiration to use catastrophe theory to illuminate two of the most remarkable crises of the nineteenth century. It is a pity, however, that at the end of a pioneering paper the author unnecessarily pulled out the rug from under his arguments. The non-numerate explanations he finally offers for the different Bank of England behaviour in the respective crises are inadequate, and in any case are not required. In terms of the author's equations, he implies that there was a low value in 1866 for θ, the discount factor which 'serves as an index of the amount of information on the relative safety of banks' (p. 69). He infers, therefore, that the failure of Overend, Gurney was, *ceteris paribus*, likely to induce a general run on banks. In contrast, he detects a high value for θ in 1890, so that the failure of Baring Brothers was less likely to have set off a bank run. It is to explain the Bank of England's refusal to save Overend's in 1866, whereas the Bank helped to rescue Baring Brothers in 1890, that he adduces political and personal factors. A closer look at the historical record may, however, suggest *low* values of θ in *both* crises. In that case, a money market collapse lying ahead would both in 1866 and 1890 have justified central bank action. A comparison of four particular aspects of the two crises seems to support that judgement.

First, the two crises posed the classic hazards: that a liquidity run arising for one reason (domestic drain 1866, foreign drain 1890) will, if handled unsuccessfully, lead to an intensified drain from elsewhere (foreign drain 1866, domestic drain 1890). The lender-of-last-resort will want to stop whatever drain occurs; it is easier to stop a domestic drain since it can create new domestic liquidity, whereas the foreign drain may be unstoppable if gold or other international means of payment are being demanded. In 1866, the domestic drain had to be checked lest it provoke a foreign drain (and there was indeed much unease abroad following the crisis), but Overend, Gurney was not an international finance house, so that there was no symbolism to be preserved by propping it up. In 1890, however, the direct danger was of a foreign drain: the collapse of confidence in sterling that, like a kind of anticipated 1931, had been feared increasingly by the Bank of England as it had watched the growth of banks of all sorts apparently outstripping its own capacity to influence them.

A second difference concerns the vulnerability of the Bank's gold reserves. They were desperately low in relation to legal requirements in 1866. Although stronger, apparently, in 1890, the great increase of foreign banking in London by then made the reserves more liable to be run down.

A third point, again external, is that the relationship between London money market rates and those of financial centres overseas seems to have become less predictable, in the context of contemporary amateurism no doubt, in the later nineteenth century. A high Bank rate could be expected to hold foreign money in 1866, judging by the previous trend of London–Paris rates. By 1890, it is difficult to see much stability in relationships between London on the one hand, and Paris, Berlin, and New York on the other. But one must also recognise two domestic constraints on higher interest rates in 1890, when Bank rate rose only to 6 per cent, compared with the 10 per cent of 1866. First, in 1888, the Chancellor of the Exchequer, G. J. Goschen, had launched the great conversion of 3 per cent Consols towards an eventual (coupon) yield of 2½ per cent. It is quite clear that he would have regarded extremely high rates as an unwelcome threat to 'Goschens' as the new Consols were known. A second hindrance to using high rates was simply that the classical era of Bank rate had not yet arrived. For about two decades, the Bank had been making greater use of open market operations than previously; this reflected the Bank's efforts to influence the market more systematically than by being a remote discount window.

Finally, a fourth aspect of the two crises is the need in both cases to maintain liquidity, albeit for somewhat different reasons. In 1866, it was the money market in general that was at hazard, whereas in 1890 it was the specific status of the bill on London, and the name of one its leading acceptors in particular, Baring Brothers.

In all this, the unmeasured variable in the equations is the significance of the Bank of England. Its policy simply cannot be treated as consistent or as gradually evolving, or as predictable. Governors served a two-year term, with rare exceptions; most were undistinguished, some downright weak, and occasionally – fortunately with William Lidderdale in 1890 – outstanding. In terms of specific policy attitudes, after the crisis of 1857, which had done no good to the reputation of discount houses, the Bank sought to keep at arm's length from them; its behaviour in 1866 must be seen partly in that light. Compare the position in 1890: a few months before the crisis, the Bank had at last reversed the post-1857 isolationism of its money market policies, in order to be in more regular contact with day to day transactions.

The equations of Roy Batchelor seem to need, in addition to lower θ values, at least two additional variables. One would take account of the relative strength of the threat, from internal and external drains, to the gold reserves. The other would encompass expectations, gloomy in 1866, less so in 1890, of the probability of Bank of England action to help financial institutions in difficulties. This second matter brings us back to the historical issue raised by the author: was the help received by Baring Brothers from the Bank exceptional and privileged? Without suggesting that the Bank's lifeboat was always at sea, have historians and others realised that it was launched quite frequently, long before the 1970s? Moreover, it took a little over four years to row Barings to safety: a remarkably short trip, compared with earlier and later rescue missions.

There is one extremely important, but often neglected, consideration with which to conclude these essentially appreciative comments on Batchelor's paper. The Bank of England, with other City institutions, successfully forestalled what could have been an open crisis of great severity in 1890. The Bank was still a private shareholders' bank. It had to safeguard that status. It had remarkably little scope in its balance sheet for massive rescue work, and there was at best only limited emergency help to be expected from overseas institutions. The problem is less that the Bank let Overend, Gurney go in 1866 and saved Barings in 1890 than that it managed with limited resources for so long; and there is an associated problem, of how the merchant and clearing banks, and the discount houses, themselves lessened their own vulnerability to the sort of catastrophes of which 1866 was the last real example in British monetary history.

3 The Summer of 1914[1]

TERESA SEABOURNE

INTRODUCTION

Although the Balkan Wars had created much political unrest in Europe, international tension was not appreciably higher in June 1914 than it had been at any time since the Agadir crisis in 1911. There had been forty years of growth since the Franco-Prussian War and nearly a century since any general European war. In Britain, the chief political concern centred on the problem of civil unrest in Ireland rather than European affairs, while in the financial world, it was very much business as usual in June 1914.

Then, on 29 June, political tension increased dramatically with the assassination of the heir to the Austrian throne. Even so, the full gravity of this event was not generally realised until a month later when Austria sent her ultimatum to Serbia on 24 July. From that moment, war between Austria and Serbia appeared inevitable, and this, together with the fear that hostilities would spread throughout Europe, produced a major financial crisis involving the complete collapse of international credit.[2]

The financial implications of war were first felt throughout the world's stock exchanges, where heavy selling in internationally traded securities caused prices to plummet.

As political tension mounted, sales increased and this in turn began to produce erratic fluctuations in the foreign exchanges beyond the normal export/import specie points. Within a matter of days one foreign Bourse after another ceased trading, exchange rates became purely nominal and the whole system of international remittance, and hence international credit, fell into paralysis.

In Britain, the financial consequences of a pending European conflict placed the London Stock Exchange under great pressure during the last two weeks of July. Of even greater concern, however, owing to Britain's position as the great international creditor, was the foreign exchange situation, since it was becoming apparent that foreign borrowers would be unable to remit in time to the London acceptance houses. With the declaration of war between Austria and Serbia on Tuesday, 28 July a rush for liquidity began. The banks started to call in loans from the Stock Exchange and discount market, further weakening the former and forcing the latter to the Bank of England for assistance. In response Bank rate was raised from 3 per cent to 4 per cent on Thursday, 30 July. With the mobilisation of German, Russian and French troops the financial situation rapidly deteriorated. On Friday, 31 July the London Stock Exchange followed the example of the foreign Bourses and closed its doors, Bank rate was raised to 8 per cent and then to the crisis level of 10 per cent the following day. Also on the Friday and Saturday, the financial situation was causing something of a panic among the general public, largely on account of the banks which, fearing an internal drain on their gold reserves, refused to pay out gold to their customers.

On Sunday, 2 August military action escalated with the formal declaration of war between Russia and Germany. Fortunately for Britain, the full financial implications of this were averted, because Monday, 2 August was a Bank Holiday. Clearly, however, the crisis could not be left to run its course and government interventicn was needed to alleviate the situation. To provide further room for manoeuvre the Bank Holiday was extended for three days and to relieve the acceptance houses from their immediate difficulties a moratorium on bills of exchange was proclaimed.[3] While financiers were engaged in frantic discussions throughout the prolonged Bank Holiday, Britain declared war against Germany at 12.00 a.m. on Wednesday, 5 August.

On 6 August, the main measures to deal with the crisis had been decided. A general moratorium was proclaimed, the 1844 Bank Act was suspended, Bank rate was reduced to 6 per cent and £1 and 10s. Treasury notes were to be issued. When the banks reopened on Friday, 7 August fears of an internal currency crisis proved unfounded and Bank rate was further reduced to 5 per cent the following day. Problems in the bill market, however, remained and had to be dealt with by direct government assistance, plans for which were announced on 13 August and 5 September.

The crisis itself had thus come and gone within a matter of days. Although the events of the crisis and the measures introduced to deal with them were not without their repercussions, the main focus of attention shifted to the central issue of how to finance the war.

To understand financial behaviour during the summer of 1914, financial and institutional conditions prior to the crisis cannot be ignored. The second section is therefore devoted to reviewing the dominant financial issue at the time, namely the controversy surrounding the adequacy of British gold reserves. This debate is important since it had a bearing on the behaviour of the banks during the crisis and the subsequent measures introduced to deal with the crisis.

In the third section the first phase of the crisis is examined. The close connection between political and financial events are stressed and the reason why Britain was militarily, but not financially, prepared for war is explained by drawing a distinction between risk and uncertainty. The events leading up to the closure of the Stock Exchange, the failure of international remittance and the internal currency problems are considered in detail. Finally in this section, the reaction of the banking sector to the crisis is assessed from both a macroeconomic and microeconomic perspective.

In the fourth section, the discussions that took place between the various financial interests of the City during the extended Bank Holiday are reviewed. During this phase of the crisis a clear distinction is drawn between internal and external currency demand and the appropriate measures needed to deal with these separate problems discussed.

The fifth section deals with the third phase of the crisis, after the Bank Holiday, when the effectiveness of the measures introduced could be assessed. That such measures proved ineffective in reviving the bill market is evident from the fact that additional assistance had to be afforded to the money market on 13 August and 5 September. The inflationary consequences of these subsequent measures are considered and possible alternatives discussed.

The sixth section concludes the chapter by reviewing the role of government intervention in the crisis and its effect on future expectations for assistance.[4]

THE CONTROVERSY OVER GOLD RESERVES

In 1914 some rivalry still existed between the various financial institutions of the City, especially between the Bank of England and the joint stock banks. The growth of joint stock banking throughout Britain[5] and especially in London after 1833[6] may have promoted competition and efficiency, but it also created much tension, since the Bank of England, obliged to perform certain public duties, could not match the dividends paid out by other banks. In turn, the joint stock banks were suspicious of the Bank. They had not forgotten the Baring crisis, when, at the request of the Governor, they had increased their balances at the Bank of England, only to discover later that the Bank had used these funds to compete with them in the discount market. This rivalry resulted in a certain lack of co-operation which had important implications for the 1914 crisis, as reflected in the banks' behaviour and the various arguments and proposals put forward to remedy the crisis.

In 1913, relationships in the City suffered a setback with the revival of an old debate concerning the adequacy of Britain's gold reserves. This issue had been continually canvassed by bankers, economists, journalists and politicians for over twenty years. Each time Britain faced the possibility of an external drain (as in 1891 and 1907 due to financial crisis, and in 1899 and 1913 because of political hostilities abroad), the adequacy of central gold reserves at the Bank of England came under critical review. The Bank of England, however, as a private profit-making institution, was naturally unwilling to bear the costs of keeping an increased gold reserve. In a farewell speech to the representatives of the London clearing bankers on 6 February 1913, the Governor of the Bank of England, A. C. Cole, tried to persuade the banks themselves to increase their balances at the Bank. He argued that the Bank had significantly increased its proportion of gold reserves to liabilities from 44.2 per cent in 1892 to 47.8 per cent in 1912, representing a 42 per cent increase in gold reserves over the past twenty years[7] and asked whether the banks had done the same.[8]

According to Sir. Edward Holden, chairman of the London City and Midland Bank, it was in response to Coles' question that the representatives of the London clearing banks decided to revive their secret Gold Reserve Committee,[9] the minutes of which have recently become available in the Midland Bank Archives.[10] Between 7 May 1913 and 22 July 1914 the secret committee,[11] under the chairmanship of Sir Felix Schuster, met eight times to discuss the adequacy of British gold reserves and formulate proposals for increasing the reserve. The Bank of England was invited to join the committee but declined to do so, much to the annoyance of the bankers.

The Gold Reserve Committee was of the opinion that when compared with other countries and the past, British gold reserves were too small in absolute size and in relation to transactions.[12] This, they argued, caused large fluctuations in the discount rate to the detriment of British trade.[13]

That central gold reserves were inadequate was a view shared by many bankers, who, as a consequence, had been accumulating private gold reserves of their own. Since the banks did not publish details of their individual gold reserves, the total amount of gold so held has previously been a matter of conjecture.[14] The Gold Reserve Committee did, however, collect data on the gold reserves held by forty-six banks in England and Wales. Although separate figures for each bank have not survived, the minutes of this committee reveal that the total gold reserves of these forty-six banks amounted to £34 824 145 on 28 May 1913. At the same time, total deposits stood at £805 385 157. Although this represents an average gold holding against deposits of 4.30 per cent this proportion varied considerably between the banks from 8.24 per cent to 0.25 per cent (see Table 3.1 for further details). The average amount of gold to deposits held by the clearing banks was 4.85 per cent.[15]

TABLE 3.1 RATIO OF GOLD TO DEPOSITS HELD BY 46 BANKS ON 28 MAY 1913

5 banks held between	5%	and	8.25%	gold to deposits.
6 ,, ,, ,,	4%	,,	5%	,, ,, ,,
6 ,, ,, ,,	3%	,,	4%	,, ,, ,,
11 ,, ,, ,,	2.5%		3%	,, ,, ,,
4 ,, ,, ,,	2%	,,	2.5%	,, ,, ,,
9 ,, ,, ,,	1%	,,	2%	,, ,, ,,
5 ,, ,, ,,	0.25%	,,	1%	,, ,, ,,

Source: Minutes of the secret Gold Reserve Committee, Midland Bank Archives, Ref. ACC 158/1.

In March 1914, the total amount of gold held by the same banks (reduced in number to forty-two through merger) had fallen slightly to £33 588 073 while total deposits had risen to £830 830 428. The proportion of gold to deposits had therefore fallen slightly to 4.04 per cent but still varied considerably between the banks from 6.34 per cent to 0.33 per cent, with the clearing banks retaining a high ratio at 4.69 per cent. Since the committee was of the opinion that these private gold reserves were inadequate to support the volume of deposits they declined to publish their findings, recommending in secret that each bank should top-up its gold reserve to a level equal to 5 per cent of its deposits.[16]

Having made this recommendation the committee then went on to consider how this gold might be used to strengthen the central reserve during a crisis.[17] They were concerned that a hostile nation might use its holding of bills on London to deplete gold reserves and precipitate a financial crisis.[18] To meet such a crisis, Holden proposed a scheme (modelled on German banking practice) whereby the banks could obtain emergency currency from the Bank of England in exchange for deposits of an equivalent amount, comprising one-third in gold and two-thirds in bills. Such a scheme, argued Holden, would not only provide the Bank with additional gold to meet an external drain but would also provide the banks with the necessary currency to meet any internal demands.[19]

The committee's views and proposals were relayed to W. Cunliffe, the new Governor of the Bank of England, who, reported Schuster, strongly criticised and disagreed with them.[20] This prompted Holden to request Lloyd George, the Chancellor of the Exchequer, to appoint a Royal Commission to investigate the gold reserve question. Lloyd George in turn requested the view of the Treasury and of Sir George Paish, the Government's statistical adviser.

The Treasury expressed total opposition to the bankers' proposal and dismissed the need to appoint a Royal Commission, arguing that the banks would be better advised to keep their gold reserves during an emergency, in order to meet customer demands, rather than exchange gold for notes at the Bank.[21] Sir George Paish *per contra* showed some sympathy towards the bankers' proposal and favoured the appointment of a Royal Commission.[22] Perhaps the most informative opinion came from Keynes who, commenting on the Treasury view, noted that the real question was not about the size of gold reserves, but where the centre of power in the London money market should lie.[23]

This then, with no financial emergency plan ready, was the state of affairs when the crisis hit London.

FIRST PHASE OF THE CRISIS

Describing the financial crisis at the beginning of the First World War, Withers (1915) writes, 'it came upon us like a thunderbolt from a clear sky . . . no credit system could have stood up to the events'; a statement which reflected the sentiments of most contemporary financiers and journalists. Exactly why the crisis took the City by surprise, given the political unrest in Europe, is a question which raises a number of issues concerning the role of expectations.

First, was a large-scale European war actually anticipated in 1914; secondly, if the possibility of war was anticipated, then was its occurrence expected to disrupt financial markets; thirdly; was the likely severity of this disruption fully appreciated? These questions are especially important given the fact that the crisis developed in London before Britain entered the war, and indeed even before a single shot had been fired in Europe.

To answer these questions it is necessary to take the existing financial and political situation into account and to draw a distinction between expectations, anticipations, uncertainty and risk. Since financial markets respond to political events and since political relations in Europe were tense, then a war and financial crisis may have been expected to occur at some future date, but because the occurrence of such an event was so uncertain it was not actually anticipated in the sense that no actions were taken to mitigate the financial risks involved.

Here Knight's (1921) distinction between risk and uncertainty is important. Risk, he argues, emerges when outcomes differ from their expected values with a known or calculable probability, whereas uncertainty arises when the distribution of outcomes is subject to unpredictable change and therefore unknown. Hence economic agents can prepare themselves for risk but not uncertainty. Since financial markets were not prepared for the crisis we can associate this with uncertainty. Keynes also makes the distinction between risk and uncertainty using a rather apt example. Speaking of uncertainty Keynes says, 'The sense in which I use the term is that in which the prospect of a European War is uncertain . . . about such matters there is no scientific basis on which to form any calculable probability whatever. We simply do not know.'[24] Keynes argued that in practice people have no choice but to ignore uncertainty and act 'as if' the distribution of expected outcomes is fixed.

Like uncertainty, expectations refer to future events about which we necessarily lack knowledge. People form expectations about uncertain future events over which they have little if any control. In economics, expectations are only relevant if they lead to anticipations, anticipations being actions taken now because something is expected to happen in the future. Expectations need not, however, lead to anticipations. Hence in 1914 people may have formed expectations about the possibility of a war and crisis, but because of uncertainty, did not actually anticipate and plan for its occurrence. As Keynes suggests, they effectively had no option but to ignore the possibility.

At first this argument does not seem tenable, since although financially unprepared for war, the great European states, including Britain, were militarily prepared,[25] each having expanded their military strength significantly since 1911.[26] In retrospect this may look like preparations for war but, as with the current arms race, was more likely at the time to be regarded by each nation as a defensive measure, designed to prevent a foreign invasion, along the lines of the now familiar deterrence argument. Also like today, Britain's own military expenditure[27] was regarded as a response to the arms build-up abroad rather than in anticipation of a pending war. From contemporary journals it is apparent that the growth in military expenditure did cause concern, not because of its threat to peace but because of its effect on the economy. Some, citing Germany as evidence,[28] argued that it stimulated growth, while others, based on John Stuart Mill's productive – unproductive capital theory, argued that it would eventually depress the economy.[29] Again it is interesting to note that similar arguments still exist today.[30] While the military build-up made war more feasible, it did not make it inevitable. Indeed, some writers argued that the armaments would never be used since no country could ever make a material gain from waging war on another due to the enormous capital wastage involved.[31] Doubtless this was a powerful and persuasive argument which did much to dampen expectations regarding the likelihood of war at the time.

There had been a number of dangerous incidents in Europe since the Agadir crisis, making war in 1914 no more probable than before. As previously mentioned, Britain was preoccupied with the Irish problem, while on European affairs Lloyd George delivered a reassuring speech in early July saying that 'there are always clouds on the international horizon', but that we could 'pull through the difficulties' which were 'no greater than those of a year ago'.[32] A. J. P. Taylor's remark that 'no war is inevitable until it breaks out',[33] can be applied to public opinion in 1914. There was a genuine belief that war in Europe could be avoided or at least contained between Austria and Serbia. A large-scale war was certainly not anticipated while British neutrality was assumed guaranteed since she was not bound by treaty to any other country.

When the British fleet was put on alert on 26 July *The Economist* termed such preparations as 'deplorable', arguing that the country would only support 'strict neutrality'.[34] Just three days before Britain entered the war Cunliffe told Lloyd George that 'the financial and trading interests of the City were totally opposed to our intervening in the war'.[35]

However, the structure of international credit was such that the crisis would have affected Britain even if she had remained neutral. Indeed, it was evident before the war that the financial institutions in London could not insulate themselves from the financial breakdown abroad. This, however, had not been generally appreciated. From the gold reserve controversy we know that bankers did anticipate a financial crisis if Britain went to war and they had accordingly formulated proposals for protecting gold reserves against an external drain by a hostile nation. Theirs was the only resemblance of an emergency plan available at the time. With the benefit of hindsight it may appear negligent that the Bank of England had not been instructed or thought it expedient to make any preparations for the strain of war. At the same time, two important considerations must be taken into account. First, if a European war was not anticipated, then neither was the need for an emergency plan and second, it was probably not clear to the authorities what type of emergency measures were required.

On the first point, the growth in international trade and credit had led to the realisation that a war would create disastrous financial disruption in general terms. This realisation itself had led to a certain complacency amongst traders and financiers that the very horror of such an event would act as a guarantee against its occurrence.[36] To understand this attitude, reference to Keynes' analysis on the weight of a probability is useful. Keynes, in his *Treatise on Probability* (1921, part 1, ch. 6, pp. 77–85), describes the weight of a probability as the degree of belief assigned to a particular outcome. As evidence accumulates and people gain confidence in their beliefs, but believe that an event is less probable, the weight increases as the probability of the event declines. A person who becomes almost certain that an event will not occur, places a high weight on a very low probability. Hence, in 1914, people were certain that a war would precipitate a financial crisis and therefore placed a high weight on this probability, but the probability of such an event actually occurring was considered so low as to make it very improbable, if not uncertain.[37]

On the second issue, the severity of the crisis and its actual effect on financial markets had not been expected since there was no historical precedent upon which to base such expectations. The last serious financial crisis in Britain, demanding of emergency measures, occurred in 1866. Since then international trade and finance had grown in extent and complexity. Sterling was a currency of unquestionable strength, with Britain supplying nearly half the world's long-term foreign investment and some two-thirds of total short-term trade credit via the bill of exchange. In many respects, the activities of the London money market and the pursuit of stable financial conditions abroad reinforced one another, since it was far easier for the London houses to extend trade credit when operating in a stable environment where uncertainty about the future could be reduced to a minimum.

In July 1914, the growing threat of war destroyed this stability. Yet as Keynes (1914b) notes, it had not been generally realised that one of the first effects of war would be the complete collapse of international credit, which was based on a comparatively small quantity of gold, of which only a fraction could be mobilised for actual payment. The continuance of the flow of international payments therefore depended on a substantial maintenance of the volume of international credit. Credit itself, however, depends on the assumption that goods produced will come to market and sums owed repayed. War weakened this assumption. The London money market, uncertain whether foreign clients would be able to remit existing sums, was naturally unwilling to extend fresh credits.

The actual failure of remittance – the root cause of the crisis – deserves further attention. Basically, the normal channels of remittance, namely the shipment of goods or gold, the sale of securities and the discounting of bills of exchange, were all rendered inoperative by the outbreak of war. The shipment of goods, besides being too slow to help out in a crisis, became prohibitively expensive because of rising insurance costs[38] and extremely hazardous due to enemy action. Gold shipments, while open to similar difficulties, were further hampered by the announcement of gold export embargoes in a number of countries.[39] Although the beginning of the crisis was marked by heavy security sales, the closure of all principal stock exchanges rendered further sales impossible while the most common means of remittance, namely the granting of new bills of exchange, was frustrated by London's unwillingness to extend fresh credits. In addition to these factors, some foreign clients, under the protection of moratoria in their own countries,[40] temporarily postponed repayment, while after 5 August sums owed by enemy debtors had to be indefinitely written off. In other cases, the movement in foreign exchange rates which, with the exception of France, all swung in Britain's favour, made it extremely difficult and expensive for foreign clients to remit.

For one reason or another, therefore, even solvent foreign debtors were prevented from remitting what they owed, placing those sections of the London money market which financed or guaranteed such credit in danger of insolvency. This actual course of events had not been anticipated or even generally expected, although there is some evidence to suggest that Cole did contemplate such an outcome and had relayed his fears to Holden sometime after mid-May 1914. Holden, in turn, had relayed them to the Gold Reserve Committee.[41] Cole's remarks, however, do not appear to have prompted any debate on the subject, the bankers being too preoccupied with the gold reserve issue. In retrospect, given the timing of Cole's warning, it is doubtful whether any constructive steps could have been taken to prevent or mitigate the effects of war on the bill market, even if the need to do so had been anticipated at the time. That this outcome had not been previously anticipated reflects the fact that forming expectations about uncertain future events is not costless, and hence there must presumably be some reward for correctly anticipating the future. Exactly how this can be achieved in a world of fixed contracts is not clear.

To summarise the arguments so far, although financial disruption was expected to accompany a European war and while the bankers at least had anticipated a crisis if Britain became involved, the war itself had not been anticipated in July 1914, nor had the severity of the crisis that developed before hostilities began. These arguments have important implications for the treatment of expectations and uncertainty in economics. If economic agents form expectations 'rationally', using all the available past information at their disposal, and act 'as if' their subjective probabilities are identical to the distribution of outcomes, then they would not have been led to anticipate a large-scale European war or severe international financial crisis in July 1914 since the necessary information, on which to base such expectations, was simply not available from past experience. Once we move from a stationary to a non-stationary world the future becomes subject to change that cannot be foreseen or predicted from the distribution of past outcomes. In addition, the close connection between political events and the behaviour of financial markets means that the former cannot be ignored in economic analysis. If, as Turner (1970) suggests, the First World War was a result of a series of tragic political miscalculations, it is difficult to see how the assumption of rationality in economic behaviour can be reconciled with the seemingly irrational and erratic behaviour in politics.

The first sign that any vague expectations about the probability of war were turning into actual anticipations came from an increased level of activity on the world's stock exchanges. During July, as relations between Austria and Serbia deteriorated, so the probability of war increased and once this outcome became more certain, so people could begin to calculate and thus prepare themselves for the financial risks involved. This they did by selling vast quantities of internationally traded securities. On Friday, 24 July Austria's ultimatum to Serbia, which coincided with the rumour that contango facilities[42] had been withdrawn, produced something of a panic. A large number of investors was reported as giving orders to 'sell at any price' and this produced the largest fall in international quotations since 1895.[43]

By Thursday, 30 July all the principal Bourses with the exception of London, New York and the official Paris Parquet had been forced to close.[44] Their closure brought a torrent of foreign sales on the London Stock Exchange where, of course, it still remained possible to obtain sterling through the sale of securities. That this happened is evident from the fact that the foreign exchanges moved in Britain's favour, suggesting that investors preferred to hold their sale proceeds in sterling rather than convert them into their own currencies. During the last week of July the volume of sales on the London Stock Exchange caused prices to plummet. Between 20 July and 30 July the value of 387 representative securities fell by a record £187 992 000 or some 5.6 per cent.[45] A fall of 5.6 per cent in just ten days was very substantial when compared with the normal monthly movement in quotations (prices fell by just 0.67 per cent over the previous thirty days), and came at a time when the market was already depressed. (See Table 3.2 for a comparison of monthly price movements.)

The London Stock Exchange began to show signs that it could not take the strain. Wednesday, 29 July was settlement day[46] and by tacit agreement jobbers in every part of the exchange declined to deal and in some cases refused even to quote nominal prices.[47] The previous day had seen one failure and Wednesday witnessed seven more. On Thursday, 30 July, the failure of an important firm, Messrs Derenburg & Co., which was largely concerned with business in Germany, brought home to members of the Stock Exchange the gravity of the situation. The Stock Exchange Committee met on Thursay afternoon and again the following morning to discuss what measures should be taken to prevent further failures. Concerned with the probable need to postpone the mid-August settlement and with the advisability of publishing official quotations in nominal prices, they decided to take the unprecedented step of closing the Stock Exchange on Friday, 31 July. This

TABLE 3.2 STOCK EXCHANGE VALUES

The following are the aggregate value of 387 representative securities as compiled by the *Bankers' Magazine*.

Date		*Value* £	*Increase/Decrease* £	*% Change*
19 December	1912	3 526 850 000	—	—
21 January	1913	3 539 166 000	+ 12 316 000	+ 0.35
19 February	1913	3 491 232 000	− 47 934 000	− 1.35
19 March	1913	3 463 139 000	− 28 093 000	− 0.80
21 April	1913	3 496 540 000	+ 33 401 000	+ 0.96
20 May	1913	3 485 174 000	− 11 366 000	− 0.32
20 June	1913	3 396 940 000	− 88 234 000	− 2.53
21 July	1913	3 385 737 000	− 11 203 000	− 0.33
20 August	1913	3 416 924 000	+ 31 187 000	+ 0.92
21 September	1913	3 434 506 000	+ 18 582 000	+ 0.54
20 October	1913	3 379 311 000	− 56 195 000	− 1.62
21 November	1913	3 364 047 000	− 15 264 000	− 0.45
18 December	1913	3 341 085 000	− 22 962 000	− 0.68
20 January	1914	3 389 478 000	+ 48 393 000	+ 1.43
20 February	1914	3 455 452 000	+ 65 974 000	+ 1.97
20 March	1914	3 407 840 000	− 47 612 000	− 1.38
20 April	1914	3 406 191 000	− 1 649 000	− 0.05
20 May	1914	3 385 562 000	− 20 629 000	− 0.61
20 June	1914	3 383 128 000	− 2 434 000	− 0.07
20 July	1914	3 370 709 000	− 12 419 000	− 0.67
30 July	1914*	3 182 717 000	− 187 992 000	− 5.58
20 January	1915	3 114 027 000	+ 68 609 000	− 0.35
19 February	1915	3 092 243 000	− 21 784 000	− 0.70
20 March	1915	3 017 660 000	− 74 583 000	− 2.41
20 April	1915	3 053 496 000	+ 35 836 000	+ 1.19

Source: Bankers' Magazine, vols. XCVII, XCVIII, XCIX. nos. 838–54, January 1914–May 1915

*Official quotations suspended until the Stock Exchange reopened on 5 January.

marked the climax of the crisis in the stock market for never before had the Stock Exchange been closed since it was founded in 1773.[48]

Leading authorities, such as Withers, Hawtrey, Clapham, Brown and Sayers, have tended to attribute the closure of the London Stock Exchange solely to the flood of sales from abroad. However, as Keynes (1914b) observed, the most immediate difficulties arose because of the liabilities of foreigners to the London Stock Exchange arising from previous purchases, together with what he termed as the 'disgraceful' action of the joint stock banks. British stockbrokers were owed vast sums of money by foreign clients on whose behalf they purchased securities. These sums were expected to be repaid at the end of a nineteen-day account which fell due at the end of July. However, the closing of the foreign Bourses, the imposition of complete or partial moratoria in other countries and finally the news that the Paris settlement would be postponed on 31 July, made such debts from foreign clients irrecoverable for the time being. Thus Keynes saw the problems in the stock market as identical to those in the bill market, namely, the inability of foreign clients to remit.

The failure of remittance in the stock market placed many brokers in a difficult position since they themselves had borrowed funds in order to finance the purchase of securities for their clients, using those securities as collateral. The total amount of loans outstanding was reported to be £81 million, of which £40 million had been lent by the joint stock banks, a further £20 million from other British and foreign banks and the remainder from the non-banking sector.[49] Most of this money had been advanced 'on margin', that is, collateral had to be deposited and maintained at approximately 10 per cent to 20 per cent above the market value of the loan. The rapid decline in security values during the last ten days of July eroded this margin and hence the banks began either to call in loans or to ask for higher margins.[50] To meet the banks' request, brokers were forced to sell some of their less gilt-edged securities which inevitably depressed prices further, not only of the stocks sold but of all stocks which fell in sympathy, and so the process went on. The banks therefore, by calling in loans undoubtedly weakened the stock market further and it was for this reason that Keynes and other contemporaries, together with subsequent researchers such as de Cecco, criticised the banks for their behaviour.[51]

The banks were further criticised for the way in which they treated their depositors during the crisis. Since Britain had not been involved in a major war for over 100 years, the reaction of the British public to the threat of war in 1914 was uncertain. However, from past history and more recent experiences abroad, the general expectation was that the public would do two things, hoard food and hoard gold.

On the first account, there was apparently a move to buy large quantities of food as evident from the sharp rise in prices, especially non-perishable food prices, in August 1914.[52] On the second account, it is more difficult to ascertain whether or not the public began to hoard gold since the crisis itself coincided with a Bank Holiday week-end when the demand for money was higher than usual. From Table 3.3, a

TABLE 3.3 BANKERS CLEARING HOUSE RETURNS IN JUNE–DECEMBER 1914 COMPARED WITH THE SAME PERIOD IN 1913 (£,000)

1914 on a Thursday		*1913 for the equivalent Thursday*
3 June	306 206	368 785
10 June	285 464	281 268
17 June	329 729	352 567
24 June	275 105	268 080
1 July	445 419	425 992
8 July	348 453	327 789
15 July	356 222	334 831
22 July	295 707	267 371
29 July	337 450	328 280
5 August	161 929	305 297
12 August	187 317	274 692
19 August	179 421	315 412
26 August	150 432	255 204
2 September	155 707	324 544
9 September	167 196	270 596
16 September	180 216	287 283
23 September	184 844	255 964
30 September	207 994	367 292
7 October	233 189	326 647
14 October	243 921	324 320
21 October	248 954	295 117
28 October	258 472	288 272
4 November	248 870	378 794
11 November	232 258	288 535
18 November	222 590	334 301
25 November	200 392	289 091
2 December	215 603	354 586
9 December	241 793	292 403
16 December	203 817	324 679
23 December	206 560	315 745
30 December	162 904	227 604

Source: Stock Exchange Official Weekly Index

comparison of weekly clearing house returns for a comparable period in 1913 suggests that the value of cheques presented or cashed during the last week of July 1914 was not excessive, although gold, of course, could have been obtained by other means.

Regardless of what actually happened, the important point is that the banks anticipated an internal drain on their gold reserves and as a consequence began to ration or refuse gold payments to their depositors, supplying instead Bank of England notes, the lowest denomination of which was £5. Although the banks were entitled to do this, such a policy opened them to the accusation of causing a panic amongst the general public. Since a £5 note was of little use for every day transactions, the public began to exercise their right to exchange notes for gold at the Bank of England.The queues that formed in Threadneedle Street on Friday, 31 July and Saturday, 1 August were, however, the only sign of a general panic, if indeed it could be termed a panic given that the public were not being unreasonable in demanding smaller denominations of currency. According to *The Times* the public behaved in an 'orderly fashion' and the Bank of England readily met all their demands for gold.[53]

While the Bank of England and Treasury were quick to criticise the banks for causing a panic among the public,[54] they were not free from that charge themselves. The rise in Bank rate from 3 per cent to 10 per cent in just ten days was bound to provoke concern, to say the least. It was most unusual for Bank rate to be altered by more than 1 per cent and this normally occurred on a Thursday. Given that a rise in Bank rate is taken as a danger signal, it was inevitable that a jump of 7 per cent made headline news, indicating to the general public that all was not well in the financial world.

The Treasury rather than the Bank must be held responsible for raising Bank rate to 10 per cent. When Cunliffe inquired on 1 August whether the usual Parliamentary indemnity would be granted, permitting the Bank to breach the 1844 Bank Act by increasing its note issue beyond the legal fiduciary limit, Lloyd George replied that as he understood it, the Bank Act had never been suspended unless Bank rate stood at the 10 per cent crisis level.[55] Thus Withers (1915) argues that 'in effect the Treasury, merely for the sake of blindly following a mouldy old precedent, practically told the Bank that the Act could not be suspended until Bank rate stood at 10 per cent (p. 10). It is difficult to find any alternative explanation since the rise was certainly ineffectual regarding the usual purpose of raising Bank rate, namely attracting gold from abroad or restricting credit at home. Keynes (1914a), in his September article, also thought this to be the case, suggesting that Cunliffe initially raised the rate to 8 per cent on 31 July in direct anticipation of Lloyd George's reply (p. 481).

Keynes, in the same article, does however offer an alternative explanation, arguing that the banks were largely responsible for the rise in Bank rate and the suspension of the 1844 Act on account of their draining the Bank's gold reserves both directly and also indirectly via the discount market (p. 472). During the last week of July the banks had been topping up their own reserves by withdrawing cash balances in gold from the Bank of England to the tune of £10 million. This prompted Keynes to accuse them of a blatant act of hoarding, arguing that 'Our system was endangered, not by the public running to the banks, but by the banks running to the Bank of England' (p. 471). Given the large gold reserves accumulated by the banks for the specific purpose of meeting a crisis, and given the concern expressed by the Gold Reserve Committee over the possibility of an external gold drain, it seems peculiar that the banks themselves chose to deplete central reserves.[56]

In connection with their operations in the London money market the banks came under further attack, this time for calling in money lent to the discount market 'to an extent which appears difficult to justify'.[57] To understand their position it is necessary to draw a distinction between the acceptance houses who guarantee bills of exchange but do not advance the capital, and the discount houses and banks who, on the strength of acceptance house guarantees, do actually advance the capital. To finance the discounting of bills the banks employ their depositors' funds, while the discount houses, in addition to their own funds, employ money borrowed from the banks at call or short notice. At the end of July 1914 the value of outstanding bills in London was approximately £350 million, of which £3–4 million fell due each day.[58]

However, as previously discussed, the failure of international remittance rendered a large proportion of this total irrecoverable from foreign clients which immediately affected the acceptance houses who, having guaranteed bills of exchange, were ultimately liable to meet them on maturity. The banks, concerned about their liquidity position, began to call in loans from the bill brokers, who, in turn, followed the traditional course and sought assistance from the Bank of England.

Bank of England weekly returns, given in Table 3.4, suggest that the Bank began to rediscount a large volume of bills during the last week of July, as indicated by the 29 July return, which shows an increase of £12 234 000 in 'other deposits' and £13 675 000 in 'other securities' in the Banking Department. It was on this basis that Bank rate was raised to 4 per cent. At first this business appeared manageable, the simultaneous growth in 'other deposits' suggests that sums advanced were being redeposited with the Bank. During the next three days the Bank advanced a further £18 044 000 of which only £2 331 000 was rede-

TABLE 3.4 BANK OF ENGLAND WEEKLY RETURNS JUNE–DECEMBER 1914

For the week ending 1914	*Notes issued* 1	*Government debt* 2	*Other securities* 3	*Gold coin and bullion* 4	*Total assets and liabilities* 5	*Proprietors capital* 6	*Rest* 7	*Public deposits* 8
3 June	52,769	11,015	7,435	34,319	77,629	14,553	3,150	17,547
10 June	53,741	11,015	7,435	35,291	76,392	14,553	3,148	16,999
17 June	55,487	11,015	7,435	37,037	77,222	14,553	3,154	17,637
24 June	56,753	11,015	7,435	38,303	80,716	14,553	3,160	18,074
1 July	56,926	11,015	7,435	38,476	89,446	14,553	3,257	17,071
8 July	56,354	11,015	7,435	37,904	74,356	14,553	3,415	12,580
15 July	56,908	11,015	7,435	38,458	73,818	14,553	3,431	13,319
22 July	57,014	11,015	7,435	38,564	73,935	14,553	3,447	13,735
29 July	55,121	11,015	7,435	36,671	85,188	14,553	3,492	12,713
5 August	44,491	11,015	7,435	26,041	86,359	14,553	3,547	11,499
12 August	50,692	11,015	7,435	32,242	109,358	14,553	3,583	7,889
19 August	55,638	11,015	7,435	37,188	139,990	14,553	3,660	13,674
26 August	61,193	11,015	7,435	42,743	166,036	14,553	3,692	23,887
2 September	65,501	11,015	7,435	47,031	180,780	14,553	3,718	28,677
9 September	65,229	11,015	7,435	46,779	173,407	14,553	3,730	24,406
16 September	66,484	11,015	7,435	48,034	172,009	14,553	3,756	18,643
23 September	69,478	11,015	7,435	51,028	179,335	14,553	3,830	28,673
30 September	70,768	11,015	7,435	52,318	177,944	14,553	3,849	22,244
7 October	74,630	11,015	7,435	56,180	182,243	14,553	3,177	17,852
14 October	77,067	11,015	7,435	58,617	180,305	14,553	3,178	23,732
21 October	77,948	11,015	7,435	59,498	176,576	14,553	3,190	15,764
28 October	79,812	11,015	7,435	61,362	169,506	14,553	3,210	24,994
4 November	87,391	11,015	7,435	68,941	174,503	14,553	3,194	16,451
11 November	87,128	11,015	7,435	68,678	174,307	14,553	3,203	19,249
18 November	90,468	11,015	7,435	72,018	181,411	14,553	3,224	16,286
25 November	90,069	11,015	7,435	71,619	192,959	14,553	3,236	18,691
2 December	89,247	11,015	7,435	70,797	198,344	14,553	3,227	12,577
9 December	89,384	11,015	7,435	70,934	183,711	14,553	3,234	45,002
16 December	90,434	11,015	7,435	71,984	183,723	14,553	3,245	43,168
23 December	88,346	11,015	7,435	69,896	170,708	14,553	3,266	37,459

For the week ending 1914	Other deposits 9	7-day and other bills 10	Government securities 11	Other securities 12	Notes 13	Gold and silver 14	Notes in the hands of the public	Gold reserve	of gold reserve to total liabilities
3 June	42,366	13	11,047	41,134	23,775	1,673	28,994	25,448	42.46
10 June	41,677	15	11,047	38,655	25,046	1,644	28,695	26,690	45.47
17 June	41,869	9	11,047	37,462	27,069	1,644	28,418	28,713	48.24
24 June	44,916	13	11,047	39,994	28,050	1,625	28,703	29,675	47.10
1 July	54,551	14	11,005	49,693	27,141	1,607	29,785	28,748	40.13
8 July	43,788	20	11,005	34,832	26,823	1,696	29,531	28,519	50.57
15 July	42,846	29	11,005	33,623	27,593	1,597	29,315	29,190	52.27
22 July	42,185	15	11,005	33,633	27,697	1,600	29,317	29,297	52.37
29 July	54,419	11	11,005	47,308	25,415	1,460	29,706	26,875	40.02
5 August	56,750	10	11,041	65,352	8,385	1,581	36,106	9,966	14.60
12 August	83,326	7	23,041	70,787	14,758	772	35,934	15,530	17.02
19 August	108, 094	9	26,041	94,726	18,451	772	37,187	19,223	15.78
26 August	123,893	11	29,779	109,905	25,621	731	35,572	26,352	17.83
2 September	133,819	13	28,024	121,821	30,213	772	35,288	30,935	19.04
9 September	130,704	14	25,747	116,923	30,008	729	35,221	30,737	19.81
16 September	135,042	15	25,669	113,792	31,862	686	34,622	32,548	21.18
23 September	125,267	12	25,682	110,733	35,275	645	34,203	35,920	23.33
30 September	137,287	11	24,732	116,820	35,793	599	34,975	36,392	22.81
7 October	146,647	14	27,971	113,894	39,801	577	34,829	40,378	24.54
14 October	138,829	13	27,571	109,716	42,400	618	34,667	43,018	26.46
21 October	143,058	11	24,074	108,788	43,149	565	34,799	43,718	27.52
28 October	126,737	12	19,427	104,869	44,699	511	35,113	45,210	29.79
4 November	140,293	12	17,204	104,905	51,861	533	35,530	52,394	33.42
11 November	137,287	15	17,004	105,091	51,609	603	35,519	52,212	33.35
18 November	147,335	13	18,601	107,103	55,155	552	35,313	55,707	34.04
25 November	156,453	16	26,286	111,315	54,754	604	35,315	55,358	31.60
2 December	167,971	16	31,290	113,121	53,321	612	35,926	53,933	29.87
9 December	120,904	18	11,959	117,600	53,633	519	35,751	54,152	32.64
16 December	122,736	21	11,969	116,482	54,842	430	35,592	55,272	33.31
23 December	115,406	24	14,806	103,294	52,126	482	36,220	52,608	34.41
30 December	128,055	24	14,808	106,236	51,343	461	36,139	51,804	33.42

Source: *Bankers' Magazine*, vol. XCIV.

posited. As a consequence, note reserves in the Banking Department fell by £17 030 000 and the central gold reserve by over £1 million. It was probably for this reason that Cunliffe sought a suspension of the 1844 Bank Act. The central gold reserve itself, which had already suffered an external drain to France[59] and an internal drain to the banks, fell from £26 875 000 on 29 July to £9 966 000 by the close of business on 1 August.

The banks were duly chastised for forcing the market to the Bank. Keynes (1914b) says they should have shown greater consideration for the bill brokers and had a greater regard for the country's reserve position (p. 471). De Cecco (1974) goes even further, arguing that 'the banks used the 1914 crisis as an occasion to ruin the Inner Circle of the City beyond repair, so that they could substitute themselves in lucrative international business' (p. 132). De Cecco, however, cites no evidence to support this contention and indeed it hardly seems tenable given the facts, for if the acceptance houses had stopped payment the discount houses would have followed suit and the whole burden of the crisis would have fallen on the banks.

While the banks as a whole may have aggravated the financial crisis in London from a macroeconomic perspective, their behaviour can be justified at the microeconomic level. As Withers, Sayers and Morgan point out, if their liquidity position is taken into account then the banks had good reason to call in loans from the stock and discount markets, withdraw gold held at the Bank of England and refuse gold to their depositors. That much of the criticism levied at the banking community was unjustified is accepted by Keynes (1921a) in his second article, where he writes, 'imperfect knowledge caused me to describe the action of the Clearing Banks, as distinguished from some other banks, with less than fairness' (p. 633).[60] Balance sheets of the London clearing banks on 30 June 1914 are given in Table 3.5 while Table 3.6 sets out the total assets and liabilities of UK joint stock banks on 30 December 1913.

The banks' chief liabilities are, of course, their customer accounts, the meeting of which is essential for survival. To meet their immediate liabilities the banks hold a variety of more or less liquid assets. Next to cash in hand and at the Bank of England, the banks' most liquid resources are money at call or short notice, bills discounted and loans and advances. In 1914, this last item included some £40 million lent directly to the Stock Exchange by the joint stock banks and a further £250 million lent against stock exchange securities.

While the banks were expecting heavy withdrawals from their depositors, a large proportion of their assets had become illiquid or of doubtful value during the last week of July. The fall in security prices had reduced the value of collateral held against loans while stockbrokers, unable to obtain funds from foreign clients, were in no position to repay the banks what they owed. The subsequent closure of the Stock Exchange prevented the banks from selling any of their securities and effectively locked up most of their longer term investments. The failure of international remittance rendered their most valued asset, the bill of exchange (some 9 per cent of total assets), illiquid. This, incidently, hit the banks on both sides of their balance sheet since they had also accepted bills of exchange (some £69 million) and were therefore ultimately liable to meet them on maturity. Given this increase in immediate liabilities and reduction in liquid assets, it was not unreasonable of the banks to mobilise their remaining resources. Expecting the demand for cash to increase, individual banks were effectively following normal banking practice by withdrawing cash held at the Bank and calling in short-term loans. In the aggregate, however, each bank pursuing such a policy excessively, aggravated the overall financial difficulties in London.

Whether the banks were justified in anticipating an internal gold drain by the public is debatable. It was certainly a fear shared by many others including Paish[61] and Alfred Marshall who, in a letter to Keynes, wrote that 'many people will go mad . . . and demand gold to bury in their back gardens'.[62] The Bank of England and Treasury did not share this view and were critical of those who did.[63] Keynes, recognising the possibility of an internal gold drain and hence the need to prevent any panic, was quick to criticise the banks for refusing gold to their depositors, saying that 'nothing could have been so well calculated to inspire the public with distrust . . . and to arouse in them the ancient instinct of hoarding' (p. 16, p. 473). Keynes did, however, recognise the need to economise on the internal use of gold in order to maintain external convertibility and to meet the future needs of war finance. In a momorandum sent to Lloyd George on 3 August 1914 he argued that, provided legal tender paper money was available in suitable denominations then, 'Gold should only be available at the Bank of England . . . banks should entirely refuse to supply gold to their customers.'[64]

Given that the English joint stock banks held private gold reserves in excess of £34 824 145, it is difficult to justify why they took additional sums from the Bank of England and then refused to use this gold to meet what were probably genuine demands for sovereigns over the

TABLE 3.5 CLEARING BANK BALANCE SHEETS AS AT 30 JUNE 1914

	Liabilities						
Clearing Banks	*Capital paid-up*	*Notes in circulation and reserve fund*	*Deposit and current accounts*	*Acceptances and endorsments*	*Undivided profits*	*Miscellaneous*	*Total liabilities*
Barclay & Co. Ltd.	3,600,000	1,600,000	61,740,267	322,131	140,670		67,403,068
Capital and Counties Bank Limited	1,750,000	800,000	40,858,543	1,680,206	103,450		45,219,199
Glyn, Mills, Currie & Co.	1,000,000	500,000	17,617,544	1,280,408	106,968		20,504,920
Lloyds Bank Ltd	5,008,672	3,600,000	106,895,364	3,890,279	426,487		119,820,802
London County & Westminster Bank Limited	3,500,000	4,000,000	90,865,122	6,384,965	270,549	332,487	105,353,123
London and South-Western Bank Limited	1,200,000	1,350,000	21,552,133	1,031,269	977,133		26,110,535
London City and Midland Bank Limited	3,700,000	4,348,650	94,636,061	7,353,110	391,378		110,429,199
London Joint Stock Bank Limited	2,970,000	1,125,000	37,107,348	2,380,076	252,156		43,834,580
Martins Bank Limited	500,000	185,000	3,151,278	327,863	42,137		4,206,278
National Bank Limited	1,500,000	1,288,242	14,470,362	91,496	522,154	9,957	17,882,211
National Provincial Bank of England Limited	3,000,000	2,000,000	71,133,338	694,369	93,027		76,920,734
Union of London and Smiths Bank Limited	3,554,785	1,150,000	41,355,157	4,756,443	433,046	49,450	51,298,881
Totals	31,283,457	21,946,892	601,409,517	30,192,615	3,759,155	391,894	688,983,530
As a % of total assets and liabilities.	4.54	3.18	87.29	4.38	0.55	0.06	

	Assets								
			Discounts and Advances		Investments				
Clearing Banks	*Cash in hand and at the Bank of England*	*Money at call or short notice*	*Discounts (where stated separately)*	*Advances, loans, etc.*	*British Government stocks*	*Bonds, stocks and other investments*	*Acceptances and endorsements (per contra)*	*Buildings and sundries*	*Total assets*
Barclay & Co. Ltd.	9,029,178	6,779,500	8,636,251	27,762,844	4,268,784	8,829,845	322,131	1,774,535	67,403,068
Capital and Counties Bank Limited	6,347,859	6,517,391	b	24,258,656	2,743,599	2,626,015	1,680,206	1,045,473	45,219,199
Glyn, Mills, Currie & Co.	2,854,103	4,607,230	b	8,523,737	912,298	1,957,144	1,280,400	370,000	20,504,920
Lloyds Bank Ltd	18,191,315	10,579,709	14,506,335	56,839,921	5,083,285	7,801,651	3,890,279	2,928,307	119,820,802
London County & Westminster Bank Limited	12,499,529	13,668,407	19,228,085	42,026,669	5,364,786	4,309,957	6,384,965	1,871,325	105,353,123
London and South-Western Bank Limited	3,403,016	3,226,566	2,955,032	10,514,975	1,854,884	1,994,984	1,031,269	1,129,809	26,110,535
London City and Midland Bank Limited	15,128,192	12,510,356	10,230,300	54,081,382	3,246,713	5,588,984	7,353,110	2,290,162	110,429,199
London Joint Stock Bank Limited	5,844,875	5,481,499	5,931,247	16,745,531	2,418,062	3,987,546	2,380,076	1,045,744	43,834,580
Martins Bank Limited	836,966	538,900	831,221	1,075,430	260,300	203,598	327,863	132,000	4,206,278
National Bank Limited	2,101,023	2,677,046	3,163,073	7,228,334	1,768,030	556,634	91,496	296,575	17,882,211
National Provincial Bank of England Limited	10,741,441	5,466,412	b	45,431,402	6,257,310	1,014,169	694,369	1,315,631	76,920,734
Union of London and Smiths Bank Limited	6,485,371	6,911,549	6,155,620	18,228,543	1,733,245	5,097,267	4,756,443	1,930,843	51,298,881
TOTALS	93,462,868	78,964,565	71,637,164	312,717,424	35,911,296	49,967,194	30,192,615	16,130,404	688,983,530
As a % of total assets and liabilities	13.57	11.46	10.40	45.39	5.21	7.25	4.38	2.34	

Source: The Economist's Banking Settlement and the *Bankers' Magazine*
(b) Discounts included in advances.

TABLE 3.6 BANKS BALANCE SHEETS AS AT 31 DECEMBER 1913 (IN MILLIONS)

	Joint stock banks of England and Wales (excluding Bank of England		*Joint stock banks of Ireland*		*Joint stock banks of Scotland*		*UK combined balance sheet (including private banks)*	
Number of banks	43		9		9		71	
Number of branches	5797		710		1240		7747	
TOTAL ASSETS AND LIABILITIES	£963.1		£90.9		£159.8		£1274.1	
LIABILITIES	£	% of total	£	% of total	£	% of total	£	% of total
Paid-up capital and reserves	82.1	8.5%	11.1	12.2%	17.3	10.8%	115.8	9.1%
Notes in circulation	0.1	0.0%	8.1	8.9%	7.7	4.8%	16.0	1.3%
Deposit, current and other accounts	809.4	84.0%	70.7	77.8%	125.9	78.8%	1059.4	83.1%
Acceptance and endorsements	61.7	6.4%	0.4	0.4%	5.5	3.4%	69.1	5.4%
Miscellaneous	9.8	1.0%	0.6	0.7%	3.4	2.1%	13.8	1.1%
ASSETS								
Cash, reserves	124.9	13.0%	10.5	11.6%	13.9	8.7%	151.9	11.9%
Money at call or short notice	110.7	11.5%	6.7	7.4%	20.1	12.6%	147.5	11.6%
Treasury bills discounted	3.7	0.4%	0.2	0.2%	0.8	0.5%	4.7	0.4%
Other discounts	88.7	9.2%	4.9	5.4%	17.2	10.8%	114.6	9.0%
Loans and advances	430.7	44.7%	43.2	47.5%	59.7	37.4%	552.3	43.3%
Acceptances and endorsements, per column	61.7	6.4%	0.4	0.4%	5.5	3.4%	69.1	5.4%
British government and government guaranteed investments	47.8	5.0%	8.6	9.5%	10.1	6.3%	70.3	5.5%
Other investments	73.0	7.6%	15.3	16.8%	27.8	17.4%	133.2	10.5%
Premises and other assets	21.1	2.2%	1.1	1.2%	4.5	2.8%	26.7	2.1%

Bank Holiday week-end. However, from Table 3.1, twenty-nine of the banks that reported to the Gold Reserve Committee held less than 3 per cent gold to total liabilities and it may well have been these banks that were led to hasty measures.[65]

Holden, in a speech delivered on 29 January 1915, offers an alternative explanation for the banks' behaviour.[66] He refers to the Gold Reserve Committee and his own proposal for depositing gold at the Bank of England in exchange for notes during a crisis. At the time, the Chancellor was favourably disposed towards this scheme and since it was the only form of an emergency plan in existence, the banks not unreasonably expected it to be adopted. In fact on Friday, 31 July, the banks did offer immediate assistance along the lines of Holden's proposal and as Sayers (1976) argues, each bank would therefore have had an incentive to retain gold in order to maximise its own contribution to the emergency pool. It was not until Sunday, 2 August that Holden's proposal was finally rejected, but by then it was too late, the damage had been done.

Overall, it would appear that much of the criticism levelled at the joint stock banks was unfair. For instance, it is not even clear that it was the British banks which were responsible for calling in stock exchange loans. Evidence suggests that it was the foreign banks in London who began to call in loans, forcing the firms affected to fall back on the clearing banks,[67] who in turn rendered every assistance.[68] In other cases the banks can be defended at a microeconomic level. Acting as individual units in a competitive environment each bank was primarily concerned with its own position. The banks had a clear incentive to protect themselves from the crisis in the interests of their shareholders and depositors.

Keynes argues that the banks should have come forward at the beginning of the crisis and assured the City of support. However, they could not have done this individually, collective action would have been required. The Clearing Houses Association could possibly have performed such a role, but given the large number of banks, it is doubtful whether collective agreement between them could have been reached in such a short period of time. Besides, the clearing banks had already offered some collective assistance in the form of Holden's proposal and this had been rejected.

The biggest failing of London as a whole was its inability to extend international credit. The banks, already suffering a loss on their bills, were in no position to discount fresh ones. Without the guarantee that new advances would be repaid, London effectively suspended her role as international creditor. During the last week of July, as those foreign clients who were able remitted funds to London, so Sterling appreciated, exchange rates became nominal and official quotations were suspended on 30 July until 26 August.[69]

The most immediate problem was to afford some relief to the acceptance houses to save them from bankruptcy. This relief took the form of a partial moratorium on bills of exchange proclaimed on Monday, 3 August. The effect of this proclamation was to enable the acceptance houses to postpone for one month payment on any bill accepted before 3 August, subject to a 6 per cent rate of interest. Although this did not relieve the acceptance houses of ultimate liability, they were for the moment saved. To decide what other measures should be taken the Bank Holiday was prolonged until 6 August.

SECOND PHASE OF THE CRISIS

On 2, 3, 4, 5 and 6 August, a conference was held at the Treasury between the various financial interests of the City. Those present included Lloyd George, Cunliffe, Bradbury from the Treasury, bankers merchants, industrialists and stockbrokers.

From the proceedings of this conference the conflicting interests and diverse opinions within the City are more than apparent. At the beginning of the conference the Bank of England and Treasury flatly refused to adopt Holden's proposal and this created much animosity between the bankers and the Bank. Lloyd George himself noted how difficult it was to reconcile the interests of the different sections of the banking community.[70]

The Clearing Bankers' Association, finding that their first scheme had been rejected, immediately submitted to Lloyd George, on 2 August, an alternative set of emergency measures. These included a suspension of the 1844 Bank Act, the issue of £1 and 10s notes, the suspension of specie payments and the proclamation of a general moratorium.[71] These proposals formed the main basis of discussion at the Treasury conference.

In the legal sense, the bankers' demand for a suspension of the 1844 Bank Act had already been met on 1 August when the bill of indemnity was issued. However, the suspension of the Act was never made operative since notes not backed by gold were not passed into general circulation.[72] Effectively, therefore, the official suspension on 1 August served no useful purpose.

The suspension of the 1844 Bank Act was rendered unnecessary by the subsequent decision to issue £1 and 10s Treasury notes. This scheme, embodied in the Currency and Notes Act, effectively satisfied the demand for internal currency. There was general agreement on the need for notes of smaller denominations and that they should be subject to a detrimental rate of interest as a safeguard against inflation. Cunliffe argued that the new notes should be issued by the Bank, but since it was doubtful whether Bank of England notes would be accepted as legal tender in Scotland and Ireland, it was agreed that the Treasury should issue the notes and the Bank distribute them. The notes were to be encashable into gold at the head office of the Bank of England.

The bankers proposed that the notes should be issued in an amount equal to 20 per cent of their liabilities, at an interest rate of 3 per cent. The Bank and Treasury thought an amount equal to 10 per cent of liabilities would be sufficient at a charge equal to Bank rate. The bankers disagreed, deadlock set in and Lord Rothschild was called in to mediate. After much debate a compromise was struck, the banks got the amount they had requested but at a charge equal to Bank rate.[73]

Under the original scheme only £13 million out of a possible £225 million (20 per cent of liabilities) notes were actually issued, suggesting that the banks had overestimated the demand for internal currency. The public quickly took to the notes and by the end of 1914 £38 million Treasury notes were outstanding. The smooth passage of the new notes into circulation demonstrated the benefits derived from a flexible note issue. If small notes had been available at the beginning at the crisis, then perhaps the banks would have been less concerned about an internal drain and more willing to assist the City and their depositors.

The banks, unwilling to pay 10 per cent interest on the Treasury notes, pressed for a reduction in Bank rate. The conference agreed that the 10 per cent crisis rate served no useful purpose, and since they were unwilling to see further disruption to trade and industry there was little objection to lowering Bank rate to 6 per cent on 6 August and then, under further pressure from the banks, to 5 per cent on the 8th, where it remained until July 1916.

It was over the question of gold convertibility that perhaps the most serious confusion arose. The bankers had always shown concern about the possible depletion of central gold reserves during a crisis. Indeed, this was the reason they had re-established the Gold Reserve Committee in 1913. In the event, their fears proved unfounded since a serious external gold drain had not materialised during the first phase of the crisis. The bankers, however, still considered a drain likely and accordingly argued for the suspension of specie payments. In analysing the crisis, the bankers failed to make a distinction between the internal and external demand for gold. They were under a misapprehension that suspending the Bank Act and suspending gold convertibility went hand in hand. Lloyd George was known to share their view, while the Treasury and Bank of England were totally opposed to suspending gold convertibility. In an effort to bring Lloyd George around to the Treasury's view, Beckett asked Keynes to write a memorandum on the subject.

Keynes[74] makes a clear distinction between the internal and external demand for gold. He treats them as two separate problems requiring different solutions. Keynes went to great lengths to stress that a suspension of the Bank Act did not necessarily have to be accompanied by a suspension of gold convertibility. On the contrary, he argued that the aim of the former was to avoid the latter by extracting gold from internal circulation. He argued that if internal demand was high, then this could be dealt with by providing additional legal tender currency, by a suspension of the Bank Act or by the Currency and Bank Notes Act, without the need to suspend gold convertibility.

With regard to the external demand for gold, Keynes did not believe the possibility of an external drain existed. In fact he argued that the reverse applied, since instead of being able to draw gold from Britain, the most formidable difficulties in the money market had arisen because foreign countries were unable to remit their liabilities to London. While Keynes considered the suspension of gold convertibility unnecessary, he also opposed it on the ground that the reputation of London as a free gold market would suffer immense damage 'if at the first sign of emergency specie payments were suspended'. Keynes therefore recommended that Britain should 'maintain specie payments, so as to meet foreign demands, while making it extremely difficult for the ordinary person to get gold'. Keynes' arguments appear to have had a great impact because Lloyd George came down firmly on the side of the Treasury and the conference decided, against the bankers wishes, to maintain gold convertibility.

Throughout the conference the bankers and discount houses had been pressing for a general moratorium. While the banks could possibly have supported an ultimate loss on their bill holdings,[75] the discount houses, whose vast bulk of assets were in bills of exchange, were on the brink of insolvency.[76] In addition, the market in new bills was at a standstill and clearly could not be revived until some form of relief had been given to the discount market. It was therefore decided to proclaim a general moratorium covering all debts over £5 except for payments in respect of wages, rates and taxes, National Health Insurance, workmen's compensation, colonial government debts and British Government Liabilities.[77]

While the general moratorium afforded relief to the banks and discount market, it did not have the desired effect of reviving the bill market where there was still a reluctance to do new business. This is one reason why the second moratorium has often been referred to as an extreme and unnecessary measure.[78] The other reason is that despite the moratorium a number of payments were actually made. However, in the absence of direct government intervention and financial aid, the discount houses would not have been able to remain solvent without the moratorium and it did help to prevent a number of bankruptcies.[79]

THIRD PHASE OF THE CRISIS

When the banks reopened on Friday, 7 August Britain was at war but, contrary to the banks' expectations, this did not prompt the public to rush for gold. The mere knowledge that Treasury notes were available was probably enough to restore confidence. The internal currency situation had therefore returned to normal, although there is some evidence to suggest that some of the smaller banks misused the discretionary powers afforded them under the general moratorium.[80]

It soon became apparent that additional measures were needed to revive the bill market. It was essential to stimulate fresh credit in order to restore the foreign exchanges and finance trade. Two separate problems required attention. The first was getting new bills accepted and the second was getting them discounted. Arguably, it was the first that was more pressing, since the money market could not function unless the deadweight of acceptances that could not be met were removed.

However, the scheme announced by the Government on 13 August dealt only with the problem of discounting. Under this scheme the Bank of England, under government guarantee, was authorised to discount any approved bill of exchange accepted before 4 August without the normal right of recourse to the holder. This was a generous offer from the Government, as it effectively enabled the banks and discount houses to turn their bills into money at a modest 5 per cent interest rate. It did nothing to rehabilitate the position of the acceptance houses.

It might have been hoped that the banks, already protected by the availability of additional legal tender and the general moratorium, would, with these latest benefits, begin to aid the acceptance houses by resuming credit facilities to their old customers and thus assist in the task of reorganising exchange and remittance. This was not to be the case and once again the banks came under attack.[81] This criticism was unfair since even if the banks were willing to discount new bills, the acceptance houses were in no position to grant new acceptances as they were still ultimately liable for all their pre-crisis business. In addition, there was no guarantee that foreign clients would be able to repay new bills and hence the acceptance houses were unwilling to guarantee them. The crisis had effectively destroyed confidence in international credit while the war rendered the future uncertain.

To remove the burden of pre-crisis acceptances, the government announced on 5 September that if acceptors were unable to meet their bills on maturity, then the Bank of England would lend sufficient funds to meet those bills at 2 per cent above Bank rate. Furthermore, it was agreed that the Bank would not seek to recover outstanding balances until one year after the war, with the Government bearing any ultimate loss.

Such government intervention in the London money market was unprecedented. The fact that assistance had to be given demonstrates just how severe the financial crisis was. The measures introduced saddled the taxpayer with a very substantial risk, but they did have the desired effect of enabling the business of exchange to get going again, albeit slowly.

Arguably, the Government should have come forward sooner and offered assistance to the City, not only in the interests of the financial sector, but also in the interests of the trade sector and employment. The failure to resume normal operations was due to a genuine inability, not the anticipation that government aid would be forthcoming. The assumption that financial institutions could, and therefore would, rectify their own difficulties was unfounded in the short run. To restore confidence and facilitate a speedy recovery, government assistance was essential. Furthermore, provided government intervention in the London money market was seen as a purely wartime expedient, there could be no danger of 'moral hazard' affecting financial operations in the future.

It may have been the short-run economic implications of financial assistance that prevented the Government from acting sooner. While government aid brought the money market back to life, it did so with a potentially inflationary glut of funds. The rediscounting of bills by the Bank significantly increased the cash base, as indicated by the massive growth *pari passu* of 'other deposits' and 'other securities' at the Bank of England. From Table 3.4 it can be seen that after August 1914 'other deposits' were some £90–100 million and 'other securities' some £70–80 million above normal. While bills rediscounted represented loans already made, exchanging these bills for book credits at the Bank of England effectively enabled new loans to be advanced against no additional security. Hence the transfer of bills to the Bank was not merely a book-keeping transaction, but an actual creation of credit. Furthermore, when 'other deposits', which primarily consist of bankers' balances, are high and therefore the supply of funds plentiful, money is cheap and hence Bank rate ceased to be effective.

The creation of base money to redress a general crisis of confidence is now a familiar macroeconomic tool, the birth of which may be traced to the 1914 financial crisis. The injection of cash restored confidence and with it the willingness to resume normal credit facilities. The authorities were widely congratulated in the financial press for adopting such bold measures,[82] while economists voiced concern about the future inflationary consequences of government policy. Keynes (1921a, p. 616) criticised the Bank of England for encouraging the rediscounting of bills of exchange[83] which, he argued, went much further than the actual till money required by the banking system. Earlier, in a memorandum written for the Treasury, on 5 August,[84] Keynes had argued that the most effective way of restoring confidence would be for the Government to guarantee all new bills of exchange. Such a scheme would have relieved the necessity to lend funds to the acceptance houses, since bills with a Treasury guarantee would have been readily discounted by banks and bill-brokers, which in turn would have enabled foreign clients to remit their original debts. Whilst this was a feasible alternative, it necessarily required the acceptance houses forming a single syndicate with mutual liability, which in the event they proved unwilling to do.

The growth in the cash base was augmented by the simultaneous increase in central gold reserves (see Table 3.4). The reserve rapidly increased during August from £9 966 000 to £26 352 000 and then to £51 804 000 by the end of the year. This was quite the opposite of what the bankers had anticipated. It was made possible by the granting of loan facilities by the Bank of England in various parts of the colonies in exchange for gold deposits. This arrangement overcame shipping difficulties and enabled exchange rates to return to former levels. On 12 August, it was announced that gold would be deposited on account for the Bank of England in Ottawa and sterling provided against it in London at $4.90:£1. This arrangement enabled New York to remit funds to London, which in turn enabled fresh credit for trade to commence.

While the moratorium had undoubtedly served a useful purpose during the height of the crisis, once financial operations began to return to normal, its continuation could only be detrimental to a full recovery. Before removing the moratorium, however, it was necessary to afford relief to stockbrokers and exporters who could not collect debts from enemy nations. In addition to the Courts (Emergency Powers) Act, passed on 31 August, which suspended the ordinary power of creditors to collect money from debtors owing to war conditions, a scheme was announced on 31 October whereby the banks, without government assistance, agreed not to call in loans from the Stock Exchange or ask for higher margins until one year after the war. To meet debts owed to the non-banking sector, the Bank of England agreed to advance up to 60 per cent of the securities held against outstanding loans (valued at mark-up prices on 29 July) at 1 per cent above Bank rate. To assist exporters, it was announced on 4 November that the banks would advance sufficient funds to meet 50 per cent of their unpaid debts, the Exchequer bearing 75 per cent and the banks 25 per cent of any ultimate loss.

Having made these final arrangements the moratorium was lifted on 4 November. On 18 November, the first Stock Exchange settlement day since July passed with relative ease. As confidence gradually returned so financial conditions improved. While the banks began to lend more freely it is evident from clearing house returns (Table 3.3) that business remained depressed. That 'other deposits' at the Bank, which carry no interest, remained high suggests that the demand for accommodation was low. This was largely because the war had significantly curtailed trade, with British exports falling dramatically by 50 per cent after the declaration of war.

Since the closure of the Stock Exchange limited trading had been conducted on the street markets, but prices gradually began to increase and by December were approaching pre-crisis values. On this basis it was decided to reopen the Stock Exchange on 4 January 1915, subject to certain trading restrictions designed to close the market to the enemy. The reopening of the Stock Exchange effectively marked the end of the financial crisis in London.

CONCLUSION

The 1914 financial crisis was unique in the sense that it was a war-related crisis, but this does not prevent some general conclusions from being made. Perhaps the most significant legacy of the episode was the realisation of how effective government intervention could be in redressing a crisis of confidence. The direct financial assistance granted to the money market, together with government intervention in other sectors of the economy, provided reformers with the necessary ammunition to argue for greater government participation in the future.

The 1914 financial crisis differed from previous crises in that the traditional expedients of redress, namely raising Bank rate and suspending the 1844 Bank Act, had little effect in resolving the difficulties encountered in 1914. The growth and complexity of international finance demanded new methods of redress. The closure of the Stock Exchange to prevent a crash, the imposition of a moratorium to prevent wide-scale bankruptcy and the issue of Treasury notes to meet internal currency demands were all innovations for Britain. The massive injection of money to restore confidence marked a further turning point in policy.

The distinctive feature of the 1914 crisis in London, from the viewpoint of gold standard analysis, was that instead of regulation there was a complete stoppage in the flow of sterling credit and a temporary suspension by London of its function as middleman in international finance. The crisis in Britain arose because of her strength as the great international creditor, not because of any weakness in the system. When Britain asked the rest of the world to repay what it owed, the rest of the world could only reply, 'But how can we unless you advance us the money first?'

NOTES

1. I would like to thank the following:
Dr Forrest Capie and Mr Geoffrey Wood for their advice and guidance, Professor Charles Goodhart for helpful comments on an earlier draft of this paper, Dr Paul Bowles for his constant support and finally the

Economic and Social Research Council for funding my Ph.D research at City University.

2. In accordance with established theory a crisis is defined here as the threat or actual inability of debtors to meet their obligations. See Kindleberger (1978) for a distinction between crises and panics.
3. A moratorium may be defined as an arrangement under which it is legally enacted that creditors cannot for a certain specified time claim payment of what is due to them. It postpones the date on which debts have to be met.
4. Throughout the paper reference will be made to the views of other writers on the crisis. The contemporary literature includes works by Sir. J. Clapham (1940) using Bank of England records, R. G. Hawtry (1938) who was at the Treasury, the journalist H. Withers (1915) and J. M. Keynes, whose most important contributions can be found in two articles he wrote for the *Economic Journal* in 1914 and (1921a). Further comments can be found in Harrod's Life of John Maynard Keynes (1951) and volume XVI of Keynes' *Collected Writings* (1921b). Much additional information and data are available in the contemporary journals. Of the above writers it is only really Withers and Keynes who go beyond a mere narration of events to analyse the crisis in detail. They critically appraise the measures introduced to alleviate the crisis and suggest alternatives. Keynes in particular is very critical of the joint stock banks which, he claims, aggravated the crisis.

   Subsequent work on the 1914 crisis has been done by W. A. Brown (1940), E. V. Morgan (1952), R. S. Sayers (1968, 1976) and M. de Cecco (1974). Brown is mainly concerned with foreign exchange during the crisis while Morgan gives a general account largely based on the works of Keynes and Withers. Morgan departs somewhat from Keynes' criticism of the banks while Sayers attempts to defend their behaviour. M. de Cecco *per contra* is very critical of the banks, accusing them of causing the crisis in London. He claims that his views are in accordance with Keynes', but this does not appear tenable since there are significant differences of emphasis between the two writers.
5. In June 1914, there were 13 London joint stock banks, 15 London provincial joint stock banks, 22 provincial joint stock banks, 18 London private banks, 2 London 'ephemeral' banks and 15 provincial private banks. In addition there were 9 Scottish banks and 9 Irish banks. Of the London banks 13 (including the Bank of England) belonged to the Clearing House Association. There were also at least 85 colonial and foreign banks having offices in London in June 1914. The information on UK banks was supplied by A. Webber of the Centre for Banking and International Finance at City University. Information on clearing and foreign banks was obtained from the *Bankers' Almanac* 1914.
6. In 1833 an Act was passed permitting joint stock banks to operate in the London area, they had previously been excluded from the 65 mile radius around London.
7. Between 1892 and 1912 the Bank's liabilities increased from £42 000 000 to £67 000 000 and gold reserves by some £13 462 000.
8. An account of this speech can be found in the archives of the Midland Bank, Ref. Acc 158/1.
9. A special subcommittee had previously been appointed by the London

clearing banks in 1907 to investigate the gold reserve question, but to the author's knowledge no records of its proceedings exist.

10. Ref. Acc 158/1. As far as the author is aware, the findings of this committee have not been published elsewhere. Holden's comment is recorded in the minutes of the first meeting of the secret committee held on 7 May 1913.
11. The committee was secret in the sense that it did not publish its findings, its existence, however, was common knowledge in financial circles. The committee's refusal to make its proceedings public alienated contemporary financiers and journalists.
12. While the Bank of England had strengthened its own position by substantially increasing the proportion of gold held against its own liabilities between 1893 and 1913, when this gold was looked upon as the ultimate reserve of the country it was considered inadequate. While the increase in gold over this twenty-year period amounted to 42 per cent the volume of trade and banking deposits had increased by over 100 per cent.
13. Britain's position was compared with France who had large gold reserves and a more stable discount rate.
14. See, for example, C. A. E. Goodhart, *The Business of Banking 1891–1914*, pp.101–5.
15. From the minutes of the second meeting of the secret Gold Reserve Committee held on 11 June 1913. Midland Bank Archives, Ref. Acc 158/1.
16. From the minutes of the seventh meeting of the secret Gold Reserve Committee, 14 May 1914. Midland Bank Archives, Ref. Acc 158/1.
17. The bankers feared that an external drain would deplete gold reserves as it had done in the past. During the 1847 crisis gold reserves fell below £1 million, in the panic of 1857 the Bank's reserves ran out and an additional currency issue of £2 million had to be provided by suspending the 1844 Bank Act, while during the 1866 crisis central gold reserves fell below £400 000.
18. From the minutes of the sixth meeting of the secret Gold Reserve Committee held on 2 April 1914.
19. Similar schemes were also proposed by Schuster and Tritton.
20. Minutes of the seventh meeting of the secret Gold Reserve Committee held on 14 May 1914. Midland Bank Archives, Ref. Acc 158/1.
21. PRO Accession no. T 170 19.
22. PRO Accession no. T 171 53.
23. Reprinted in J. M. Keynes, *Collected Writings* (1921b), vol. XVI.
24. 'The general theory of employment', in the *Quarterly Journal of Economics* 1937, as reprinted in Keynes' *Collected Writings*, vol. XIV, pp. 113–14.
25. The contrast between financial and military readiness for war may simply reflect the difference between political and financial circles.
26. The build-up of arms started before this date but was accelerated after the Agadir incident by Germany's determination to achieve a 2:3 ratio of capital ships with the British Royal Navy. Concern over Germany's growing military strength led France, Russia and Britain to increase their military power.
27. Actual military expenditure on the army and navy amounted to £77 179 000 for the fiscal year 1913–14. This represented 39 per cent of total Government expenditure, compared with 34.4 per cent in 1911.
28. Germany, with the highest proportion of military expenditure to total

expenditure in Europe (some 47 per cent in 1914), had reached the apex of her strength in 1914. She was the world's second largest steel producer, and coal production had risen 500 per cent since 1900 while there had been a great expansion in her textile, mining, electronic, chemical and optical industries.

29. For further details of this debate see, for example, 'The burden of armament', *The Statist*, 1914, vol. LXXIX and *The American Bankers' Magazine*, 1914, vol. 88, pp. 429–34. Also see J. S. Mill, *Principle of Political Economy*, Book I, especially ch. iv.
30. See for instance the recent report published by the Society of Civil and Public Servants entitled, 'Defence, expenditure and employment'.
31. For example, 1914, vol. LXXIX see N. Angell, *The Great Illusion*, Also see *The Statist* and *The American Bankers' Magazine*, 1914, vol. 88.
32. As reported in *The Times* 18 July 1914. Lloyd George was referring to October 1913 when Austria dispatched an ultimatum to Serbia giving her one week to withdraw her troops from Albania. Serbia, under pressure from Russia, agreed. It is argued that if Russia had been willing to back Serbia on this occasion then war would have broken out in 1913.
33. A. J. P. Taylor, *The Struggle for Mastery in Europe 1848–1918*.
34. *The Economist*, 1 August 1914.
35. Lloyd George, *War Memoirs*, vol. 1, p. 40.
36. This view was often expressed in contemporary journals. See, for example, 'The great crisis', the *Bankers' Magazine* 1914, vol. XCVIII, no. 846 p. 318.
37. Note that Keynes makes a distinction between very improbable and uncertain in his *General Theory*, 1936, p. 148.
38. At the outbreak of war insurance rates increased dramatically. On 28 July the rate was 5s per cent, this shot up to 80s per cent on the 31st, 10 guineas per cent on 4 August and then to 20 guineas per cent on 6 August. At this point the War Risks Office intervened, offering a uniform rate of 5 guineas per cent which was reduced to 4 guineas per cent the following day.
39. Fearful of external drain and aware of the future internal needs of war finance, gold export embargoes were immediately declared in Germany and Russia when they entered the war. The Russian State Bank suspended specie payments on 27 July, the Reichsbank on 4 August and the Bank of France on 5 August. The Bank of France also refused to deliver gold except for reasons it regarded as satisfactory, and in the United States a *de facto* gold export embargo was established.
40. France imposed a moritorium on all negotiable instruments on 1 August which lasted until 1 March 1915, Russia established a partial moratorium on bills of exchange on 2 August to the end of the year, and Italy placed moratorium on bills and a partial moratorium on bank deposits from the outbreak of war until 31 March 1915. In addition, Argentina, Austria-Hungary, Belgium, Brazil, Egypt, Greece, Norway, Peru, Portugal, Roumania, Sweden and Switzerland all had moratoria in one form or another.
41. Cole had asked Holden what would happen to the vast sums of foreign bills held by the banking system if war broke out. Recorded in the 8th meeting of the secret Gold Reserve Committee held on 22 July 1914. Midland Bank Archives, Ref. Acc 158/1.
42. On the Stock Exchange contango facilities refer to a sum of money paid by

a buyer or seller for the right to defer delivery of securities until the next account period.
43. *The Economist*, 1 August 1914, p. 229.
44. On 25 July the Berlin exchange postponed settlement. On 27 July the Vienna, Budapest, and Brussels Bourses closed while the unofficial Coulisse market in Paris temporarily suspended all transactions. On 28 July the Barcelona Bourse closed and on the 29th the St Petersburg Bourse closed.
45. The *Bankers' Magazine*, August 1914.
46. Settlement days are pre-set in advance by the Stock Exchange and clearing banks and mark the end of a nineteen-day account when funds borrowed to finance the purchase of securities are settled.
47. *The Economist*, 1 August 1914 p. 221.
48. Even during the Napoleonic Wars the London Stock Exchange remained open, but at that time trading was a purely domestic affair and hence the market was shielded from external influence.
49. *Journal of the Institute of Bankers* vol. XXXVI, part 2, February 1915.
50. Evidence from contemporary journals suggests that the banks began to call in loans from the stock market on Tuesday, 28 July. See, for example, *The Economist* 8 August.
51. See pp. 103–5 for further discussion and a defence of the banks.
52. The monthly price index of forty-five commodities as compiled by *The Statist* while falling by 3.25 per cent between January and June 1914, rose by 1.48 per cent in July and by a further 6.67 per cent in August.
53. *The Times*, 1 August 1914.
54. See, for example, the correspondence between Keynes and Bradbury at the Treasury, reprinted in J. M. Keynes (1921a) *Collected Writings*, vol. XVI, p. 3.
55. Lloyd George, *War Memoirs*, vol. 1, p. 103.
56. See pp. 102–3 for a possible explanation.
57. *The Times*, 1 August 1914.
58. *The Economist*, 8 August 1914.
59. France, with large deposits in London, was in fact the only country in a position to take gold from the Bank of England. During the last week of July some £4 million in gold was exported to France.
60. Keynes' attitude towards the clearing banks apparently changed after a meeting with Schuster. Unfortunately, the conversation was never recorded. The clearing banks may have been in a position to weather the crisis better than some other banks since they held substantially higher gold reserves.
61. PRO Accession no. T 170 14.
62. Reprinted in vol. XVI *Collected Writings*, p. 32.
63. PRO Accession no. T 170 14.
64. PRO Accession no. T 170 39, reprinted in vol. XVI *Collected Writings, p*. 12.
65. See note 59.
66. Reported in the *Journal of the Institute of Bankers*, vol XXXVI, part IIV, 1915, p. 110.
67. Morgan, citing evidence from Lloyds Bank, argues that the foreign banks were ruthlessly calling in stock exchange loans.

68. *The Times History of the War*, fol. 1, pp 179–80.
69. London exchange quotations on continental centres became nominal from 28 July in St Petersburg; from 29 July in New York, Montreal and Genoa; from 30 July in Paris, Brussels, Berlin, Vienna, Amsterdam, Zurich, Madrid, Stockholm and Lisbon. Before the suspension of official quotations, the Sterling exchange rate rose from 4.86 to 6.35 against the dollar.
70. Lloyd George, *War Memoirs*, vol. 1, p. 106.
71. PRO Accession no. T 170 14.
72. In a sense the Act was technically violated since 43 043 000 notes beyond the fiduciary issue were advanced to bankers on 8 August, but these had all been returned by the 10th and never reached the public. (Hansard, 9 November 1915, col 1002.)
73. After 20 August the interest charges were dropped.
74. Reprinted in vol. XVI *Collected Writings*, pp. 7–15.
75. Keynes believed they could. See Keynes (1914a) 'War and the financial system: August 1914', *Economic Journal*, vol. XXIV, p. 469.
76. Had the acceptance houses collapsed, the discount houses would have been liable for any bills they had rediscounted. To give some idea of the sums involved, on 30 June 1914, the three discount companies (as distinguished from the private discount houses) had discounted £58.2 million bills, of which £14.4 million had been rediscounted. This was against total capital and reserves of only £3.6 million.
77. The moratorium, proclaimed on 7 August originally covered a period of one month and was subsequently extended until 4 November.
78. Morgan argues that relief would have been better afforded under the Courts (Emergency Powers) Act since the general moratorium damaged internal confidence and external prestige. Withers doubted the need for a general moratorium and would have preferred to see the Bank Holiday extended further.
79. R. S. Sayers (1976) *The Bank of England 1891–1944*.
80. Holden's assistant, J. Murray, recorded a number of incidents in his diary of the Midland Bank cashing cheques which other banks had refused. For example, a branch of the Lanchashire and Yorkshire in Rochdale refused to cash one of their customers cheques for £10, giving him only £3 – he had a balance of between £300–£400. Other stories include the District Bank in Rochdale who paid a wage cheque for £450 in three notes of £100 and three at £50. J. Murray's diary is in the Midland Bank Archives.
81. Lloyd George criticised the banks in the House of Commons, which prompted *The Economist*, 29 August to publish an article in their defence saying that the banks should not be pressurised into making loans against bad security or no security at all.
82. See, for example, 'The great crisis', *Bankers' Magazine*, November 1914, vol. XCVIII, no. 848.
83. On 29 September the Bank posted a notice which read, 'in order to avoid possible disappointment, those who wish to avail themselves of the arrangement for discounting premoratorium bills at the Bank of England are invited to send in their applications without delay!'
84. Reprinted in vol. XVI, *Collected Writings*, pp. 16–19.

REFERENCES

Ashworth, W. (1952) *A Short History of the International Economy Since 1850* 3rd ed. 1975 (Harlow: Longman).

Bankers' Magazine, 'The great crisis', a series of monthly articles commencing in vol. XCVIII, no. 846, September 1914.

Beales, F. S. (1915) 'The war and the gold problem', *Journal of the Institute of Bankers* XXXVI (III): 142–7.

Brown, W. A. (1940) *The International Gold Standard Reinterpreted 1914–1934*, vol. 1 (New York: National Bureau of Economic Research).

Burton, T. E. (1902) *Financial Crisis* Repr. 1971 (New York Books for Libraries Press).

Churchill, Sir W. S. (1931) *The World Crisis 1911–1914* (London: Thornton Butterworth).

Clapham, Sir J. (1940) 'Account of the financial crisis in August 1914', in Sayers, R. S. *The Bank of England 1891–1944*, Appendix 3 (Cambridge: Cambridge University Press, 1976).

de Cecco, M. (1974) *Money and Empire* (Oxford: Basil Blackwell).

Fisher, I. (1923) 'The business cycle, largely a dance of the dollar', *Journal of the American Statistical Association*. Vol. 18.

Fisher, I. (1925) 'The unstable dollar and the so-called business cycle', *Journal of the American Statistical Association*, Vol. 20.

Fisher, I. (1933) *Booms and Depressions* (New York: Adelphi Co.).

Gold Reserve Committee, Minutes of Meetings 1913–1914, Midland Bank Archives, Ref. Acc 158/1.

Goodhart, C. A. E. (1972) *The Business of Banking 1891–1914* (London: Wiedenfeld & Nicolson, 1972).

Hawtrey, R. G. (1938) *A Century of Bank Rate*, 2nd ed. (London: Frank Cass, 1962).

Harrod, R. F. (1951) *The Life of John Maynard Keynes* (Harmondsworth: Pelican Books, 1972).

Jackson, H. F. (1914) 'Gold reserves', *Journal of the Institute of Bankers* XXXV (VI): 435–41.

Keynes, J. M. (1941a) 'War and the financial system, August 1914', *Economic Journal*, vol. XXIV (Sept.): 460–86.

Keynes, J. M. (1914b) 'The prospects of money, November 1914', *Economic Journal* XXIV (Dec.): 610–34.

Keynes, J. M. (1921a) *Treatise on Probability: Vol. VIII, Collected Writings* (London: Macmillan, 1971).

Keynes, J. M. (1921b) *Activities 1914–1919. The Treasury and Versailles: Vol. XVI, Collected Writings* (London: Macmillan, 1971).

Kindleberger, C. P. (1978) *Manias, Panics and Crashes: A History of Financial Crises* (London: Macmillan, 1981).

Knight, F. H. (1921) *Risk, Uncertainty and Profit* (Boston). (Reprint 1965, New York: Harper & Row).

Lloyd George, (1933) *War Memoirs*, vol I (London: Ivor, Nicholson & Watson).

Meltzer, A. H. (1982) 'Rational expectations, risk, uncertainty, and market response', in Wachtel, P. (ed.) *Crisis in the Economic and Financial Structure* (New York: Lexington Books).

Minsky, H. P. (1972) *Financial Stability Revisited: The Economics of Disaster* (Washington: Washington Press).

Morgan, E. V. (1952) *Studies in British Financial Policy 1914–1925* (London: Macmillan).

Sayers, R. S. (1968) *Gillets in the London Money Market* 1867–1967 (Oxford: Oxford University Press).

Sayers, R. S. (1976) *The Bank of England 1891–1944* (Cambridge: Cambridge University Press).

Sheppard D. K. (1971) *The Growth and Role of UK Financial Institutions 1880–1962* (London: Methuen).

Sykes, E. (1915) 'Some effects of the war on the London money market', *Journal of the Institute of Bankers* XXXVI (2): 68–84.

Taylor, A. J. P. (1957) *The Struggle for Mastery in Europe 1848–1918* (Oxford: Oxford University Press).

'*Times*' *History of the War* (1921) (London: Times Books).

Tobin, J. (1982) 'The commercial banking firm: a simple model', *The Scandinavian Journal of Economics* 84 (4): 495–530.

Turner, L. C. F. (1970) *Origins of the First World War*. Repr. 1980 (London: Edward Arnold).

Withers, H. (1915) *War and Lombard Street* (London: J. Murray).

Comments on 'The Summer of 1914'

CHARLES GOODHART

This is an excellent chapter, combining thorough knowledge of secondary sources and good judgement with impressive research into the primary material, culminating in the most valuable and relevant discovery of the Minutes of the banks' Gold Reserve Committee. In my view this paper is, and may permanently remain, the most authoritative account of financial developments in these crucial months.

I have very few critical comments, or even differences of emphasis or nuance to offer. I wonder, however, whether the author, perhaps still under the remaining influence of Keynes' initial, perhaps not-fully-considered waspish comments on the banks' behaviour, and also of de Cecco's subsequent exaggeration of conflicts and rivalries within the City, does not still slightly overstate the importance of such inherent rivalry. Thus she notes the rivalry, 'especially between the Bank of England and the joint stock banks'. On the other hand, she may not have given quite sufficient weight to the accidents of personalities. If A. C. Cole, a wise and competent Governor, had still been in office in the Bank of England, rather than Cunliffe, who could not be so described, might not the crisis have been surmounted more quickly and smoothly? Yet even so, the main impression that Miss Seabourne's chapter leaves (and I am sure that it is correct impression) is that the crisis arrived with totally unexpected, indeed unimagined, ferocity; and that faced with such pressures, problems, breakdowns and disturbances, the authorities and the City together, after a, perhaps, understandably hesitant start, coped really rather well. Indeed, the author also explains sensibly why there was so little contingency planning. Consider a horrifying modern-day equivalent: nuclear war between the USA and Russia that just happened to leave London unscathed.

Would we now do any better in dealing with the subsequent financial crisis?

The initial problems and financial disturbances were partly due, as demonstrated by the author, to disagreements over the one contingency plan that was then ready, that of the main joint stock banks, which was to centralise their gold holdings with the Bank of England – together with an accompanying proportion of earning assets – in return for an issue of emergency currency notes. This had the twin advantage of centralising the gold holdings of the country in the Bank of England, where it would be more useful and usable in order to offset an external drain, while at the same time providing the joint stock banks with additional currency in order to meet an internal drain. Despite its apparent advantages, this entirely sensible plan appeared to run into strong opposition from the authorities. Basil Blackett in the Treasury wrote a paper that was not only notable for its bad economics, failing to distinguish between the requirements to meet an external as compared with an internal drain, but also argued against the scheme on the standard Treasury argument that it might cost the Government something. Cunliffe also apparently 'strongly criticised and disagreed' with these proposals. Perhaps he was also concerned with the parochial question of the Bank's own profits. Even Keynes appeared to find favour with the proposals, according to the author, mainly on the grounds that it would strengthen the political position of the Government, rather than that it would deal with both the possibility of external and internal drains.

The banks' expectation that this sensible scheme might well be adopted could account in part for the banks' actions in refusing to pay out gold on Friday, 31 July, an action that was with hindsight almost certainly unwise, and one for which they have been roundly condemned subsequently. (One minor point, that does not change the argument, is that not all of the gold held by the joint stock banks was usable for paying out to the general public, since some considerable proportion of it was in the form of either gold bars or foreign coins, rather than of gold sovereigns.) But even if this sensible scheme had been adopted instantaneously, it would not have dealt with the central problem that the outbreak of hostilities posed. This was the complete breakdown of the system of the provision of international credit, of which London formed the centre, and the inability of debtors to make transmission to London of funds to repay their debts. With, or without, a quicker and more deftly handled means of meeting internal drains in the form of additional demands for currency, there would still have been a need for moratoria with respect to bills and acceptances, and, no doubt, a need for a temporary closure of the Stock Exchange. These were the main problems, and, all things considered, Miss Seabourne's paper suggests that, after a short early hiccup, the authorities dealt with them really rather successfully, given the scope of the problems involved.

Undoubtedly, one of the facets of the programme for dealing with the crisis would have to have been provision of more currency notes, to meet the internal drain, by one route or another. One point that Miss Seabourne does not deal with adequately, in my view, is whether the route that was taken led subsequently to far too large an upsurge in currency notes. The high-powered monetary base expanded at an enormously fast rate during the next few months. Whereas some initial additional increase in notes was undoubtedly necessary, the route that was taken seemed to encourage and allow the authorities to finance the early period of the war by an inflationary expansion in the note issue. Could this have been avoided by some preferable procedure? For example, Miss Seabourne comments that, 'The creation of money to redress a general crisis of confidence is now a familiar macroeconomic tool, the birth of which may be traced to the 1914 financial crisis.' But, whereas the initial injection of extra notes was undoubtedly desirable, the continued subsequent injection could be more strongly criticised. Again, in an earlier passage, she states that, 'The smooth passage of the new notes into the system demonstrated the benefits derived from a flexible note issue.' Apart from questioning exactly what she means by 'a flexible note issue', it is possible to argue that perhaps the new system was *excessively* flexible, in that there was no check on the continuing and very sizeable injection of additional notes into the economy in the UK.

Finally, the resumption of the continuing working of the financial system, after the moratoria, required the authorities to take over the debts on bills and acceptances, which were effectively bad, in that they were never likely to be recovered from payers in hostile countries, and others whose conditions were permanently changed by the outbreak of hostilities. I would have liked to have learnt how much these losses eventually amounted to, and how they were ultimately absorbed by the Government. Perhaps, some future day, Miss Seabourne will do some additional research, on what happened to those bills and acceptances assumed by the Government at the outbreak of war.

4 What Happened in 1931?

FORREST CAPIE, TERENCE MILLS, GEOFFREY WOOD

In 1931 Britain left the gold standard. Why? Was sterling pushed off gold by the backwash of the banking crisis in continental Europe? Was the UK rendered illiquid as a result of the loss of reserves experienced by the primary producers of the Empire as their terms of trade worsened? Or did the cause lie rather in UK policy, in the overvalued sterling exchange rate or the large budget deficit?

These causes are, of course, not mutually exclusive – they all may have played some part. Whether they did, and if so what was their relative importance, is a problem of considerable interest – first in itself, and second in helping to understand why Britain left the gold standard, as opposed to devaluing but staying on gold. If the system were brought down by a crisis, then abandoning gold is readily comprehensible. But if the UK's problem was UK policy, why was sterling not just devalued?

This paper explores these issues, using recently available data and some aspects of economic analysis which, although by no means new, have not previously been brought to bear on this episode.

The argument is in four main sections. First we describe what is usually meant by a financial crisis, and proceed to consider whether there is any evidence that the crisis of continental Europe spread to the UK financial system. We then examine (as far as the data allow) the impact, and timing of this impact, of the worsening terms of trade of primary producers on their London financial assets. That clears the way for consideration of domestic UK policies. Was the budget deficit excessive in any sense? Was the exchange rate the problem Keynes (and many subsequently) made it out to be?

FINANCIAL CRISIS

Is the financial system fragile or robust? Some favour the latter and claim that no crises are possible so long as the money supply is controlled by a set of rules, markets are left to function efficiently, and exchange rates allowed to move to purchasing power parity. On that view, crises are only possible when governments depart from sensible rules. There are those who believe, however, that it is difficult to set the rules and that in the short run financial crises are possible. But what is a financial crisis? One suggestion is that it can be identified when owners of wealth shift quickly out of one type of asset into another. The lender-of-last-resort function consists of 'providing the sought-after liquid assets in abundant amount, and this slows down the stampede'.

Drawing on the work of Minsky (1972), Kindleberger (1982) has elaborated the anatomy of a typical crisis. According to this analysis the crisis starts with an exogenous shock such as a harvest failure; prices rise, new opportunities present themselves and a boom is fed by an expansion of bank credit. Further price rises in turn lead to new profit opportunities and new investment, and a general state of euphoria. There follows speculation on price increases, and as some see others making profits they follow. In other words, a crisis is characterised by a certain amount of irrationality. In the boom interest rates rise, velocity of circulation of money increases and prices rise. Then at some point insiders decide to take their profits and get out. There is a hesitation in the market, prices level off, and a race to get out of real assets begins. A specific signal may be the failure of a bank. Finally, prices fall so low that people once more move back from cash into less liquid assets. Certainly many of these features, in that sequence, were present in the financial crises that occurred in the nineteenth century. But does this anatomy of a crisis in any way describe the events in Britain in 1931?

A FORMAL MODEL

Most work by economists (and others) on crises has been verbal rather than mathematical. This in part reflects that until recently most such work has been by writers who were at least as much practical men, men of affairs, as they were scholars. Walter Bagehot is an excellent example. Mathematical techniques, or at any rate their use in print, were confined largely to scholars. The above typology of a crisis continues that tradition, drawing as it does on the work of economists whose studies are rooted in economic history – and often particular episodes in history – rather than in formal economic analysis.

In this section a rudimentary formalisation of these ideas is set out. Doing so inevitably loses the richness of detail which characterises the work of these scholars – and also the vividness of narrative. But that loss can bring gain; the main, the central and essential features of a crisis can be laid bare.

This will enable a test to be developed which will separate 'crises' from other events – it will lead to a formal definition of a crisis. Whether the test can be applied to the problem of the current paper will then be considered.

The Approach

It is the characteristic of a crisis that it be unexpected. It strikes suddenly, and cannot be anticipated – it can be prepared against only by being continually in readiness. In Frank Knight's terminology, it is associated with uncertainty, *not* with risk. There is no probability distribution, whether known *a priori* or from experience, on the basis of which the likelihood of a crisis occurring on any one day, or at any one time in the future, can be calculated. It is an unexpected change in the model which generates events.

As is now fairly well established the 'best' (defined below) way to model any process which generates a series of future events is to construct a statistical model of the time series. This may not supply a behavioural explanation, but strictly in terms of forecasting it is the 'best' – that is, most accurate – approach. Such time-series models use all the information which went into generating the series. A crisis can then be viewed as unpredictable change in the time series.

The Model

A very straightforward example can be found in Meltzer (1982).

Suppose that a variable X is generated by a process such that X at any time (i.e. X_t), is $A_t e^{a(t)t} u_t$ (1) where A, a, and u are random walks, with (for example) $\ln u_t \sim N(o, \sigma_u^2)$.

If A_t and $a(t)$ are constants $\ln X_t$ is expected to change at a constant rate through time. Hence X (whatever it is – share price, national income) will deviate randomly form a constant, stationary trend. In any one period there is risk of departure from trend, but the trend is constant and the expected value at any one time (or an average over time) is known. So far, there is *risk*, but not *uncertainty*.

Uncertainty can now be introduced.

The expected value of log X at $t + j$ is not just a random walk around a trend.

$$E \ln X_{t+j} = E \ln A_{t+j} + E\, a_{t+j}(j-t) \tag{2}$$

A and a are assumed to be random walks.

$$E\Delta \ln X_{t+n} = E\Delta \ln A_{t+n} + E\,(\Delta a_{t+n}\,(n-t) + a_{t+n})$$

Changes in A change the level of X, but not the trend. Changes in a alter the trend rate of growth. X_t therefore changes in three ways – transitory random deviations about the trend line, given by u_t; permanent changes in level, given by $\Delta \ln A_t$; and permanent changes in growth rate, Δa. The diagram summarises the three effects.

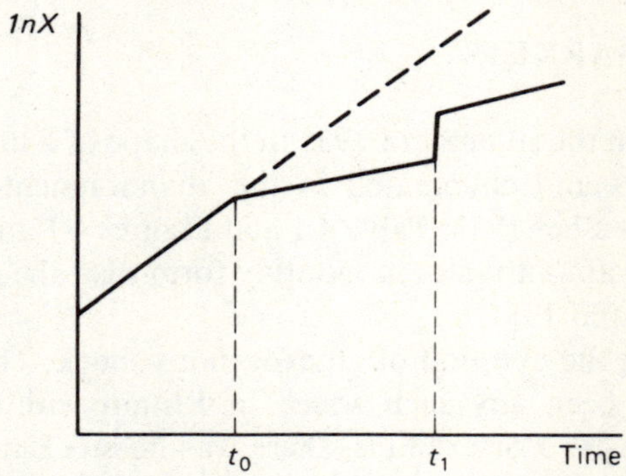

The solid line is the actual path of X. Should neither A nor a change, it would continue beyond t_0 along the dashed line. But a fell at t_0, and A changed (increased) at t_1.

Neither of the events could be anticipated before t_0, because they had not been observed, and we had assumed they could not be deduced *a priori*. Only the actual values of A, a and ln u_t were known. A sudden change in A or a is, in the definition above, a *crisis* – although whether large or small depends on the size of the change (inter alia).

Application

In the present chapter, part of the question addressed is whether there was a crisis in any part of the UK financial system. Series examined for this are prices and various interest rates. We do not formally apply the above test, looking for changes in A or a, because of the small number of observations in each time series. Rather they are examined informally for evidence of such change. This is admittedly non-rigorous, but the non-rigorous application of the above analysis is forced on us by data limitations. If (as turns out to be the case) we reject the hypothesis of a crisis in the financial system on this informal basis, and are incorrect to do so in the sense that a formal test, had it been possible, would have supported the hypothesis, the probability is that the 'crisis' was so small as to be one only in the above, statistical, sense, and not in any practical sense.

The above analysis is also applied formally (modelling A and a as potential crises in a time series) to the behaviour of prices and a proxy for price expectations. Was the abandoning of gold preceded, or followed, by a 'crisis' in either of these series?

FINANCIAL MARKETS

The crisis came in the summer of 1931 in the shape of a loss of Bank of England reserves and culminated in the abandonment of the gold standard in September 1931. Table 4.1 and Figures 4.1 and 4.2 present some of the relevant variables in monthly form over the course of the two years, 1930 and 1931.

We begin with the question of an exogenous shock. There does not appear to have been any such shock in Britain within reasonable distance of a 'crisis'. For example, there was no stock market experience comparable to that of the United States. An index of ninety-two industrial security prices shows that these had risen from the base of 100 in 1924 to a peak of 149 in January 1929, but drifted downwards in the course of the rest of that year. There was a major case of fraud that broke on the market in September 1929. The Committee of the Stock Exchange suspended dealings in the shares of the Hatry group of companies. Spurious scrip and duplication and triplication of shares was discovered and the initial impact was to curb activity in almost all securities. The collapse of the Hatry group was regarded by some as the expected sequel to the speculative 'boom' in new company flotations in 1928. (A similar case erupted in France in November – the Oustiric scandal – ruining many banks and scaring investors.) But the markets were quiet in 1930.

Stock market prices drifted downwards that year (from 129 to 99 between January and December); this hardly spells panic or doom, but

TABLE 4.1 MONEY, PRICES AND INTEREST RATES 1930–31

	Total bank deposits £.mill.	*Prices & cost of living (1924 = 100)*	*3-Month bank bill rate*	*Consol yield*
1930				
January	2230.7	94.0	3.938	4.329
February	2162.1	92.0	3.438	4.630
March	2126.0	90.0	2.344	4.386
April	2162.3	89.0	2.422	4.567
May	2196.7	88.0	2.125	4.454
June	2252.4	88.5	2.219	4.525
July	2253.2	89.5	2.282	4.525
August	2224.0	89.5	2.047	4.494
September	2225.2	89.0	2.125	4.484
October	2257.4	89.5	2.063	4.348
November	2266.6	88.5	2.173	4.283
December	2306.0	87.5	2.297	4.340
1931				
January	2304.8	87.0	2.469	4.310
February	2242.3	86.0	2.672	4.425
March	2177.3	84.0	2.594	4.386
April	2145.7	84.0	2.563	4.274
May	2150.2	83.0	2.079	4.158
June	2204.2	84.0	2.063	4.132
July	2211.6	83.0	4.344	4.310
August	2160.9	83.0	4.251	4.348
September	2121.6	83.0	5.813	4.717
October	2136.7	83.5	5.594	4.425
November	2116.1	84.5	5.844	4.739
December	2153.4	84.0	5.625	4.545

Sources: Capie and Collins, *Inter-war Economy* (1983); Capie and Webber, *Monetary History* (1985).

it is rather a reflection of the generally pessimistic mood of the first full year of economic depression.

So there was no exogenous shock such as would have led on from the 'peak' year 1929 to a boom–panic–crisis sequence. Neither was there any unusual expansion of bank credit nor rise in prices such as would have characterised a typical crisis. Bank deposits did rise from £2250m at the beginning of 1930 to £2300m at the end, but that hardly constitutes an expansion of bank credit on the scale suggested by Kindleberger. In the course of 1931 bank deposits were on a downward trend. Similarly with prices. Prices (as measured by the cost of living index) had been stable or slipping down for some years and slid down throughout 1930 and 1931. The index fell from its highest point of these

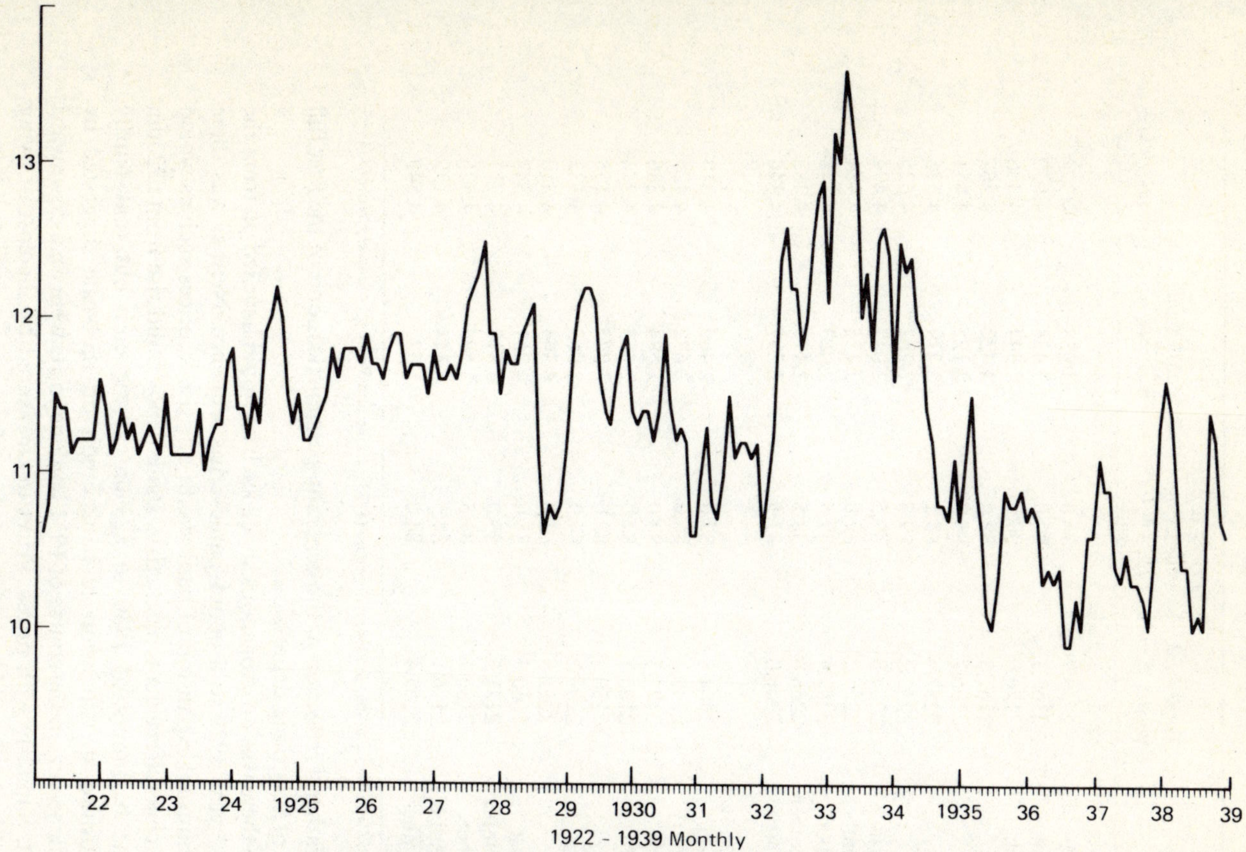

FIG. 4.1 Total Reserves/Total Deposits Seasonally Unadjusted

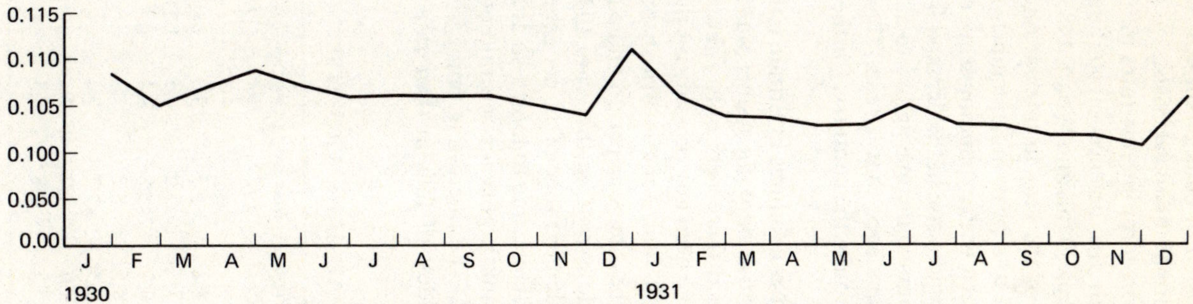

FIG. 4.2 Reserve/Deposit ratio of the London Clearing Banks.

two years, in January 1930 (94) to a trough of 83 in late 1931. In short, there is neither the expansion of bank credit nor the rise in prices that are associated with a 'normal' financial crisis.

There was a rise in short-term interest rates in mid to late 1931 but that was associated with the defence of sterling, rather than any internal problems (see Capie, Mills and Wood, 1983, 1). In midsummer (July), the first increase of the year in interest rates is observed, and rates kept rising through to a peak in September–November of 1931. This rise was not associated with expanding bank credit arising out of new profit opportunities and a rise in the demand for money. Unfortunately, there are no sub-annual income figures to allow a calculation of velocity but there is no evidence that it rose. There was certainly no euphoria in any market – quite the contrary, for the climate was one of gloom.

Finally, there were no bank failures in Britain either. This is perhaps not surprising for the British banking system was by this time dominated by the 'Big Five' and there were only a few other banks. There does not even seem to have been any pressure on the banks. Figure 4.1 shows that reserve/deposit ratio for the British banking system was fairly stable throughout the inter-war period and although the greatest movement is, as we would expect, in the years 1931–3, even here the ratio did not move outside the range of 11 per cent to 13 per cent.

In this connection it is interesting to look also at bank profits. Table 4.2 shows commercial bank profits for several countries for selected years from 1925 to 1932. The interesting point is that British banks experienced only the mildest of falls in their rate of profit, whereas

TABLE 4.2 COMMERCIAL BANK PROFITS*

	Profit or loss as percentage of capital and reserves				
	1925	*1929*	*1930*	*1931*	*1932*
Austria	8.2	5.5	5.0	L 34.4	L136.0
Germany	7.5	7.0	4.5	L118.1	L 15.0
France	10.1	8.8	8.4	L 7.0	6.3
England/Wales	8.5	8.2	7.3	7.9	6.9
Scotland	7.5	7.7	7.4	7.2	7.2
United States	9.0	9.7	7.4	1.7	L 4.9
Australia/New Zealand	7.5	6.8	5.3	3.6	2.7

*These are not intended to be in any sense precise but simply an indication of the broad outline of the movements in profits.

Source: League of Nations.

Europeans suffered substantial losses, and there were losses in the United States.[1]

RESERVE LOSS

It seems clear that there was no financial crisis in the Kindleberger/Minsky sense within the UK. That particular problem was not transmitted directly from continental Europe. There were, however, other countries, further afield, which experienced great economic problems. Some of these countries had intimate financial ties with the UK. Did the UK import problems from them?

Many of the world's primary producers were at this time still part of the British Empire, and maintained, originally for historical reasons but by this time for convenience, substantial holdings of financial assets in London. These countries did in some cases suffer substantial falls in real income in this period. Their terms of trade worsened sharply, and trade volumes were sluggish. This decline in income would, one would expect, lead to a running down of financial assets, for it would be quite rational for primary producers to anticipate that the decline in income was a cyclical phenomenon; there had been many cycles in the past. Such a run-down could have drained assets from the British banking system, and put financial markets generally under strain as assets were liquidated in large amounts. This could have left British financial markets nervous, exposed to speculative panics, and highly illiquid. Did it? There is only a small amount of data on reserve holdings in London by primary producers of the Empire. These data are shown in Table 4.3, below. (Ideally a set of balance of payments accounts for the sterling/non-sterling area should be drawn up but so far this has proved too difficult.)

This table suggests that whatever difficulties these countries experienced had a trivial impact on their London reserve holdings. Indeed, the fluctuation of 1931 was no larger than fluctuations that had occurred in the past without causing any problems for the financial system.

Further, even if some countries had withdrawn reserves from London on a significant scale, there is nothing to show that these reserves may not have been redeposited in London, changing ownership but remaining at a leading financial centre.

Accordingly, therefore, it cannot be shown that the difficulties of the primary producers at this time caused problems for the UK via the

TABLE 4.3 GOLD RESERVES OF EMPIRE PRIMARY PRODUCERS ($m.)

	Australia	*New Zealand*	*South Africa*	*India*
1925	162	38	44	109
1926	110	38	37	109
1927	106	38	40	119
1928	109	35	39	124
1929	89	28	37	128
1930	75	32	33	128
1931	51	28	43	162
1932	41	21	36	162

Source: L of N. *International Currency Experience* (1944): 233–40.
T. E. Gregory, *The Gold Standard and its Future* (1932): 112–15.

financial connections between primary producers and the UK. That position can still be maintained – but doing so would entail neglecting what evidence there is (how representative that evidence is, it should be stressed, we have no way of knowing), and would also involve arguing that the funds withdrawn from London were largely deposited elsewhere by their recipients.

The defence of that position must therefore rest entirely on conjecture. The balance of available evidence and of argument is in our view tilted to rejection of that position; the problems of the primary producers did not push the UK off gold.

This finding has implications for the hypothesis that the UK was pushed off gold by the drain of reserves from the sterling area as a whole. If reserves were not drained through the Empire's primary producers, the strain must have been directly on the UK. By ruling out, as far as the data allow, a drain through the primary producers, one is thrown back to examining the UK itself. Ruling out the primary producers also rules out the broader, but related, sterling area hypothesis.

UK INTERNAL POLICIES

Two aspects of UK domestic policy have been considered candidates for the role of having pushed the UK off gold. These are budgetary policy, and the choice of exchange rate in 1925.

(a) Budgetary Policy

The Government of the day was concerned by the size of their deficit. Efforts, including cuts in unemployment benefit, were made to reduce it. Can the UK's problems be ascribed to the budgetary position? There are two interrelated grounds for saying that they cannot.

First, the budget deficit was not growing at a rate so rapid that monetisation with eventual inflation, was inevitable. (For a detailed description of this process, see, for example, Sargent and Wallace, 1984.) Indeed, a good part of the deficit was cyclical, and therefore transitory.

Unemployment stood in 1931 at about 3 million, 21 per cent of the insured workforce – equivalent on the definition of unemployment now in use to an unemployment rate of around 16 per cent. This manifestly contributed to the deficit. Ideally, to ascertain whether the budgetary position was transitory or permanent – permanent in the sense that it required policy action rather than economic recovery to correct – one should calculate the constant employment budgetary position. Only that can really reveal whether a surge in the deficit in any one year is an economy-induced fluctuation, or a shift of policy to a new, and conceivably unsustainable, course. Budgetary calculations of that nature are not straightforward and results can differ widely. There are in existence, however, two independent calculations of the constant employment budgetary position of the UK in the 1920s and 1930s – the work of T. Thomas (1979) and Roger Middleton (1981). Fortunately, these studies produce similar results. The main focus of these studies was to consider whether fiscal policy was operated in what is generally viewed as a stabilising way – deficits varying counter-cyclically. As a preliminary to that both authors calculate constant employment deficits. Both find that, on a constant employment basis, the deficit was low – indeed, in 1931 the Budget on that definition was in small surplus.

This indicates fairly clearly that the *underlying* budgetary position was not at fault in pushing the UK off gold.

What of the *actual* budgetary position? Could that be responsible? There are strong analytical grounds for arguing that it could not. Under a fixed exchange rate system, a budget deficit financed by the issue of interest-bearing debt attracts rather than repels funds. Interest rates are driven up (perhaps only very briefly, if capital markets are sufficiently responsive) and capital attracted from the rest of the world. A budgetary deficit, so long as it is not so large as to presage monetisation and subsequent inflation, cannot lead to pressure to abandon or devalue a pegged exchange rate. The UK's budgetary position cannot be blamed for the abandoning of gold.[2]

(b) A Sterling Overvaluation

One version of the exchange rate story runs as follows: the proximate source of the financial pressure is found in Central Europe where first the Austrian banks were unable to meet the demands on them and the Credit-Anstalt closed in May. Pressure moved to Germany where the Danatbank closed temporarily in June. There followed a scramble for liquidity throughout Europe. London had short liabilities greatly in excess of gold and foreign exchange reserves in the Bank, a situation that was known in international financial circles at the time. The same had been true prior to 1914 when the international system seemed to work smoothly, but on this occasion several factors shook the confidence of foreigners. There was the growing feeling that sterling was overvalued. (As early as October 1929 Norman voiced fears that sterling would be forced off gold.) Then there was the publication of the Macmillan Report (13 July) which brought out the damage done to London and revealed the extent of the short-term liabilities. Further, there were growing fears abroad over the extent of the budget deficit. Although this was not large by recent standards, and as argued above fears were not objectively justifiable, it nonetheless worried foreigners and permeated the atmosphere in all financial markets at the time. Foreigners began withdrawing balances from London, and in spite of American and French credits the Bank was left with insufficient reserves with which to defend the exchange rate. A final straw is said to have been the Invergordon Mutiny on 15 September, and Britain left gold on the 21 September 1931.

An alternative explanation of the exchange rate crisis is that sterling would have been under extreme pressure anyway because of the weakening balance of payments position, deriving specifically from the poor performance of invisibles. Moggridge (1970) points out that in 1931 Britain's current account balance moved into deficit as a result of the deterioration in invisibles, in part a product of the contraction of world trade. Falling interest rates reduced receipts from overseas investments and the contraction of trade reduced income from shipping and financial services. In this account the scramble for liquidity only brought matters to a head.

In an attempt at bringing some rigour to this investigation Cairncross & Eichengreen (1983) recently sought to distinguish between the 'liquidity' cause and the 'balance of payments' cause. To this end they examined the determinants of the official settlements balance arguing that it was that balance rather than any one of the components that determined the extent of reserve flows. [At the same time they conceded the knowledge that a particular component of that balance (in this case the invisible balance) exhibited the largest swing prior to the crisis may be helpful for interpreting the results.]

There are many difficulties with his approach – difficulties that range over the data, the econometrics and the theory of the balance of payments; and in the end the exercise yielded no unambiguous advance on our understanding of the episode.

Some insights can, however, be gained by examining certain consequences of the exchange rate movement after the gold standard was abandoned.

EXCHANGE RATE BEHAVIOUR

Over the three months from September 1931, sterling fell by some 25 per cent against the US dollar, and by somewhat less on a trade-weighted basis. There is a widely accepted view of the effects such a move is likely to have.

Some domestic prices will rise almost mechanically, as tradable goods are marked up in home currency terms to keep their foreign currency prices unchanged. This impact on prices affects inflationary expectations, and in turn affects long-term interest rates and wage claims. This widely accepted view does seem to capture the 'stylised facts' of, for example, post 1945 UK experience. (See Williamson and Wood, 1976 for a discussion of the model underlying that view, and an examination of how well it fitted in the UK between 1945 and 1975.) Simple examination of the data on prices and interest rates (see tables) suggests that view does not match the stylised facts of the 1930s. Is this traditional description of devaluation experience still incorrect when the data of the 1930s are examined rigorously? If so what is the explanation?

To investigate whether there was actually anything to be explained, we analysed the time-series behaviour of prices and of interest rates – the latter being both long bond yields, and, for completeness, short-term interest rates, to see whether the abandoning of gold (or any of the precursive events) affected any of the series. (Using interest rates in this way does not, of course, commit us to the full Fisher hypothesis;

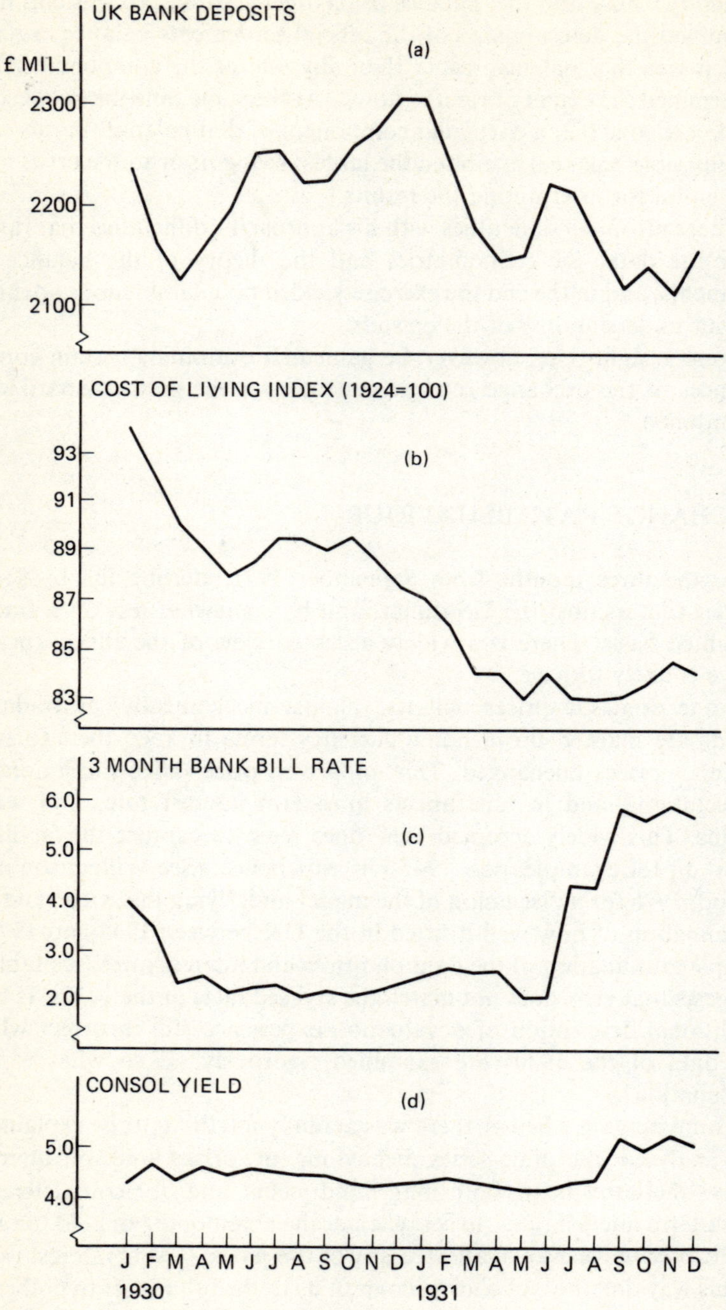
UK BANK DEPOSITS
(a)
£ MILL
2300
2200
2100
COST OF LIVING INDEX (1924=100)
(b)
93
91
89
87
85
83
3 MONTH BANK BILL RATE
(c)
6.0
5.0
4.0
3.0
2.0
CONSOL YIELD
(d)
5.0
4.0
J F M A M J J A S O N D J F M A M J J A S O N D
1930
1931

all we need assume is that a change in inflationary expectations has some effect on interest rates.)

The two interest rates examined were the Consol Yield denoted *RC*, and the rate on three month bank bills denoted *RB*. The price series employed was the Ministry of Labour Retail Price Index (Cost of Living), which is denoted *P*. Initially, ARIMA models were built for each series (using the techniques popularised by Box and Jenkins (1976) over the period January 1927 to December 1937, a total of 132 observations. Such a period was considered to provide an adequate number of observations both before and after the period in question, while avoiding other periods of economic upheaval.

Thus a monthly series $x_t = (1-B)^d(1-B^{12})\ ^D Y_t$, transformed to stationarity, is modelled as:

$$\varphi_p(B)\varphi_P(B^{12})x_t = \Theta_q(B)\Theta_Q(B^{12})a_t \qquad (1)$$

where B is the lag operator, a_t is a sequence of independently distributed normal variables having mean zero and variance σ^2, and the $\varphi(B)$'s and $\theta(B)$'s are polynominals in B of degrees p, P, q and Q respectively, all of whose roots lie outside the unit circle. The series Y_t is then said to be modelled as an ARIMA $(p, d, q)\ (P, D, Q)_{12}$ process.

Both interest rate series were adequately fitted by (non-seasonal) ARIMA (0, 1, 2) processes, the estimated models being

$$(1-B)\ RC_t = (1 - \underset{(.08)}{.16B} + \underset{(.08)}{.29B^2})\ a_t\hat{\sigma} = .102 \qquad (2)$$

$$(1-B)\ RB_t = (1 + \underset{(.08)}{.09B} + \underset{(.08)}{.27B^2})\ a_t,\ \hat{\sigma} = .382 \qquad (3)$$

standard errors being shown in parentheses.

The price series displayed a seasonal pattern and required an ARIMA (0, 1, 0) (0, 1, 1)$_{12}$ model, the estimate being

$$(1 - B)(1-B^{12})\ P_t = (1 - \underset{(.07)}{.74B^{12}})\ a_t,\ \hat{\sigma} = .673 \qquad (4)$$

The economic events occurring during 1931 and 1932 may be regarded as non-repetitive exogenous interventions. When the *exact* timing of such interventions are known their effects can often be accounted for by using the intervention analysis techniques proposed by Box and Tiao (1975).[4]

In the present circumstances, however, the exact timing and influence of the interventions are uncertain and the sequence of such shocks may make it difficult to identify correctly the separate dynamic responses. As a consequence, analysis based on the residuals from the fitted models (2) to (4) was first undertaken to identify possible outliers and isolate significant interventions.

Following Hillmer, Bell and Tiao (1981), we define two types of outliers, additive and innovational. An additive outlier (AO) is defined as

$$x_t = \frac{\theta(B)}{\varphi(B)} a_t + \omega_A \xi_t (t_0) \tag{9}$$

and only affects the level of the t_0th observation. An innovational outlier (10) is defined as

$$x_t = \frac{\theta(B)}{\varphi(B)} (a_t + \omega_1 \xi_t^{(t_0)}) \tag{10}$$

and hence represents an extraordinary shock at t_0 influencing x_{t_0}, $x_{t_{0+1}}$, ... through the memory of the system described by $\theta (B) / \varphi(B)$.

If t_0 and all the time-series parameters of the model (1) are known, then, by defining the residuals

$$e_t = \frac{\varphi(B)}{\theta(B)} x_t = \pi(B) x_t \tag{11}$$

we have, for an AO

$$e_t = \omega_A \pi(B) \xi_t^{(t_0)} + a_t \tag{12}$$

and for an IO

$$e_t = \omega_1 \xi_t^{(t_0)} + a_t \tag{13}$$

From least squares theory, estimators of the impact, ω, of the intervention and the variances of these estimators are

$$\hat{\omega}_A = \pi^2 (F) e_{t_0} \text{ Var. } (\hat{\omega}_A) = \rho^2 \sigma^2 \tag{14}$$

$$\omega_1 = e_{t_0} \text{ Var } (\hat{\omega}_1) = \sigma^2 \tag{15}$$

where $\rho^2 = (1 + \pi_1{}^2 + \pi_2{}^2 + \ldots)^{-1}$ and $F = B^{-1}$. Thus the best estimate of the effect of an IO at time t_0 is the residual e_{t_0}, while the best estimate of the effect of an AO is a linear combination of e_{t_0}, e_{t_0-1}, ... with weight depending on the structure of the time-series model. Likelihood ratio test statistics for these outliers are straightforward to construct. If the null hypothesis is that x_{t_0} is not an outlier, then a test that it is an IO is given by $\lambda_1 = \hat{\omega}_1 / \sigma$, while a test that it is an AO is given by $\lambda_2 = \hat{\omega}_A / (\rho\sigma)$, both statistics being distributed as $N(0,1)$.

In practice, of course, t_0 and the time-series parameters are unknown. If only t_0 is unknown, we may proceed by calculating λ_1 and λ_2 for each t, making decisions based on the sampling properties of the test statistics given above. However, the time-series parameters (φ's, θ's and σ) are also unknown and estimates of these parameters, particularly σ can be seriously biased by the existence of outliers. This would suggest that decisions should be made more informally on the basis of size and patterns of the statistics.

Table 4.4 lists these statistics for the three series over the years 1931 and 1932. For the *RC* series there is a suggestion of two outliers, the first an *AO*, the second an IO, during the summer of 1931. There is also a pattern of negative statistics in the first half of 1932, culminating in large *AO*'s in May and June and large IO in July. This provides confirmation of the significant stock conversion intervention found in

TABLE 4.4 OUTLIER TEST STATISTICS

	RC		*RB*		*P*	
	λ_1	λ_2	λ_1	λ_2	λ_1	λ_2
Jan 1931	−.01	.76	.36	.55	.77	1.54
Feb	.87	.32	.42	.62	−.36	.34
Mar	−.24	−1.43	−.34	−.49	−.16	1.68
Apr	−1.38	−2.08	−.16	−1.22	.83	.26
May	−1.29	−.67	−1.16	.12	−.89	.32
June	−.07	1.24	.11	4.58	.48	.98
July	2.11	3.06	6.28	3.89	−2.05	−1.57
Aug	.73	1.39	−.84	1.07	−.21	.25
Sept	2.14	1.41	2.46	1.08	−.71	.06
Oct	−2.57	−.66	−.57	−.24	−.39	−1.45
Nov	1.77	.42	.04	.49	1.71	1.26
Dec	−.88	−2.08	.42	−1.21	.24	.42
Jan 1932	−1.82	−2.52	−1.28	−4.21	1.32	1.37
Feb	−1.34	−1.64	−4.02	−4.12	.47	.58
Mar	−1.26	−.96	−2.72	−1.24	1.39	2.40
Apr	−.23	−.96	.93	−.71	−.87	−.40
May	−1.18	−2.94	−1.88	1.37	.08	1.23
June	−1.59	−2.99	−.16	−.26	−.39	.88
July	−3.48	−2.09	−.29	−.31	−1.53	−.25
Aug	.35	−.26	.07	−.36	−.16	.46
Sept	.35	−.21	−.25	.43	.96	.72
Oct	−1.62	−.09	.49	.46	1.03	−.03
Nov	1.67	1.20	1.09	.26	−.22	.14
Dec	.04	−.21	.48	1.07	.18	.35

Capie, Mills and Wood (1983). Indeed, on estimation only this intervention was found to be significant, the finally chosen model being

$$\underset{}{(1-B)\,RC_t} = -\underset{(.10)}{.22}(1-B)\,1_t + (1-\underset{(.09)}{.20B}+.30B^2)\,a_t,\ \sigma=.100$$

where $1_t = \eta_t^{\,66)}$, *a* 'step' intervention at June 1932. Thus the shock conversion had an immediate permanent affect on the *RC* series, reducing the level of the series by 0.22 percentage points. No shock in 1931 produced a significant effect on the time-series behaviour of the series, either permanent or transitory.

For the *RB* series, patterns of large statistics are found in the middle of 1931 and the first three months of 1932. Large *AO*s are found at June and July 1931, the second month having an even larger IO. These outliers correspond to the Austrian banking crisis and the May Committee. There is also a suggestion of an IO in September 1931, the month when the UK came off the gold standard. Large AO's are found in January and February 1932, and large 10's in February and March 1932. These outliers have been interpreted in Capie, Mills and Wood (1983) as a reaction to exchange rate pressures.

On estimation of an intervention model for *RB* the sequence of shocks in 1931 was found to be most adequately modelled by an 'extended pulse' intervention between July and November. The intervention in early 1932 was modelled as a step at February, with the response spread over two months. Thus the model finally selected was

$$(1-B)\,RB_t = \underset{(.23)}{1.14}(1-B)\,1_{1t} - (\underset{(.33)}{1.80} + \underset{(.32)}{1.00}B)(1-B)\,1_{2t}$$
$$+(1+\underset{(.09)}{.22}B^2)a_t\sigma=.316$$

where $I_{1t} = \varepsilon_t^{(55,59)}$ and $I_{2t} = \eta_t^{\,(62)}$. Thus the sequence of shocks during 1931 had a net effect of increasing the level of *RB* by 1.14 percentage points between July and November, while the shocks in early 1932 permanently reduced the level of the series by 2.80 percentage points.

For the price series no strong evidence of outliers of either type was found for the period and hence the shocks of 1931 and 1932 had no impact on the general level of prices. These results are puzzling at first glance, being quite plainly at variance with what is generally accepted as post 1945 experience. They suggest that the abandoning of the gold standard was not significant for any aspect of the UK financial system; there was no consequent or associated fundamental crisis for the UK banking system, financial markets, or the price level.[5]

They also raise the question of why this result was found, and before concluding it is useful to consider why the devaluation had such an insignificant effect on prices.

POSSIBLE EXPLANATIONS

There are five explanations of interest, four of one type and one of another. The devaluation may have been fully anticipated; it may have been expected to be transitory; some other movement may have occurred to offset it; or, the return to gold in 1925 was thought even at that time to be transitory. These four are considered in order, before we consider the fifth, which rejects the above described connection between exchange rate changes and price level changes.

(i) Anticipated

There were undoubtedly forebodings before the event. But did they affect any objective indicators? As discussed above, we tested for the existence of outliers in the series of prices and interest rates, so as to allow for the possibility that one or other item of news affected the series before the abandoning of gold. No outliers were found which could be related to the publication of any report, or to any other item of news which would have led to anticipations of the UK leaving gold. Accordingly, whatever forebodings were expressed, they were not acted on to an extent sufficient to affect significantly any financial markets, and they did not affect either the general level of prices.

(ii) Permanent *v* Transitory

Was the devaluation expected to persist? Had the abandoning of gold been widely believed to be temporary, it is quite possible that it would not have affected either prices or inflationary expectations.

The very strenuousness of the efforts made to remain on gold indicate that the authorities feared leaving it to be an irrevocable step. Two participants were quite explicit in stating that they believed a fall in the rate would last. Siegman (of the Bank) accepted that $4.86 was gone forever, and Niemeyer rejected the idea of pegging at a new rate. There were also discussions of future policy. By December, Norman had formulated plans. Howson says:

> We should eventually return to gold, not necessarily at the former parity but we could not decide the rate until we had
>
> (a) an active trade balance
> (b) a settlement of reparations and war debts
> (c) a budget balanced now and in the future, and
> (d) a competitive price level.
>
> The Governor was not in agreement with those who thought that we must wait until there was an agreement on the part of other countries to 'play the gold standard game according to the rules', whatever this exactly might mean. Foreign lending would begin when confidence was restored. . . . It would be dangerous to make any statement as to the time or rate of stabilisation. . . . It must be recognised that we have not the means to peg exchange.
>
> As for liaison between the Bank and the Treasury, 'the Government entirely agreed with this proposal and arrangements will be made accordingly'. (Howson, 1975)

From then on, the problem was seen as that of 'managing the sterling exchange so as to give more benefit to British industry than had been possible under the gold standard' (Howson, 1975).

These views all indicated recognition that a fundamental and irrevocable step had been taken. Belief in the transitoriness of the new rate and any expectation of return to the old level can certainly not be invoked to explain the behaviour of prices and interest rates.

(iii) Offsetting Events

There are two events which could have offset the effects of the exchange rate movement – a sharp monetary contraction, or a sharp fall in the price of imports.

The first can be rapidly dismissed. Money growth accelerated soon after the abandoning of gold – initially not by much, but even in 1931 manifestly a movement in the wrong direction.

What did the reduction in the price of imports do? Table 4.5 shows the behaviour of a price index for UK imports. This index was falling but the fall of 1931 to 1932 was, while large, certainly not large enough to offset the effects of the devaluation of sterling (on a trade weighted basis) on the level of prices. Further, it should be recollected that the proxy we have used for inflationary expectations also did not respond; even, then, if the terms of trade effect *had* been substantial it would be

TABLE 4.5 PRICE INDEX FOR UK IMPORTS
(1963 = 100)

1925	155
1928	138
1929	134
1930	118
1931	96
1932	89

Source: Key Statistics 1900–1970.

necessary to explain why it was expected to have a persistent effect on the inflation rate, as opposed to a once-for-all effect on the price level. The behaviour of the index may help explain the behaviour of the price level, but it does not explain *all* of the behaviour of the price level and explains *none* of the behaviour of interest rates.

(iv) Was 1925 Transitory?

A fourth explanation for the abandoning of gold and subsequent devaluation having no apparent effect is that it was fully anticipated – fully in that when the UK returned to gold, this return was not expected to last, so that the new parity and new commitment had no effect on any economic time series. (We adopt this definition of anticipation since we found no evidence of anticipation of devaluation between 1925 and 1931.)

It is not possible to test statistically for this possibility, for the return to gold was in effect implemented gradually. There had been much discussion in advance (for example, by the Cunliffe Committee), and the exchange rate gradually drifted towards its pre-war parity, the final step on repegging being a small one. A study of contemporary opinion is therefore necessary. The two main opponents of the return to gold, both in their evidence to the Bradbury Committee and elsewhere, were Keynes and McKenna.

Despite their criticism of the decision, that a return to the gold standard would persist was clearly the view of them both; indeed to some extent that was the basis of their criticism. When the decision was taken Keynes immediately switched to advocating policies based on the presumption that the system would persist. We had gone back at too high a parity; that parity would persist; measures, for example protectionism, should be taken to alleviate the consequences. Not only was Keynes critical of the short-term effects of overvaluation: he was fearful also of the long-term consequences. He feared there would be inflation in the US, which would lead to an inflow of gold to the UK, and subsequently to inflation (Pigou papers, evidence of J. M. Keynes to the Chamberlain–Bradbury Committee). In his evidence to the same committee, McKenna was less clear cut. He appeared to differ from some of the proponents, unlike them thinking that the City would prosper without it. He resisted deflation to achieve parity with the US; but, like Keynes, expected US prices to rise until the UK could safely peg. Underlying that position must be the belief that, once restored, the system would last. One of the main protagnists, Montague Norman, clearly expected the system to last, and indeed ascribed its collapse to policy failures *after* 1925.

> Yes, I have made mistakes also. I am now accused for having gone back to the Gold Standard. It was probably a mistake. And still in those circumstances I should do the same thing again. It is easy to see it afterwards. *But a great deal of what has happened in the meantime was not necessary but depended on policy.* It might have been different. (E. E. Jucker-Fleetwood, 'Montagu Norman in the Per Jacobson Diaries', *National Westminster Bank Quarterly Review*, November 1968, emphasis added.)

Certainly there seem to have been no doubts about the desirability of the gold standard *system*. There were doubts in advance, but only about the parity. The durability of the system was taken for granted – sometimes with trepidation for the inflationary consequences – even by the critics of the system. There is no evidence in the historical record for arguing that the 1925 return was expected to be transitory.

A RESOLUTION

There appears to be a paradox – a major devaluation which affects neither prices nor price expectations, and yet not accompanied by any offsetting factors. There is, however, a resolution of the paradox, and one which sheds light on why the gold standard was abandoned by the UK. The resolution involves rejecting the existence of a link between exchange rate changes and subsequent price level movements.

The view of the relationship set out above is essentially a description of what happens when a country moves from one pegged rate to another. At the second peg, just as at the first, monetary policy has to be *accommodative* to the rest of the world's inflation. Consequences for the rate of inflation arise not from the devaluation but from the necessity to conduct monetary policy so as to make the new exchange rate sustainable.

In contrast, when, as the UK did in 1931, a country moves from a peg to a float, the behaviour of the exchange rate is in the long run irrelevant, and the behaviour of the price level determined in the long run by the behaviour of the stock of money.

As noted above, monetary policy eased after 1931, but very modestly. Hence the apparent paradox can be resolved. After 1931 monetary policy was domestically determined and the exchange rate in the long run irrelevant. Domestic monetary policy clearly was not inflationary in 1931, so neither prices nor inflationary expectations surged on the abandoning of gold. But it should be observed that the theory relates to the long-run, equilibrium, result. The theory does *not* say that there is no transitory effect, some prices rising sharply as a result of devaluation and others falling only slowly so that there is a transitory upward boost to the domestic price level. Indeed, this transitory boost to the price level is inevitable unless domestic prices respond within the period of observation to the monetary squeeze, the fall in the *real* stock of money, created by devaluation.

There seems to have been no such transitory effect on prices in the UK. Taken at face value, this suggests considerable – indeed, rather surprising – price flexibility. It would make 'sticky price' explanation of the Great Depression difficult to accept, and, important for the present purpose, it undermines the notion of a *sustained overvaluation*. After all, if prices responded within a quarter in 1931, a 10 per cent overvaluation which existed in 1925 is unlikely to still be around in 1931! (As Sayers (1976) implicitly assumed.)

There must, however, be two qualifications. Just as Cairncross and Eichengreen's (1983) study was undermined by, among other factors, the scarcity of data, so the above finding is 'softened' by the composition of the price index, and by currency invoicing practices.

The index was composed to a much greater extent than its present-day contemporary counterpart of primary commodities – notably food. These goods are flex-price goods, whose price responds very quickly to clear markets. (See McKinnon, 1979; Carse, Williamson and Wood, 1980.) Hence our results are not so clear cut in their implications as the same results on, say, a present day CPI would be.

A second qualification arises from currency invoicing practices. If most primary products were invoiced in sterling, then the impact effect of a sterling devaluation on the UK price index would be diminished, changes in the prices of these goods feeding through not mechanically as a result of the changed exchange rate, but only as these prices responded to the changed balance of supply and demand. It is the conventional wisdom that a good part of primary product trade was invoiced in sterling in the 1920s and 1930s. There is, however, no evidence; and it was, until the publication of Grassman (1973) and Carse, Williamson and Wood (1980), conventional wisdom that in the 1960s and 1970s the bulk of world trade was invoiced in US dollars.

The second 'softening' must be noted as a possibility, but one not supported – or refuted – by the data.

All that said, the finding does add weight to the rejection of overvaluation as a cause of Britain's leaving gold.[6] In this it supports studies that have gradually reduced the estimate of the overvaluation – from the 10 per cent suggested by Keynes in 1925, to around 8 per cent now. The last is still an 'overvaluation' but not so large as to be conclusive, given the margin of error associated with PPP calculations.

A SUMMING UP

The banking crisis of continental Europe did not impose strains on the internal financial system of the UK. The impoverishment of some gold holders in the Empire may have led to increasing illiquidity of the UK financial system, but what data there are do not suggest this is important. UK budgetary policy was certainly not inconsistent with a fixed exchange rate. It appears that UK prices were sufficiently flexible that any overvaluation there may have been in 1925 could not have persisted until 1931.

When then was the gold standard abandoned? Partly by elimination of other arguments, we are driven back to the view that the cause was the continental European banking crisis. This, as a result of national central bankers failing to act as lenders-of-last-resort followed as individual bankruptcies turned into a national banking crisis and then an international banking crisis. There was a scramble for gold; the Bank of England, because of its low level of reserves, and because of the attention drawn to the low level, was caught up in this scramble; and the two major *national* gold holders, France and the USA, failed to follow Bagehot's guidance on how a central bank should act at a time of crisis. The abandoning of the gold standard was the result.

The argument has the appeal of explaining why parities were not just adjusted; that would not have worked in a crisis of the international system. It has the appeal of showing France behaving consistently with its behaviour in the 1920s (see Clarke, 1967), building up its gold holdings without regard to the effect of this on the gold standard system as a whole. And it has the appeal, too, of showing the Federal Reserve acting internationally in the same, deficient, way as Friedman and Schwartz (1963) showed it to have acted domestically. It failed to act as lender-of-last-resort.

But that does prompt a question, one which has troubled many commentators on the gold standard. In principle, the system does not need a dominant central bank to act as Bagehot required – but in practice it appears to, for the system seemed to work best when the Bank of England did fill that role (1870–1914). There is plainly an issue for further research here, but at this point we would offer a conjecture. Just as a domestic banking system can work well without a lender-of-last-resort when there are no strains, so can an international fixed rate system. But when there are pressures, when small lenders are no longer ready to respond in their thousands to small movements in interest rates, a lender-of-last-resort is necessary. Bagehot may have international as well as domestic implications. But to develop that argument is for a separate paper.

We would summarise the conclusions of this paper as follows.

What happened in 1931 was a crisis, not just the result of overvaluation. That is why the system was abandoned, rather than restructured at different parities. What happened in 1931 was that the world saw the consequences of central bankers not understanding central banking.

NOTES

1. It has been drawn to our attention by Michael Wagner that the losses shown by the Austrian banks in 1931 and 1932 in fact occurred before 1925, but only appeared in their accounts in 1931 and 1932. The losses of these two years are spurious, in the sense that they were carried forward from earlier years. Why the banks did not show them earlier or why they showed them when they did is not clear.
2. This does lead to two issues, which are taken up briefly below. There was clearly a scramble for liquidity on the Continent. Under a fixed rate system, this would tend to push up interest rates in the UK. The deficit would have

the same tendency. But the authorities were keen to see rates come down (see Capie, Mills and Wood, 1983). This may have increased willingness to break financial links with the rest of the world, and thereby alleviate domestic interest rate pressures. Second, markets may have taken fright, irrationally on the above arguments, because of the deficit. There is under the gold standard an appropriate central banking response to such an irrationality. The actions of central banks other than the Bank of England are discussed in the final section of this paper.

4. As an illustration, suppose that an intervention occurs at time t_0. Then its effect can often be modelled as

$$x_t = \frac{\omega(B)}{\delta(B)} \mathrm{I}_t + \frac{\theta(B)}{\varphi(B)} a_t \tag{5}$$

where $\theta(B)=\theta_q(B)\theta_Q(B)$, $\varphi(B)=\varphi_p(B)\varphi_P(B)$ and $\omega(B)$ and $\delta(B)$ are polynominals in B, their ratio describing the dynamic behaviour of the intervention I_t, which can usually take one of three forms (i) a 'step' at t_0 defined as

$$\mathrm{I}_t = \eta_t^{(t_0)} = \begin{matrix} 0 \text{ for } t < t_0 \\ 1 \text{ for } t \geqslant t_0 \end{matrix} \tag{6}$$

(ii) a 'pulse' at t_0, defined as

$$\mathrm{I}_t = \xi_t^{(t_0)} = \begin{matrix} 0 \text{ for } t \neq t_0 \\ 1 \text{ for } t = t_0 \end{matrix} \tag{7}$$

or (iii) an 'extended pulse' between t_0 and t_1

$$\mathrm{I}_t = \varepsilon_t^{(t_0, t_1)} = \sum_{s=t_0} \xi_t^{(s)} = \begin{matrix} 0 \text{ for } t < t_0 \text{ and } t > t_1 \\ 1 \text{ for } t_0 \leqslant t \leqslant t_1 \end{matrix} \tag{8}$$

5. This is certainly not to say that the move was of no consequence for the UK economy. Indeed, it was soon to prove of great importance, for it ensured that the severely contractionary monetary policies pursued in the USA were not imported into the UK.
6. This is aside from the problem that overvaluation can explain devaluation but is not enough by itself to explain the collapse of the system. Consider the Bretton Woods system. There were, as Triffin frequently observed, fundamental flaws in the Bretton Woods system which gradually destroyed it. That system was not wrecked by a set of misaligned parities; (although parity misalignment certainly affected the timing and probably the manner of its end).

REFERENCES

Blinder, A. and Solow, R. M. 'The analytical foundations of fiscal policy', in '*The Economies of Public Finance*', ed. G. F. Break (Washington, DC:): 3–115.

Box, G. E. P. and Tiao, G. C. (1975) 'Intervention analysis with applications to economic and environmental problems', *Journal of the American Statistical Association* (70): 70–9.

Box, G. E. P. and Jenkins, G. M. (1976) *Time Series Analysis: Forecasting and Control* Revised ed. (San Francisco: Holden Day).

Break, G. F. and Peachman, J. A. (1974) *The Economics of Public Finance* (Studies of Government Finance, The Brookings Institution).

Cairncross, A. and Eichengreen, B., (1983) *Sterling in Decline* (Oxford: Basil Blackwell)

Capie, Forrest and Collins, Michael (1983) *The Inter-war British Economy: A Statistical Abstract* (Manchester University Press).

Capie, F., Mills, T. C. and Wood, G. E. (1983) 'Was the war loan conversion operation a success', The City University, Centre for Banking and International Finance, *Monetary History Discussion Paper 5.*

Capie, Forrest and Webber, Alan (1985) *A Monetary History of the UK, 1870–1982, Data Sources Methods* (London, George Allen & Unwin).

Carse, S., Williamson, J. and Wood, G. E. (1980) *The Financing Procedures of British Foreign Trade* (Cambridge: Cambridge University Press).

Clarke, S. V. O. (1967) *Central Bank Cooperation 1924–31* (New York: Federal Reserve Bank of New York)

Friedman, M. and Schwartz A. J. (1963) *A Monetary History of the United States* (Princeton UP, for the NBER).

Grassman, S. (1973) *Exchange Reserves and the Financial Structure of Foreign Trade* (Farnborough: Saxon House).

Gregory, T. E. (1932) *The Gold Standard and its Future* (London: Methuen & Co.).

Hillmer, S. C., Bell, W. R. and Tiao, G. C. (1983) 'Modelling considerations in the seasonal adjustment of economic time series', in A. Zellner (ed.) *Proceedings of the Conference on Applied Time Series Analysis of Economic Data* (Washington: US Bureau of the Census).

Howson, S. (1975) *Domestic Monetary Management in Britain 1919–1938* (Cambridge: Cambridge University Press).

Keynes, J. M. (1925) *The Economic Consequences of Mr Churchill* (London: Hogarth Press).

Kindleberger, C. P. (1978) *Manias, Panics and Crashes* (London: Macmillan).

Kindleberger, C. P. and Laffargue, J. (1982) *Financial Crises: Theory, History, and Policy* (Cambridge: Cambridge University Press).

McKinnon, R. J. (1979) *Money in International Exchange: The Convertible Currency System* (New York: Oxford University Press).

Meltzer, A. H. (1982) 'Rational Expectations, Risk, Uncertainty, and Market Responses' in Wachtel, P. (ed.), *Crises in the Economic and Financial Structure* (Lexington: D. C. Heath).

Middleton, R. (1981) 'The Constant Employment Budget Balance and British Budgetary Policy, 1929–39', *Economic History Review*, xxxiv, 2, May.

Minsky, H. P. (1972) 'Financial stability revisited: the economics of disaster', in Board of Governors of the Federal Reserve System (ed.), *Reappraisal of the Federal Reserve Discount Mechanism*, Vol. 3 (Washington: Federal Reserve).

Moggridge, D. (1970) 'The 1931 financial crisis – a new view', *The Banker*, Vol. 120 (August).
Moggridge, D. (1972) *British Monetary Policy 1924–1931* (Cambridge: Cambridge University Press).
Sargent, T. J. and Wallace, N. (1984) 'Some unpleasant monetarist arithmetic', in B. Griffiths and G. E. Wood (eds) *Monetarism in the United Kingdom*, (London: Macmillan).
Sayers, R. S. (1976) *The Bank of England 1891–1944* (Cambridge: Cambridge University Press).
Thomas, T. (1979) 'Aggregate demand in the United Kingdom 1918–1945', in R. Floud and D. McCloskey (eds) *The Economic History of Britain Since 1700* (2) (Cambridge: Cambridge University Press).
Williamson, J. and Wood, G. E., (1976) 'The British Inflation: Indigenous or Imported?', *American Economic Review*, 66, 1976: 520–31.

Comment on 'What Happened in 1931?'

TIM CONGDON

In their interesting paper, Capie, Mills and Wood ask big questions and reach unexpected answers. They suggest that Britain's departure from the gold standard in 1931 stemmed from a 'scramble for liquidity' probably occasioned by the Central European banking crisis. This is not a particularly surprising conclusion, although a more conventional account would place greater emphasis on the unneighbourly conduct of France and the USA in accumulating excessive gold reserves in the late 1920s and 1930. They make only a passing reference to France and the USA towards the end of the paper. More provocative is the claim that abandoning the gold standard 'was not significant for the UK economy' which they amplify to mean 'there was no consequent fundamental crisis for the financial system, financial markets or the price level'. This claim is counter-intuitive, to say the least. I shall argue that it is, in several important respects, very misleading.

Capie, Mills and Wood consider several candidate explanations for leaving the gold standard. But, of course, in one sense there is nothing to be explained. Britain broke the link with gold because, by September 1931, the drain on the Bank of England's reserves was irresistible. To organise a discussion of the problem we may usefully draw on insights from the monetary approach to the balance of payments. According to this theory, changes in a nation's reserves reflect imbalance between changes in the demand for and supply of high-powered money.[1] The distinction generates a question to ask about the 1931 crisis. Was the attack on Britain's reserves caused by changes in the demand for high-powered money or by changes in the supply? As we shall see, the answer is the key to understanding events after the departure from gold and to solving some of the puzzles raised in the paper.

There is no reason to think that the supply of high-powered money was excessive or threatened to run out of control. As the authors note, 'the budget deficit was not growing at a rate so rapid that monetisation, with eventual inflation, was inevitable'. If central bank credit to the public sector was under firm restraint, so also was central bank credit to the private sector. The Bank of England's holdings of commercial bills showed no systematic tendency to expand in 1930 and 1931, hardly surprising in view of depressed economic conditions and weak loan demand.

The trouble did not stem from the supply side, but from the demand side. At the exchange rates ruling in early 1931 economic agents were unwilling to hold the quantity of sterling balances actually in being. This unwillingness led to a fall in the demand for high-powered money issued by the Bank of England and so to intolerable pressure on the reserves. The absence of serious banking difficulties suggests that the origin of the disequilibrium was not domestic, but external. The inappropriateness of the $4.86 rate against the dollar set in 1925 was obviously part of the story and has often been noticed, but its significance can be overdone. Although the USA was a net gold importer over the 1925–31 period, there were phases of gold export. A much bigger absorber of gold in the critical period leading to Britain's abandonment of the standard was France. Over the five year period from 1925 to 1929 the USA imported $306m. of gold; over the two and half year period from 25 June 1928 to 26 December 1930 the Bank of France's gold holdings soared by 24 643m. francs – or almost $1000m.[2] France, described at the time by one Treasury civil servant as 'the queen of gold bugs', continued to pile up more of the precious metal throughout 1931.[3] With so much gold destined for the central banks or France and the USA, the Bank of England was in an impossible position.

Contemporaries were well aware that the delinquent behaviour of the French – and, to a much lesser extent, of the Americans – would cause inconvenience for Britain. A perceptive analysis was given in the Macmillan Report. It noted that the stabilisation of the franc in 1926 had 'left the French price level considerably below that in the outside world'. Consequently, there would be 'readjustment of the per capita holding of currency so as to bring the amount into line with normal needs'; and this increased demand for currency had 'to swell the aggregate demand for francs which could only be supplied by the Bank of France'.[4] In technical terms, there was heavy excess demand for French high-powered money. The inflows were reinforced by a law of June 1928 which mandated that the Bank of France's liabilities had to be at least 35 per cent covered by gold. With the pound and the franc both on the gold standard, the exchange rate between them was fixed and the excess demand for high-powered money in France necessarily involved deficient demand for high-powered money in Britain. Keynes – who was, of course, a member of the Macmillan Committee – wrote several trenchant indictments of French policy. In July 1926, he warned that franc stabilisation at too low a rate would be bound to lead to a higher price level and 'in due course this rise in prices may require an increased note issue'. In September 1928, he was more outspoken. 'It is evident that if every country were to lock away 35 per cent of the sight liabilities of its state bank and then hold some substantial amount in excess of this in order to feel comfortable, there would be a steady deflationary pressure which, failing wiser courses, might continue over a long period. At any rate the future of gold now lies in the hands of the Bank of France as well as those of the Federal Reserve System.'[5]

It may seem lop-sided to dwell so much on French monetary policy. But the evidence given here, selective though it is, suggests the hypothesis that the actions of the French authorities were the main cause of the Bank of England's embarrassment from 1926 onwards. This claim is consistent not only with the scale and pattern of gold flows in the five years up to 1931. It was also the view held at the time by Montagu Norman and Hawtrey as well as Keynes.[6] The emphasis in most later work on the overvaluation of sterling against the dollar may be exaggerated. Perhaps more damaging for Britain's export industries was the overvaluation of sterling against the franc and, indeed, several other European currencies.

If French monetary policy was the culprit for Britain's departure from the gold standard, much of the analysis given by Capie, Mills and Wood appears a little off-beam. For example, changes in London balances by British Empire countries were negligible in comparison with the Bank of France's activities. It may be reasonable to interpret the Central European banking crisis, which engendered an intensified demand for high-powered money in general and for high-powered money free from devaluation risk (dollars, francs and gold) in particular, as the final trigger for the September 1931 crisis. But the root-cause of the Bank of England's plight can be dated back to 1925 and, more especially, to 1926. It is also quite clear that these difficulties were due to a decreasing demand for its liabilities, not to excessive expansion of its domestic credit to either the public or private sectors.

The identification of trouble in the demand for, not the supply of, sterling high-powered money is critical to understanding economic developments after September 1931. Capie, Mills and Wood express some surprise that the devaluation had little effect on either inflationary expectations and interest rates or, indeed, the price level.

In fact, there is nothing surprising about the absence of any rise in interest rates if the original disequilibrium consisted in a contracting demand for high-powered money. This disequilibrium would, if maintained, have caused falling prices and *deflationary* expectations, leading to lower interest rates.[7] Inflationary expectations would have been justified only if the devaluation had been attributable to excessive growth of the Bank of England's assets or, in other words, to disequilibrium in the supply of high-powered money. But there was no such disequilibrium. A Labour Government had just fallen because of its determination to keep the budget balanced and, despite many alarmist newspaper stories, the National Government was very unlikely to lose control of public sector finances. It therefore made little sense for bondholders to fear that the devaluation of September 1931 would initiate an inflationary spiral.

However, the abandonment of the gold standard should have had a once-and-for-all impact on the price level. As Capie, Mills and Wood comment, some prices 'will rise almost mechanically, as tradable goods are marked up in home currency terms'. But the retail price index may – at least over a short period and possibly over several years – behave quite differently from tradable goods prices. The distinction is necessary because, in their econometric work, Capie, Mills and Wood use the retail price index to validate their assertion that the September 1931 devaluation had no effect on the price level. A more detailed examination shows that there definitely were effects and they were of the kind normally associated with devaluation. The prices of tradable goods rose sharply between August 1931 and November 1931, while over the period from September 1931 to June 1933 retail prices were declining and wholesale prices – with their larger imported component – were broadly stable. The figures are presented in Table 4.6.

The reason for the apparent failure of devaluation to affect the price level more noticeably is, in fact, rather straightforward. The two years from September 1931 saw heavily falling prices of all goods in foreign

TABLE 4.6 THE IMPACT EFFECT OF DEVALUATION ON THE PRICES OF TRADABLE GOODS IN LATE 1931

1924 = 100	*Index value in: August 1931*	*November 1931*	*Change between August and November*
Tradeable categories in wholesale price index:			
Cereals	53.0	64.0	+20.8%
Other foods	67.3	71.3	+5.9%
Other metals and minerals	64.6	72.2	+11.8%
Cotton	37.9	42.9	+13.2%
Other textiles	44.2	50.2	+13.6%
Wholesale price index (1924 = 100)	59.9	64.1	+7.0%
Retail price index (July 1924 = 100)	145	146	+0.7%

THE RELATIONSHIP BETWEEN WHOLESALE AND RETAIL PRICES, SEPTEMBER 1931—SEPTEMBER 1934

	Wholesale prices (rebased to September 1931 = 100)	*Retail prices (rebased to September 1931 = 100)*	*Ratio of wholesale prices to retail prices*
1931 September	100.0	100.0	1.00
December	106.7	102.1	1.05
1932 March	105.5	100.7	1.05
June	98.8	97.9	1.01
September	102.8	97.2	1.06
December	101.8	98.6	1.03
1933 March	98.3	95.9	1.03
June	102.5	93.8	1.09

Note: The original retail price index was not given to one decimal place. The decimal points in the rebased series should not be taken too seriously.

Source: Cmnd. 5144 *Statistical Abstract for the United Kingdom* (London: HMSO, 1936):239, 137.

currency terms. A decline in the value of sterling against foreign currencies did not, therefore, require a rise in the British price level to maintain equilibrium. It should be noted here that sterling touched its lowest point against the dollar in November 1932 at a rate of \$3.14½, over a third lower than before leaving gold. If foreign currency prices had been stable, a big jump in Britain's prices should have occurred. Fortunately, international price deflation was most pronounced in primary commodities, of which Britain was a major importer. So extreme was the collapse in commodity prices that Feinstein's index of import prices, calculated in sterling terms, fell in 1932 and 1933 despite devaluation.[8] Although the drop in import prices in the two years together was less than that in either 1930 or 1931 individually, it is remarkable that there was any drop at all in view of the exchange rate movements. In 1933 and 1934 the pound advanced strongly and persistently against the dollar to reach a rate of \$5.10 in January 1935, slightly higher than the \$4.86 rate associated with the gold standard before September 1931. So it seems supererogatory to carry out a statistical analysis of the potential inflationary effects of devaluation extending until December 1937, as Capie, Mills and Wood have done.[9]

By severing the link with gold, Britain was able to avoid the worst of the international price deflation of 1931–3. In that sense, the events of September 1931 were highly beneficial for the price level and the economy.

But to limit the discussion to price level changes is too restrictive. Until September 1931 the Bank of England was obliged, by the rules of the gold standard game, to keep interest rates high enough to sustain the demand for sterling balances and so, ultimately, for its own liabilities. In an environment of falling prices these interest rates were a serious burden on all debtors, notably manufacturing industry. After September 1931 the Bank of England – with the Treasury's full endorsement – could allow interest rates to fall substantially, irrespective of the exchange rate consequences. According to Howson, the cheap money regime inaugurated by the fixing of 2 per cent Bank rate on 30 June 1932 was deliberate Treasury policy to promote exports, ease the slump and reduce unemployment.[10] Certainly it became feasible for the Bank of England to expand its balance sheet without disturbing monetary equilibrium (i.e. endangering the reserves) because national income, and hence the demand for high-powered money, recovered after Britain left the gold standard. In the six years to the third quarter 1931 high-powered money fell fractionally from £536m to £524m; in the six years from the third quarter 1931 high-powered money increased by over 33 per cent to £698m.[11] Without this easing of the monetary strait-jacket Britain is unlikely to have had the quite brisk upturn in output, employment and living standards experienced in the 1930s.

The view that 'the abandoning of the gold standard was not significant for the UK economy' is surely untenable, unless intended in a much qualified form.

NOTES

1. This is the version expounded by H. G. Johnson in 'The monetary approach to balance-of-payments theory' pp. 229–49, in his *Further Essays in Monetary Economics* (London: Allen & Unwin, (1972). Other versions are looser – for example, that 'the balance of payments' (undefined) depends on the demand for money relative to the supply.
2. Cmnd. 3897 *Report of the Committee on Finance and Industry* (the Macmillan Report) (London: HMSO, 1931), p. 306 and p. 75. For purposes of comparison it should be noted that the Bank of England's gold holdings hovered around £150m, or less than £570m, for most of 1930 and 1931. R. S. Sayers *The Bank of England* (Cambridge: Cambridge University Press, 1976), Appendixes, pp. 354–5.
3. Sayers, *Bank of England*, vol. 1, p. 231.
4. *Macmillan Report*, p. 73.
5. D. Moggridge (ed.) *The Collected Writings of John Maynard Keynes: Vol. XIX Activities 1922–29* (London: Macmillan, 1981), pp. 567 and 759–60.
6. See pp. 228–32 of Sir Henry Clay, *Lord Norman* (London: Macmillan, 1957) for details of a lively exchange in May 1927 between Norman and Moreau, Governor of the Bank of France. Norman was very conscious of the damage the sterling/franc exchange rate was doing to British industry. 'It is the condition of British industry which is in fact the tragic feature of the ... situation' (p. 231). A paper by Hawtrey formed the basis for the Macmillan Committee's remarks.
7. The contracting demand for high-powered money required, with the fixed exchange rate, a contracting supply. That, after all, was the cause of the reserve drain. The smaller supply of high-powered money was accompanied by downward pressure on the price level.
8. C. H. Feinstein, *Statistical Tables of National Income, Expenditure and Output in the UK 1855–1965* (Cambridge: Cambridge University Press, 1976), p. T139.
9. Sayers, *Bank of England,* vol. 2, p. 467. But during the mid-1930s the

pound/franc rate was the focus of most Bank of England foreign exchange intervention.

10. S. Howson, *Domestic Monetary Mangement in Britain 1919–38* (Cambridge: Cambridge University Press, 1975), p. 89.
11. Howson, *Management*, pp. 148–9.

Comments on 'What Happened in 1931?'

MICHAEL WAGNER

The reasons for Britain leaving the gold standard in 1931 have attracted much interest among economic historians. Various explanations have been offered, none of which seems to be entirely convincing. Thus I appreciate the attempt of Capie, Mills and Wood to put some of the more prominent hypotheses about 1931 to an empirical test. It is the rather rigorous design of their tests which I find a particular gratifying feature of their paper. Moreover, the authors' main conclusion, that it was the failure of central bankers to implement adequate rules of proper conduct under a gold standard which was to blame for the crisis of 1931, will certainly stimulate further controversy.

Given the formidable task the authors have set themselves, it is hardly astonishing that their paper is long and difficult. It is certainly the result of much research, only part of which, I suspect, is described in the paper at hand. I am sure that Capie, Mills and Wood originally developed their arguments in a macroeconomic model of the British economy of the 1930s; nevertheless, I would have found my way easier through their analysis (which is really four analyses), if they had cared to write down their background model in a more explicit manner. In particular, it would have been easier to assess how much weight their time series analysis (of price and interest rates) carries with respect to the main thrust of their argument.

Since I am basically in agreement with the paper's test design and its conclusions, there is only a minor point left on which I like to comment. The issue is the use of published balanced sheets of joint stock banks as a source for calculating rates of profit in banking.

I know for certain that the figures on commercial bank profits (Table 4.2 in the paper) are grossly misleading for Austria; and I suspect that the same holds true for Germany. Though this does not imply, as far as I can see, a major revision in the line of arguments which Capie *et al.* follow, it nevertheless bears directly upon a general issue of this conference, namely, how the banking system deals with problems caused by financial distress of some of its members.

In the case of Austria, bankers followed a simple rule after the First World War. Whenever a major bank faced financial distress, its fellow competitors would rather come to its rescue than let it go under. For all financial intermediaries suspected that even a minor incident could trigger off a major run on commercial and savings banks. Since most of the problems Austrian banks faced after the war proved to be permanent, their fellow bankers, who at first had meant to provide only temporary support, later on had to accept a conversion of their loans into equities of the joint stock banks to which they had made advances. This induced a series of takeovers, reducing dramatically the number of Austrian private and joint stock banks especially after the hyperinflation (and the *hausse* at the Viennese Stock Exchange) had been brought to a sudden halt. By the late twenties, only four major commercial banks had survived these mergers.

Their financial position did not look too bad, that is to an outsider. Their true status, particularly that of the Boden-Credit-Anstalt and the Credit-Anstalt, was dangerously close to insolvency, partly because the interests they held in manufacturing industries drained their resources. More important, however, was probably the fact that the managing directors refused to value the securities of the banks (and other joint stock companies) they had taken over previously at their true value. This would have implied writing off major part of the items on the asset side of their financial statement. For political as well as commercial reasons the managing directors showed little inclination to risk such a step; and there was no public agency that could force them to do so.

It was not until the crash of the Credit-Anstalt, when the foreign creditors called in a Dutch expert to serve as internal accountant, that the true financial position of the only remaining major Austrian commercial bank was made known to the public. At this point of time, all the losses which had been incurred over the previous decade showed up in official publications.

This course of events not only explains why League of Nations tables on bank profitability can be quite misleading; it also highlights how risks can get quite out of hand if financial crises get solved by takeovers within the banking system. It might be sometimes less costly to the public purse, if an imprudent banker gets bailed out by the Government than if losses are allowed to be accumulated (rather than absorbed) by fellow bankers. Though the Austrian central bank had never taken on the final responsibility for rescue operations during the twenties, it had in the end no other choice than to serve as lender-of-last-resort to the Credit-Anstalt. This led to a rather remarkable situation: financial bills issued by the Credit-Anstalt made up the better part of the assets against which the central bank created high-powered money.

5 Walter Bagehot and the Theory of Central Banking[1]

HUGH ROCKOFF

INTRODUCTION

In the debate in monetary economics over 'rules' versus 'discretion' there is one issue that receives little attention because it appears to have been settled long ago – what to do in a crisis. Here, the textbooks tell us, Walter Bagehot proved that there is one and only one correct course of action – 'lend freely at high interest rates'.[2] The appropriate policies for non-crisis periods are debated, and the appropriate arrangements for assuring that the monetary authority has the power to act on Bagehot's principle are debated, but the rule itself and Bagehot's case for it are seldom discussed.

Part of the reason, I think, is that Bagehot dazzles us. He had in Clapham's (1944, V. 2, p. 283) words 'as good a head and as good a pen as any in England'. His works bristle with brilliant epigrams – his collected works contains an index of them, surely unique for an economist – while they display deep practical knowledge of the money market. He wrote widely on literature and politics as well as economics, and *The English Constitution* has attained a status in political science that rivals that of *Lombard Street* in economics. He was the confidant of the leading businessmen and statesmen of the day. Indeed, he was known as the 'spare chancellor', a phrase that became the title of one of his biographies (Buchan, 1959). No wonder we are tempted to accept his word on things. This, I hope to show, is unfortunate because *Lombard Street* contains a subtler analysis, and raises more questions than our memory of Bagehot's epigram suggests.

The main problem, I believe, is this. There are really two Bagehots, even though we remember only one. There is, of course, the Bagehot who tells us to 'lend freely at high rates' in a panic, but there is also the Bagehot who tells us to 'protect the reserve' when the market is merely apprehensive. Both speak authoritatively, but to whom should we listen? It is here that Bagehot fails us, for nowhere does he supply an explicit guide for recognizing the state of the market that calls for one policy rather than the other.

This weakness is not obvious when we confine ourselves to the theoretical parts of *Lombard Street*, but it becomes apparent when we turn to the historical parts. Indeed, I will argue below that when we compare Bagehot's descriptions of the nineteenth-century crisis with those of other analysts, particularly those of Clapham based on the records of the Bank, the conclusion that forces itself upon us is that the problems of the Bank were seldom if ever due to an unwillingness to lend in a panic. Rather the problem was typically one of recognising the right moment for extreme actions, and of avoiding being pushed to take actions it thought were unnecessary. *Lombard Street*, in other words, for all its excellent qualities, and I will have occasion to notice many of them, did not create an exception to the general rule of monetary economics. In this area, as in others, the crucial issues are still controversial.

It is always worthwhile to take a fresh look from time to time at our economic classics. But current policy discussions make a fresh look at *Lombard Street* seem particularly worthwhile. There exists a mounting concern that the world financial system has grown fragile, while the inability of the less developed countries to meet their obligations has increased the probability of a shock to the system. Plans for reforms of the system are discussed frequently. One argument, pressed perhaps most notably by Charles Kindleberger (1978) for example, is that what is most needed is an international lender-of-last-resort with the freedom and power to follow Bagehot's formulae. At the other end of the spectrum is the school of thought that would have us return to the gold standard in order to return to a lost world of monetary stability. Bagehot wrote about a world on the gold standard in which the Bank of England was (it could be argued) in a position to perform as an international lender-of-last-resort. It makes sense, therefore, to attend closely to what he had to say about that world.

I have divided the paper as follows. In the next section I review the central themes of *Lombard Street*. In the third section I then review some of the traditional criticisms, and the weaknesses that I think have been neglected next in the fourth section. In the fifth section I examine Bagehot's use of historical evidence. In the sixth section I review the remainder of the nineteenth century to see to what extent later episodes also reveal shortcomings in Bagehot's analysis. In the seventh section I take up the role of the gold standard. And in the eighth and final section I set out my main conclusions.

THE CENTRAL THEMES OF *LOMBARD STREET*

Bagehot began writing *Lombard Street*, he tells us (1873, p. 46), in the autumn of 1870. The reason is not hard to find. The Franco-Prussian War had forced the Bank of France to suspend specie payments. Now more than ever any great demand for gold, including an indemnity, would fall on the Bank of England. The appropriate response was for the Bank of England to hold a larger reserve. But Bagehot was not convinced that this was appreciated at the Bank. The point had to be driven home to the Bank and to the world of opinion. Hence, *Lombard Street*.

The lend-freely rule was, in fact, a secondary theme of *Lombard Street*. This was the lesson that later writers, such as Hawtrey (1933), distilled from Bagehot. But they were writing with a different financial system in mind, with different preconceptions about how the economy works, and with different social concerns. The Bank had stilled the panic that followed the failure of Overend, Gurney & Co. in 1866 by lending freely, and had even admitted its responsibility to do likewise in future crises. There had been some backsliding in the form of statements by Thomson Hankey, one of the directors of the Bank, who denied the Bank had an unequivocal duty to lend widely in panics. And Bagehot intended to set this right in *Lombard Street*. But the point at which he hammered away the most, because he thought it was the least understood, was the duty of the Bank to maintain a large reserve in all 'seasons of trouble'.

There is obviously a potential contradiction between maintaining or augmenting a reserve and lending it freely. Bagehot resolved this conflict by distinguishing between periods in which the market was merely apprehensive and periods in which it was in a panic. When the market was apprehensive the chief concern in the City was, according to Bagehot, with the level of the Bank of England's reserves. The appropriate policy was to protect and if possible augment them by raising the discount rate and restricting credit. Higher reserves would calm the market's fears and restore credit to normal. But, if the Bank failed to calm the market and if apprehension became panic, then the only plan open to the Bank was the 'brave plan', to lend freely. In a panic each man fears that the next deny him credit if he cannot show that he has money. Only when he gets cash, and sees that men in debt to him can get it, will the panic end.

It was altogether natural that Bagehot should make a psychological distinction the key to his theory. As Keynes (1915) pointed out long ago, it is Bagehot's psychological approach that provides the common thread of his seemingly diverse interests. He was best, moreover, in Keynes' view, at analysing men like himself, active self-confident men of business or politics.[3] But note that Bagehot's schema makes everything depend on the Bank's 'psychoanalysis' of the market. If the Bank mistakes apprehension for real panic and lends freely, then the reserve will fall and the level of apprehension will rise. On the other hand, if the Bank mistakes panic (significantly, Bagehot referred to it as a species of 'neuralgia') for mere apprehension, the Bank will starve the market of funds and the panic will intensify.

Although he was confident that the psychology of the market could be accurately read, and the appropriate medicine prescribed, Bagehot was not confident that the Bank of England as it was then constituted could do it. It was for this reason that he suggested his famous reforms of the Bank of England. There should be, he thought, a permanent Deputy Governor, to provide a clear head in a crisis – when the Governor and the Directors might be engaged with their own affairs. (Did he have himself or, more likely, a friend in mind?) And he thought that bankers, as well as brokers and exchange dealers, should be admitted to the 'court' – the flow of correct information to the Bank was crucial.

Bagehot's policy, it should be noted, was harder to apply than one which simply held that the Bank's reserves could be gradually augmented in 'normal' times and then used when troubles loomed. Bagehot, for example (1861, pp. 20–22), favoured a policy of augmenting the reserve in ordinary times, but it is clear from his analysis of historical episodes that this would not necessarily be enough. There were also sensitive periods when the market was close to panic, and yet when the correct policy was a further augmentation of the reserve.

The distinction between augmenting the reserve in normal times and augmenting it in periods of trouble was stressed earlier by Henry Thornton (1802, pp. 161–7), and the contrast between his analysis and Bagehot's helps to clarify the distinction.[4] Thornton, writing in the aftermath of the crisis of 1797, saw no reason to augment the reserve once the feeling was widespread that the reserve was inadequate; this was like trying to increase the supply of grain when there was already a shortage. Thornton simply had not conceived of it as a purely psychological problem in which the state of credit was closely tied to the level of reserves. There was more sense, Thornton thought, in the idea that the Bank of England should have tried to increase the reserve in more normal times. But this was ruled out, Thornton believed, by the cost to the shareholders of the Bank. The shareholders had a right to a normal return, and this would have been precluded by a build-up of reserves.

Given the crucial role of a larger reserve in Bagehot's schema, it is surprising that he did not consider some way of defraying the costs of accumulating gold. It would be natural to argue that since the economy as a whole benefits from a larger reserve at the Bank, the Treasury should subsidise the reserve. The costs of such a subsidy might be met in turn through a tax on the joint stock banks since the larger reserve is going to be of greatest benefit to them. Implicit taxes had been imposed on the joint stock banks before to the benefit of the Bank of England – the limitations on the note issue. But such a recommendation might have seemed out of place in the heyday of *laissez-faire*. In any case, Bagehot noted the profit problems of the Bank (1873, pp. 66–7). But he evidently believed that it was sufficient to point out to the Bank its appropriate duties. This decision may have been based on a close reading of the kind of men that directed the Bank. But in retrospect it appears to have been a mistake to ignore the profit problem. As we will see below, it was years before the Bank accumulated the additional reserves that Bagehot advocated.

TRADITIONAL CRITICISMS

Bagehot is not without his critics. Perhaps the point made most frequently is that the existence of a lender-of-last-resort creates a problem of moral hazard. If the banks know that someone is there to bail them out in a crisis, they are likely to take more chances – reserve ratios will be reduced, dividend pay-outs will be increased, risky loans will be undertaken – and as a result, panics will be more frequent than they would otherwise be.[5] Charles Kindleberger (1978, pp. 215–20) has referred to it as a familiar argument, although he does not put much weight on it. He has argued, for example, that the presence of a lender-of-last-resort may actually reduce the frequency of panics by removing fears that a rapid business expansion must end in a liquidity crisis.

How would Bagehot have responded to this point? Hirsch (1977) argues that Bagehot implicitly assumed that the problem could be solved through the paternalistic leadership of the Bank within the narrow confines (social as well as physical) of Lombard Street. This seems to be a good suggestion. It fits well with Bagehot's neglect of a mechanism for providing the Bank with a financial incentive for holding more reserves. Men who had been to the right schools could be counted on to do the right thing once it was pointed out to them. But we also have some direct testimony in *Lombard Street* that shows that Bagehot thought this to be a minor point in any case. Moral hazard was the heart of Thomson Hankey's objection to the Bank committing itself to the role of lender-of-last-resort, the statement that so irritated Bagehot. Bagehot's answer was simply that the joint stock banks already acted on the principle that the Bank was there to bail them out. Their reserves were already reduced to the point where they were insufficient to meet the extra demands of a panic (1873, pp. 133–5). Any further movement of the joint stock banks in the direction of greater risk probably did not seem very important to Bagehot, especially because panics were as likely to be started by an external shock – war, a bad harvest, and so forth – as by bad banking.

A number of other reservations have been expressed. Mints (1945, p. 249) and Sayers (1957) expressed a concern that Bagehot's recommendation of a high discount rate sometimes did more harm by keeping up rates than good by slowing the loss of bullion from the Bank or by drawing fresh supplies from abroad.[6] And Kindleberger (1981, pp. 297–300) has noted that there may be a problem of mopping up excess liquidity after the panic has subsided. But despite the willingness of many economists to think critically about Bagehot's message, the literature seems to ignore a number of thorny problems that follow from a policy that grants the Bank – and more particularly the 'permanent deputy governor' – unrestricted authority to declare a crisis and to shift radically the Bank's policies.

SOME NEGLECTED PROBLEMS

A panic, Bagehot evidently believed, was something to be read from the furrowed brows of the brokers in Lombard Street, not something to be deduced from quantitative indicators. With only one exception, the reserve of the Bank, the variables that play such a large part in modern discussions of monetary policy – the stock of money, interest rates, the supply of credit, and so on – are ignored. Bagehot apparently assumes that it is easy (at least for the right man) to intuit the state of the market. And when it comes to a certain kind of crisis, he is probably right. If the market is sailing along smoothly, and suddenly without warning a giant bank with a reputation for soundness fails, and if there is a sudden demand for cash, there is not likely to be much disagreement with labelling the situation a panic. As it turns out, the crisis of 1866, the one that was one of the provocations for *Lombard Street*, could be described in these terms without doing very much violence to the facts; it was very much a bolt from the blue. But in earlier crises, I will try to show below, it was not so easy to decide the state of the market.

The problem with leaving the definition of a panic to the discretion of the Bank is that without objective criteria it becomes extremely difficult for the Bank to resist political pressures to define any period of distress as a panic. As a matter of political survival the Bank is likely to find itself embarking on a policy of lending freely when it doesn't want to. As we will see below, Bagehot criticised the Bank for having allowed its reserves to become dangerously low in pre-1866 crises. But he is somewhat vague on why these mistakes were made. A closer look at these episodes shows that the reason was that there were many qualitative signs of a panic, and the Bank was under strong pressure to act as if there was one.

A second difficulty with Bagehot's set of proposals, is that it assumes that the market always responds in a simple and predictable way to the policy chosen by the Bank. Thus, it ignores the likelihood that the market will learn to anticipate the sharp changes in Bank policy that Bagehot advocates. Once it is established that the Bank has adopted a Bagehotian policy, Lombard Street is likely to watch the Bank closely and react, possibly in counter-productive ways, to changes in the Bank's official perception of the market.[7] The decision to raise the discount rate in an apprehensive market may further alarm the market once it is understood that this is the Bank's standard policy in an incipient crisis.

In short, the psychological states of the market that lie at the core of Bagehot's schema appear to have been harder to diagnose, and less stable than Bagehot suggested.

Bagehot was aware that the market watched the Bank closely. But he tended to ignore the implications of this for his own proposals. This was especially true in his discussion of the Bank's reserve. Bagehot argued that the main cause of apprehension in the market in past crises, before the point of actual panic, was a concern with the level of the

Bank's reserves. He believed that at the time when he was writing apprehension would become acute when the reserve in the Banking Department reached £10 000 000. This was the 'apprehension minimum'. To prevent this level from ever being approached he suggested an effective minimum of £15 000 000. The reserve had been £10 320 000 in 1869, close to the apprehension minimum, and averaged £12 259 750 in the years 1869–73. So Bagehot was advocating an increase of perhaps £3 000 000, about 25 per cent. He undoubtedly had figures of this sort in mind. A figure of £10 million was also mentioned by Thomas Tooke (1838, V.2, pp. 330–1), and Bagehot may have been influenced by him, or the figure may have simply been part of the lore of the market.

In any event, the crucial question is what would have happened if the Bank had adopted these figures as a guide to policy? The obvious answer is that once the market learned that whenever the reserve approached £15 000 000 the Bank would take restrictive actions – raising the discount rate, allowing bills to run-off, and so on – the market would react to the approach of £15 000 000 by limiting credit. The approach of the minimum would itself produce a crunch. Bagehot recognised this problem in a slightly different context. In considering the American plan of fixed legal reserve ratios he pointed out that if this plan were adopted by the Bank of England then, 'In a sensitive state of the English money market the near approach to the legal limit of reserve would be a sure incentive to panic; if one-third fixed by law, the moment the banks were close to one-third, the alarm would begin and would run like magic (1873, p. 216). Granted that a legal reserve ratio would be worse than a voluntary level of reserves, why would not this argument apply to Bagehot's proposal as well, even if on only a limited scale?

Thus Bagehot failed to solve the classic problem of defining the appropriate guide for monetary policy. In the case of panics he proposed giving the monetary authority complete discretion without giving them any bulwark against pressures to upgrade periods of stress to the status of panics. In the case of apprehensive markets he proposed a guide, the level of reserves, but one which on his own reasoning was not likely to work well.

BAGEHOT AS ECONOMIC HISTORIAN

Because the state of the market, in Bagehot's schema, is something to be recognised intuitively, the ex-post definition of the state of the market can become a mere tautology. If we observe a period in which the Bank followed a policy of liberal lending, and we observe that things got worse, we can say that the market was merely apprehensive, and the Bank should have been concentrating on building up its reserve. If we observe a period in which the Bank holds on to its reserve, and we observe that things got worse, we can say that the market was in a panic, and the Bank should have been lending freely. At points Bagehot comes very close to this sort of reasoning.

He supports his case with an examination of the five crises, after the restriction, that preceded *Lombard Street*: 1825, 1939, 1847, 1857, and 1866. The crisis of 1825 was, next to 1866, his most persuasive example. His analysis of 1825 is simple. The Bank failed to protect its reserve and so produced a panic. The reserves (total bullion in the Bank) fell from £10 721 000 in December 1824 to £1 260 000 in December 1825 and, to quote Bagehot, 'the consequence was a panic so tremendous that its results are well remembered after nearly fifty years' (1873, p. 138). The Bank then took the correct action and lent freely. In a passage that has become famous he quoted Jeremiah Harman.[8]

> 'We lent it,' said Mr. Harman, on behalf of the Bank of England, 'by every possible means and in modes we had never adopted before; we took in stock on security, we purchased Exchequer bills, we not only discounted outright, but we made advances on the deposit of bills of exchange to an immense amount, in short, by every possible means consistent with the safety of the Bank, and we were not on some occasions over nice. Seeing the dreadful state in which the public were, we rendered every assistance in our power.' (1873, p. 73)

But what was going on in 1825? Why did the Bank's reserve decline so precipitously? Well before December of 1825, and the fall of Sir Peter Pole & Co. that is associated with the actions that Harman mentions, there were signs of strain in the banking system. Clapham (1944, V.2, p. 98) writes of abnormal bankruptcies beginning at the end of September. Tooke and Newmarch (1838+, v.2, p. 184) suggest that there were runs on the country banks by small noteholders 'after the summer' of 1825 (although the evidence they cite mentions the end of the year). Now couldn't we argue as follows, using Bagehot's own principles? The reserve had fallen from £11 787 430 in August 1824 to £3 634 320 in August 1825, and perhaps this was a mistake, perhaps the drain was an external one that could have been stopped without alarming the money market. But beginning in the fall of 1825 there was an internal drain prompted by the fears of noteholders that could only be stayed by following the policy of lending freely. I think that we could reason along these lines; the only problem is that the crisis got worse. It is only in hindsight that it is clear that the Bank was following the wrong policy by lending freely in the fall of 1825.

In recounting the crisis of 1825 Bagehot made an instructive error stressed by Frank Fetter (1967).[9] Bagehot refers to a letter from Peel to Wellington discussing the Government's quandary over whether to issue more Exchequer bills, to make borrowing from the Bank easier, or whether to force the Bank into lending directly on goods, the course ultimately followed. Bagehot suggests that this letter refers to the same moment in the crisis as the statement by Harman quoted above. In fact, Peel's letter refers to events some months later. It is a natural error, and perhaps Bagehot is not to be faulted too much for making it. But it does illustrate the problem of defining a panic. Should the Government have gone to any length to make borrowing easier, or was it right in allowing other concerns (in this case a rather dubious concern with out-of-pocket expenses) to take precedence? The heaviest demands on the Bank had passed, but failures were still high. The pressure on the Government to define the situation as one requiring extreme measures was obviously great.

To be sure, the Bank could not use the discount rate during the crisis in the manner suggested by Bagehot due to the usury law. The rate was kept at 4 throughout 1825 until it was raised to 5 per cent in December. Bagehot could have argued consistently that an earlier and more vigorous increase in Bank rate, had it been legal, might have reduced the outflow of cash from the Bank. But what would have been the effect of a rapid increase in the discount rate in 1825, and in particular what would have been the effect if the public realised that this was a sign that the Bank thought its own reserves were inadequate?

Of the crisis of 1839 all that Bagehot tells us is that 'the Bank was compelled to draw for £2 000 000 on the Bank of France; and even after that aid the directors permitted their bullion, which was still the currency reserve as well as the banking reserve, to be reduced to £2 404 000: a great alarm pervaded society' (1873, p. 138). Clapham (1944, V.2, p. 166) is more circumspect, but he also criticises the Bank for 'a rather shortsighted complacency [about reserves]' from the autumn of 1938 on.

The moment that Bagehot has in mind is July 1839. Before that date, presumably, the Bank should have been defending its reserve. But if we look at the period before the final humiliation (the loan from France!), it is easy to point to a number of similarities to a 'panic', and to show that the Bank was following the policy that Bagehot recommended for a panic. (1) There was a banking panic on the Continent in 1838 marked by a major suspension of payments by a bank in Belgium, a run on a banking house in Paris, and a collapse of credit and wave of failures throughout France (Clapham 1944, V.2, p. 166). The Bank of England was not under any obligation in Bagehot's scheme to act as an international lender-of-last-resort. But the linking of currencies under the gold standard created strong pressures on the Bank to operate in this way. (2) Two years earlier there had been significant closures in Britain and the circumstances had suggested that British firms were vulnerable to financial instability centred in other countries. It seems possible that the English market remained sensitive to any evidence of an unwillingness on the part of the Bank to lend when financial conditions in a major trading partner were deranged.

With these events in the backround, the Bank followed essentially the sort of policy Bagehot recommended for a panic. (1) It raised the discount rate from 4 to 5 per cent in May 1839 and from 5 to 5.5 in June. (2) In February it repeated its offer to lend on securities other than bills of exchange, and in general it followed a policy of 'allowing the public to act upon the bank' – as the policy was later described to Parliament (Clapham 1944, V.2, p. 166). From the outward course of events, in other words, we can argue that the Bank was behaving as an international lender-of-last-resort, and we can regard the Bank's difficulties as a failure of that policy. In retrospect, of course, we can also argue with Bagehot that there was no genuine panic in late 1838 or early 1839, and that the Bank followed the wrong policy. But the point is how was the Bank to know, and how was it to avoid the pressure for labelling this as a period when lending should be easy?

'The next trial,' according to Bagehot (1873, p. 138), 'came in 1847, and then the Bank permitted its banking reserve (which the law had now distinctly separated) to fall to £1 176 000; and so intense was the alarm, that the executive government issued a letter of license, permitting the Bank, if necessary, to break the new law, and, if necessary, to borrow from the currency reserve.' Again, Bagehot has the most dramatic moment in mind, the 'week of terror', 16–23 October 1847. But there were signs of a crisis well before October. Failures of major commercial houses, according to Clapham (1944, V.2, p. 203), began in August, when Bank rate was raised from 5 to 5.5. On 1 October, the Bank announced a number of actions to defend its reserve – a rate of 6 per cent for bills longer than a month, and a discontinuance of loans on stock or Exchequer bills. And it was these actions which at the time were blamed for producing the panic (Clapham 1944, v.2, p. 205), rather than the fall in the Bank's reserve cited by Bagehot; a fair illustration of the potential for Bagehot's formulae to prove counter-productive.

With hindsight we can argue that it was too late to defend the reserve at the end of September, and that the time had come to lend freely. But again the question is how could the Bank have divined this at the time? There is nothing in Bagehot's schema to help the Bank to decide on which course to follow.

The panic of 1857 was the first observed directly by the mature Bagehot; he was then 31, and would become director of *The Economist* two years later. But he argues in the same way about this crisis as about earlier ones. In *Lombard Street* (1873, p. 138) he shows the banking reserve falling from £4 024 000 on 10 October 1857 to £957 000 on 13 November. The result was that 'a letter of licence like that of 1847 was not only issued, but used'. The clear implication of this passage is that the Bank should not have 'let' the reserve fall. At the time, incidentally, Bagehot wrote a piece for the *National Review* (1858) in which he took a more moderate view. He then argued that the panic was aggravated by Peel's Act, and that some regular way for relaxing it was needed. But he did not directly criticise the Bank for allowing the reserve to fall, although he may have done so indirectly in one hard to interpret passage (1858, p. 69).

But why, to return to the main point, were there such stupendous demands on the Bank during this period? The answer, which by now should be obvious, is that the panic was already on, and the Bank was trying to put out the fires. The panic began, it appears, in the USA in September. Late in October the Liverpool Borough Bank went down. The Bank of England was clearly following Bagehot's lend-freely policy. The discount rate was raised from 6 to 7 to 8 in October, and then to 9 and the unprecedented figure of 10 in November. The Bank used its reserves as 'bravely' as possible, but its resources proved inadequate. The crisis dragged on even with the help of the letter of licence to break the Act of 1844. Finally, Bank rate was lowered from 10 to 8 on Christmas Eve, and this may be taken as a symbol of the end of the acute phase of the crisis (Clapham 1944, V.2, pp. 227–34).

Bagehot could have argued that the Bank was remiss in not building up its reserves over the years after the crisis of 1847. Or he might have argued that the letter of licence should have been issued earlier, although this course of action seems less consistent with his basic faith in the long-run usefulness of the gold standard. But it is hard to credit the argument – implicit in his discussion of the movement of reserves in October and November – that the Bank should have prevented the crisis by refusing to lend. The Bank, in other words, was listening to the Bagehot who says to lend freely in a panic; it is just that in retrospect this was the wrong Bagehot.

The panic of 1866, the one immediately preceeding *Lombard Street*, raised the fewest questions about Bagehot's schema, and one cannot help thinking that his theory was essentially a generalisation of this experience. It would be wrong to suggest that there were no signs of danger before the failure of Overend, Gurney & Co. Ltd on 11 May 1866. Yet it appears that 'panic, true panic, came with unexpected violence that day' (Clapham 1944, V.2, p. 263). Bagehot did not blame the Bank of England's reserve policy for contributing to the crisis (1873, p. 140), and he thought (1873, p. 79) the Bank's response, on the whole, was correct, although it may have erred in permitting a rumour to circulate that it was not accepting consols.

If all crises were as simple as the crisis of 1866, then Bagehot's schema might be adequate. But our review of the earlier crises shows that despite Bagehot's jamming and pushing not all of them can be made to fit into the 1866 mould. In some cases the crisis struck first in foreign countries or at the English country banks. Was this a situation that demanded action by the lender-of-last-resort? Sometimes the crisis grew slowly over months or even years. Again, when did the situation change from 'apprehension' to 'panic'? Is it any wonder that in these periods of uncertainty the Bank allowed its reserves to fall, when perhaps it should have been conserving them against a more acute demand. Without an explicit guide for defining a panic, Bagehot's analysis really helps in only a small number of cases, and may make it harder to follow an appropriate policy in others.

THE REMAINDER OF THE NINETEENTH CENTURY

What happened after *Lombard Street*? Did the Bank follow Bagehot's recommendations?[10] It is easiest to speak about the call for higher reserves. In the sixteen years between the publication of *Lombard Street* and the Baring crisis, the average yearly reserve exceeded Bagehot's minimum of £15 000 000 only four times: in 1876, 1880, 1881, and 1885. In those sixteen years, the Bank's reserves averaged £13 376 000 compared with £12 693 000 during the years *Lombard Street* was being written. Indeed, in half those years the Bank's reserves averaged less than they had when Bagehot was working on *Lombard Street*. After the early 1890s the reserve began to grow rapidly. But this was clearly due to the flood of gold from South Africa, Australia, the US, and elsewhere, and owed nothing to Bagehot. At least in the long run Bagehot's call for higher reserves went unheeded.

The reason was probably the mundane factor which Bagehot decided not to pursue in *Lombard Street*: the cost to the Bank of holding larger reserves. The sums involved do not seem large. Holding an extra £2 000 000 in gold during these years might have cost the Bank, say, £100 000 per year, and so reduced its annual dividend (about £700 000), if it were all to come out of dividends, by about 14 per cent. Not a high price for Britain to pay for a smaller chance of a financial crisis, but too high a price for the shareholders to pay.

In the years closer to *Lombard Street* there were some spells of trouble in the money market. And Bagehot was able to assimilate those that came in his time (he died in 1877) within his system. There was a crop of commercial failures in 1875 – although none of the order of Overend, Gurney & Co. – but the Bank was never faced with a panic. Bagehot (1875, 1876) claimed that this was because the Bank had maintained a large reserve. But the reserve was not really larger than it had been in the years when he was writing *Lombard Street*: the reserve averaged £10 037 000 in 1874, barely above the apprehension minimum, and £11 597 000 in 1875. Perhaps it was true that the reserve was large given the demands placed upon it.

But the plain fact was that these years, as might be said of the rest of the century, were relatively free of the sort of crisis that had repeatedly shaken the system before *Lombard Street*. The reason is not really clear, although I would lean to the view expressed by R. C. O. Matthews (Kindleberger and Lafargue 1982, p. 2) that the relative absence of major wars played a part, along with perhaps the rising supply of gold at the end of the period. The next real test of the Bank came with the Baring crisis in 1890, a crisis similar to 1866 in the sense that it involved the sudden (although not completely unanticipated) failure of a giant house in London.

The reserve on the eve of the Baring crisis was only £10 815 000, close to the apprehension minimum defined by Bagehot seventeen years earlier, and well below the working minimum of £15 000 000 he had laid down. Bagehot could well have berated the Bank once again for maintaining an inadequate reserve, but further events moved along lines that Bagehot had not foreseen. Bank rate was raised from 5 to 6 per cent in November when the Bank learned of the difficulties of

Barings. But Clapham (1944, v.2, p. 330) conjectures that the Bank didn't want to raise the rate further because it might alarm the City, once again illustrating the problem of unwanted announcement effects that Bagehot had ignored in *Lombard Street*. Once bills on Barings began to come in it was time for the Bank, according to Bagehot, or more properly to one of the Bagehots, to stem the crisis by lending freely. Instead, the Bank resorted to a device completely outside Bagehot's rules – a collective guarantee of the liabilities of the Barings, provided by the Bank, the government, and leading financial institutions. As it turned out this device was effective, and a panic was avoided (Clapham 1944, V.2, 326–39; Presnell, 1968). The success of the guarantee showed one way towards greater financial stability. But it was not a triumph for Bagehot.

THE GOLD STANDARD AND BAGEHOT'S DILEMMA

The weaknesses in Bagehot's schema which I have been discussing are clearly a product of the gold standard. It is the finite limit to the stock of high-powered money that forces the Bank of England constantly to look over its shoulder at its reserves. Under a fiat standard, by way of contrast, the Bank could never run out of high-powered money. It could always lend freely in a crisis.

If the Bank could draw on some other large supply of gold besides its own reserves, then it would be in a position to act something like a central bank with fiat powers. Several possibilities have been suggested to me as ways of reconciling Bagehot's two rules, but all seem to me to miss one of the main points of *Lombard Street*, that the supply of gold was truly limited. It could be argued, for example, that Bagehot counted on Peel's Act being suspended in a panic. Indeed, Bagehot argued, as we have seen, that there should be some formalised means of suspending the Act, and in parliamentary testimony he conceded that the Act might have to be suspended. But it is clear from his remarks on the crises of 1847 and 1857, quoted above, that he regarded the suspension of the Act as a failure of policy. Nor is it clear that suspending the Act would always have the desired effect. The amount of gold in the Bank would still be limited, and the alarm of the financial community, particularly note holders, might increase. Only going off gold altogether would really help and this was clearly anathema to Bagehot.

It has also been suggested to me that Bagehot might have been assuming that an increase in the discount rate could bring in gold, allowing the Bank to follow a lend-freely policy without worrying about the level of its reserves. But attracting gold to London was not the same as attracting it to the Bank. In these years, as Cramp (1961) has shown, the participants in the market treated an increase in the discount rate as a signal that stormy weather lay ahead. Firms tried to strengthen themselves, and one result was to pull gold from abroad. But the same consideration that led firms to bring gold home led them not to deposit it with the Bank. The Bank, as Bagehot repeatedly argued, was the one great reserve of gold in the world. It could not readily augment that reserve in times of trouble because there was no place for the gold to come from.

The gold standard, by linking currencies together, tends to force any national bank that acts as a lender-of-last-resort to act as an international lender-of-last-resort. It may choose to build its reserves to the point where it can act alone, or it may choose to act in concert with other central banks, but it cannot remain aloof from crisis in other countries. Bagehot was not comfortable, I believe, with this aspect of the gold standard. Consider, for example, his evident disgust when the Bank of England was forced to borrow from the Bank of France during the crisis of 1839. It would be fair, I think, to infer that Bagehot believed that as long as panic was confined to foreign countries, or even to the British countryside, the Bank of England should look towards its reserves; only when the panic spread to Lombard Street should the Bank begin to lend freely. But that this is the best course of action is, of course, an empirical proposition. By then it might be too late. And it is clear that the Bank would be under strong political pressures to abandon its defensive posture long before the panic hit the City itself.

Under a fiat standard, it might be thought, Bagehot's two rules (1) lend freely and (2) defend the reserve are effectively reduced to one, and the problem of deciding which to apply disappears. Undoubtedly, the eclipse of the gold standard explains why modern students of banking tend to remember only one of Bagehot's rules. But even under a fiat system a central bank is likely to have goals, such as maintaining the trend growth of the money supply, that conflict with its lender-of-last-resort duties when the latter are broadly defined. Typically, the central bank will find itself under heavy pressure to upgrade each period of stress to the status of panic. But if this is done repeatedly the long-run goal may be lost.

Thus, the dilemma posed by Bagehot's policy is in great measure a function of the attempt to formulate an adequate policy under a gold standard. In a world of fiat monies and flexible exchange rates it would be easier to play the role of lender-of-last-resort. The immediate relevance, then, of a closer look at Bagehot is to the case for returning to a gold standard. Advocates of a return might argue that the nineteenth-century gold standard was plagued by crises, but that modern theories of central banking derived from Bagehot provide an adequate means for managing such crises. My point here is that Bagehot provides a clear guide only to the most obvious situations. Ambiguous cases will remain so even after they are examined in the light of *Lombard Street*. We cannot rely on central banks to prevent crises under a new gold standard.

CONCLUSIONS

The problem I have been discussing may be put this way. In Bagehot's day the Bank of England had to be concerned with its own liquidity as well as that of the rest of the financial system. Bagehot's advice was for the Bank to protect its reserve when the state of the reserve was the major source of alarm on Lombard Street (a period of apprehension), and to lend freely when the main source of alarm was each firm's fear that its own reserve would soon prove inadequate (a panic). But how was the Bank to distinguish between these two delicate states of the market? And how could it be sure that actions taken to cure an apprehensive market wouldn't produce a panic? The most one can derive from *Lombard Street* is the implicit assumption that the right course of action would be obvious once the facts were examined.

In a few cases this appears to have been true. In the crisis of 1866, one that hit almost without warning, few would dissent from Bagehot's prescription of 'lending freely'. But other cases were ambiguous. Sometimes the crisis evolved slowly (1837–9), and sometimes it was centred initially in foreign countries (1857) or outlying regions of the UK (1825). It was not clear which Bagehot the Bank should have listened to, and the pressure was to listen to the one who advised 'lend freely'. As it turns out, *Lombard Street* argues that this policy was the wrong one. But it is hard to see how the Bank could have avoided the course it chose on these occasions without an explicit guide to fall back on.

One approach to try to rectify this weakness might be to attempt to frame an explicit definition of a financial panic. It would be possible, for example, to 'fit' a definition to the historical episodes that Bagehot described as panics. Such a Bagehotian definition would be extremely narrow by some modern standards. Panics requiring free lending would be brief moments, not long periods. They would be domestic, rather than international; indeed it would not be a true panic until the crisis hit the financial centre itself. And they would be moments when the payments mechanism itself would be in danger, when the demand was for the means of exchange. But even such an explicit definition leaves considerable room for discretion and promises difficulties as the moment for switching policies approaches.

There is much to be said, therefore, for relying on a quantitative guide such as the stock of money even during a financial crisis. This would provide the central bank with some defence against the pressure to redefine the crisis as a panic. ('Our monetary aggregates remain within their targeted range despite the unfortunate recent events on the continent!') And it would provide for the automatic increase in the means of payment as the demand for it increased. But the main point is simply that when we begin to think about the practical problems in applying Bagehot's formulae, we are led back to the standard debates on monetary policy.

The gold standard, I should reiterate, is at the heart of Bagehot's dilemma. In his day the Bank of England could run out of base money. In an emergency Peel's Act could be suspended. But even this would not eliminate the strait-jacket imposed by the gold standard. That could be achieved only by eliminating convertibility, but Bagehot evidently believed that the gold standard was such an integral part of the system of credit that had grown up in England that any abridgement of it would impose serious costs on the financial system. Today, a central bank can adopt the 'lend freely' policy more frequently and with greater vigour than it could in Bagehot's day. But a similar problem remains. The modern central bank has goals, such as maintaining a low trend rate of growth of the stock of money, which are analogies of Bagehot's goal of maintaining the reserve.[11] Bagehot, in modern terms, advises the Bank to abandon such policies in a panic. The problem is to recognise when an apprehensive market has degenerated into a panic, and to avoid announcement effects that cause the very transformation of the market the Bank seeks to prevent. The solutions to these problems, unfortunately, are not to be found in *Lombard Street*.

I have been rather critical of *Lombard Street*. I have argued that Bagehot should have proposed a system of taxes and subsidies to assure that the Bank would accumulate the additional reserves he thought necessary. I have argued that he should have proposed better guides for recognising the states of the market that were crucial to his theory. And I have argued that he should have proposed ways of preventing the potentially destabilising announcement effects that might have been created by adopting his policies. But I do not mean to disparage Bagehot's achievement. By asking the central questions – what is the Bank of England, and what should it do – and by providing a clearly stated answer, Bagehot made one of the most important contributions to the development of the theory of monetary policy in the nineteenth century. Rather, my point is that *Lombard Street* is a far more subtle book, a harder book to use Keynes' (1915) term, than the one suggested by the epigram 'lend freely at high rates'. After all, what better praise can there be for an author than to say that people are still thinking about his work more than a century after it was written?

NOTES

1. I would like to thank Anna Jacobson Schwartz, Richard Sylla and Eugene White for a number of thought-provoking comments on an earlier draft. They are not responsible, of course, for any remaining errors.
2. I first learned to pronounce Bagehot's name correctly in a class given by Professor Stigler. He explained that despite the spelling, the name was not pronounced, as most Americans supposed, as Baggy-hot.
3. Bagehot came from a banking family (indeed, he was literally born in a bank), and he maintained an active interest in the firm. So his adult observations of the money market, made from his post at *The Economist*, were joined by personal observations, some possibly from far back in his childhood. See the biography by Norman St John-Stevas (1959) for a brief well-written account of his life.
4. Thornton and Bagehot were treated by Humphrey (1975) as co-founders of the concept of the lender-of-last-resort. How much, if anything, Bagehot owed to the earlier writer, however, is unclear. In this and similar cases it should be remembered that Bagehot was not an academic, and was not concerned with intellectual precedence.
5. Roger Hinderliter and I (1976) once tried to examine the effects of the Bank of England behaviour on reserve ratios in a comparative context.
6. The high discount rate that Bagehot recommended for panics probably played several roles in his thinking. But the most important was simply that of providing some protection for the reserve (1873, p. 187). Gold or notes would be given to those who were truly desperate.
7. The argument that participants in the market form expectations and base their behaviour in part on what they perceive the policies of the Government to be has, of course, become a central issue in modern macroeconomics. The classical reference is perhaps Lucas (1976). Intuitively, central banking seems to be a clear case where considerations of this sort appear to be highly plausible.

8. This passage is quoted, for example, by Friedman and Schwartz (1963, p. 395).
9. This error was also noticed by Hawtrey (1933, p. 122), but he did not draw any conclusions from it.
10. See Fetter (1965, chapter 9) for a more positive view of Bagehot's impact.
11. In the draft of the paper presented at the conference I went a bit further in pressing this analogy than was warranted, and this was the basis of some of the comments.

REFERENCES

I have listed the references to Bagehot's writings separately so that I could cite them by their original date in the text. All are available in his *Collected Works*.

Bagehot, W. (1858) 'The monetary crisis of 1857'. Originally published in the *National Review*, reprinted in the *Collected Works of Walter Bagehot*, edited by Norman St John-Stevas, vol. 10 (London: *The Economist*, 1978): 49–76.

Bagehot, W. (1861) 'The duty of the Bank of England in times of quietude', reprinted in the *Collected Works of Walter Bagehot*, vol. 10: 20–2.

Bagehot, W. (1873) *Lombard Street: A Description of the Money Market* (London: H. S. King) Reprinted in the *Collected Works of Walter Bagehot*, vol. 9: 45–233.

Bagehot, W. (1875) 'The lesson of recent events in the money market', reprinted in the *Collected Works of Walter Bagehot*, vol. 11: 48–53.

Bagehot, W. (1876) 'The use of a large bank reserve', reprinted in the *Collected Works of Walter Bagehot*, vol. 11: 54–6.

Buchan, A. (1959) *The Spare Chancellor: The Life of Walter Bagehot* (London: Chatto & Windus).

Clapham, Sir J. (1944) *The Bank of England: A History*. 2 vols. (Cambridge: Cambridge University Press).

Cramp, A. B. (1961) *Opinion on Bank Rate, 1822–60* (London: The London School of Economics and Political Science).

Fetter, F. W. (1965) *Development of British Monetary Orthodoxy, 1797–1875*. (Cambridge, Mass.: Harvard University Press).

Fetter, F. W. (1967) 'An historical confusion in Bagehot's *Lombard Street*', *Economica*, New Series, 34 (February 1967): 80–3.

Friedman, M. and Schwartz, A. J. (1963) *A Monetary History of the United States* (Princeton: Princeton University Press).

Hawtrey, R. G. (1933) *The Art of Central Banking* (London: Longmans, Greene).

Hinderliter, R. and Rockoff , H. (1976) 'Banking under the gold standard: an analysis of liquidity management in the leading financial centres', *The Journal of Economic History* 36 (June 1976): 379–98.

Hirsch, F. (1977) 'The Bagehot problem', *The Manchester School of Economics and Social Studies* 45 (September 1977): 241–57.

Humphrey, T. M. (1975) 'The classical concept of the lender of last resort',

Federal Reserve Bank of Richmond, *Economic Review* 61 (January/February, 1975): 1–7.

Keynes, J. M. (1915) 'The Works of Bagehot', *The Economic Journal* 25 (September 1915): 369–75.

Kindleberger, C. P. (1978) *Manias, Panics, and Crashes* (New York: Basic Books).

Kindleberger, C. P. (1981) *International Money: A Collection of Essays.* (London: George Allen & Unwin).

Kindleberger, C. P. and Laffargue, J. P. (eds) (1982) *Financial Crises: Theory, History, and Policy* (Cambridge: Cambridge University Press).

Lucas, R. E., Jr. (1976) 'Econometric policy evaluation: a critique', in *The Phillips Curve and Labor Markets*, edited by K. Brunner and A. H. Meltzer. Carnegie–Rochester Conference Series on Public Policy, vol. 1: 19–46.

Mints, L. W. (1945) *A History of Banking Theory in Great Britain and the United States* (Chicago: University of Chicago Press).

Pressnell, L. S. (1968) 'Gold reserves, banking reserves, and the banking crisis of 1890', in *Essays in Money and Banking in Honour of R. S. Sayers*, edited by C. R. Whittlesey and J. S. G. Wilson (Oxford: Clarendon Press).

St John-Stevas, N. (1959) *Walter Bagehot* (London: Eyre & Spottiswoode).

Sayers, R. S. (1957) *Central Banking after Bagehot*. (Oxford: Clarendon Press).

Thornton, H. (1802) *An Enquiry into the Nature and Effects of the Paper Credit of Great Britain*, edited by F. A. Hayek. (New York: Farrar & Rinehart, 1939).

Tooke, T. and Newmarch, W. (1838 +) *A History of Prices, and the State of the Circulation from 1792 to 1856* (London: Longman, Orme, Brown, Green, and Longman) Reprinted with an introduction by T. E. Gregory (New York: Adelphi, 1928).

Comment on 'Walter Bagehot and the Theory of Central Banking'

KURT SCHILTKNECHT

In his paper, Hugh Rockoff shows very clearly the weakness of Bagehot's proposal 'to lend freely at high interest rates'. I share Rockhoff's view that Bagehot failed to solve the problem of defining the appropriate guide for monetary policy before and during a panic. But is this problem solved today? Does a central bank really know how to respond to a financial crisis? Hugh Rockhoff seems to have some doubts, at least his remark that 'even under a fiat system a central bank is likely to have goals that conflict with its lender-of-last-resort duties' gives the impression that monetary authorities have plenty of discretion to play the role of a lender-of-last-resort.

In my view there is no conflict between the ultimate goal of a central bank, namely price stability, and its lender-of-last-resort duties. In the following I would like to elaborate on this point a bit. In addition – and I think this is the main reason for my being invited to contribute to this discussion – I shall comment on the position of the Swiss National Bank with respect to its role as a lender-of-last-resort.

To begin with, I would like to define the monetary characteristics of a panic. In principle a panic in the monetary sector is characterised by a sharp increase in the demand of the public and the banks for base money. The public withdraw deposits from banks and transform them into currency. In order to prepare for such operations, banks increase the demand for reserves. Such an increase is, however, only possible for banks with no solvency problems and no credibility gap. For all the others it is extremely difficult to improve their reserve positions even if they offer interest rates above the market levels. Both developments, the transformation of deposits into currency and the increase in the demand for bank reserves, have a contractionary effect on the money stock. A shrinking money stock certainly does not serve the ultimate goal of a central bank. Therefore, a central bank has to supply more base money in order to offset the deflationary effect of the exogenous increase in the demand for base money. Given the difficulties in estimating the size of the shift in the demand for base money, the best solution for a central bank is temporarily to abandon the money stock target and to shift to an interest rate target. After a while, however, the central bank has to focus on the monetary aggregates again. The target for a narrow aggregate has to be revised upwards in order to satisfy the higher liquidity preference during a crisis. When the crisis is over, the increase has to be offset. Of course, such an approach leaves some room for discretion. But in my view such a strategy minimises the risk with respect to both the deflationary impact of a panic and the inflationary impact of the increase in the monetary base.

The specific nature of the crisis determines how the monetary base is increased during a panic. As a first step, a central bank has to supply liquidity for banks in trouble. The Swiss National Bank has made it clear to the banks that it would be in their own interest to hold assets that allow them to use the rediscount and lombard facilities offered by the National Bank. On average, the Swiss banks are very well equipped with such assets. Deposits of the Govenment with banks short of liquidity are another way to solve liquidity problems of individual banks. This approach was quite often and successfully applied during the crisis in the thirties. The Government can either raise the liquidity in the market, if the supply of base money is already high enough, or it can borrow from the Swiss National Bank.

Much better, and this is fully in line with the idea of Bagehot, is to prevent a panic. This can be done if a central bank immediately responds to the first signs of a crisis. The recognition of these first signs of a monetary crisis is much easier for the central bank if it follows a monetary base approach and if banks have under normal conditions no access to the rediscount and lombard facilities. In a country where commercial banks have virtually unlimited access to the rediscount and lombard facilities, the actual demand for reserves corresponds more or less to the amount of required reserves. Excess reserves are then quite low, because the holding of excess reserves is not attractive for the banks, as long as they can borrow base money from the central bank at a rate close to the current official rates. Even if a bank expects some difficulties, it will not increase its reserve holdings. Therefore, a central bank has no possibility of recognising the first signs of a crisis. In Switzerland, where the Swiss National Bank does not serve as a lender-of-first-resort, the response of a bank is different. If a bank expects problems, it would first try to improve its reserve position, in order to be prepared for the monetary impact of the crisis. Since the only possibility for a bank to increase its reserves is to attract base money from other banks, a shift in the demand for reserves is immediately transmitted into higher interest rates in the money market. For a central bank, a sudden, unexpected and large rise of interest rates signals that some kind of a crisis in the monetary sector may have developed. An analysis of the individual reserve positions of each bank may help to locate the problem in the banking system. In addition, a comparison between the actual and the predicted demand for reserves may enable the central bank to distinguish between random fluctuations in the demand for reserves and systematic shifts. If the change in demand is identified as systematic, the central bank has to make offsetting operations.

Of course, the most natural behaviour of a bank facing a liquidity problem is to inform the central bank about its difficulties. Then it is up to the central bank to decide whether an increase in the monetary base is necessary. During the so-called Chiasso fiasco of Credit Suisse the Swiss National Bank was faced with such a situation. Since that episode sheds some light on the practical problems of monetary management, I shall briefly discuss it.

As a result of the difficulties faced by Credit Suisse in May 1977, the Swiss financial community became concerned that the public would lose confidence in the banking system and that large-scale withdrawals of deposits would ensue. These concerns prompted the commercial banks to augment their demand for precautionary reserves. If the Swiss National Bank had refused to supply additional base money to the banking system, the scramble for reserves would have caused a sharp contraction in the money supply. In order to forestall this, the Bank decided to increase the monetary base at a rate faster than originally planned. Despite this flexibility of the Swiss National Bank, however, the expansion in bank reserves was, as we realised later, not sufficient to accommodate fully the shift in demand. For this reason, short-term and medium-term interest rates rose markedly. This rise induced a slower growth of M_1. Later in the year, it became known that the Credit Suisse would be able to absorb the losses of its Chiasso branch without much difficulty. Since the commercial banks no longer faced the prospect of large-scale deposit withdrawals, they gradually restored their normal levels of reserves and the National Bank could reduce the growth of the monetary base to its planned level.

This episode shows that targets for the money stock and monetary base must be handled in a flexible manner if a central bank is to prevent unexpected shifts in the demand for base money ffrom exerting harmful effects on the economy.

To conclude my remarks I would like to comment briefly on one of the traditional criticisms of Bagehot's proposal. Hugh Rockhoff writes that 'perhaps the point made most frequently is that the existence of a lender-of-last-resort creates a problem of moral hazard. If the banks know that someone is there to bail them out in a crisis, they are likely to take more chances – reserve ratios will be reduced . . . risky loans will be undertaken – and as a result, panics will be more frequent than they would otherwise be'. This traditional criticism is misplaced. The role of a lender-of-last-resort only implies that a central bank may provide liquidity during a crisis in order to prevent a shrinking of deposits. In general, a central bank supplies liquidity against sound assets. The provision of base money against bad assets takes place in extreme situations only. But in such a case the risk of the bad assets remains with the bank. As long as the losses on the assets of the banking system are not taken over by the central bank, it is wrong to consider lender-of-last-resort activities as bailing out operations. The possibility of making a loss in fulfilling the role of a lender-of-last-resort has in any case to be weighed against the possibility of a contraction in the money supply. In the short run, priority has to be given to the protection of the money stock under all circumstances, while in the longer run the central bank has to take care that losses are covered by the banking system.

If a central bank does not leave any doubt that the banks have to cover the losses, it is hard to understand why banks should grant riskier loans when it is known that the central bank will serve as a lender-of-last-resort. Especially under a strict monetary base approach an over-extension of loans is not very profitable.

I would like to summarise my comments in three points:

1. Within an explicit money supply framework it is possible to develop a lender-of-last-resort strategy which is in line with the ultimate goal of a central bank.
2. A monetary base approach, contrary to the gold standard, facilitates the prevention or solution of a financial crisis.
3. Central banks must distinguish explicitly between solving a liquidity crisis and bailing out the banking system.

'Walter Bagehot and the Theory of Central Banking': A Comment

J. S. FFORDE

I have read Hugh Rockoff's paper with considerable interest. It invites questions about how central banks should best respond in today's monetary policy environment, with today's institutional framework, either to the onset of conditions which threaten a financial crisis or to the actual occurrence of such a crisis. I would like to attempt some comment on one or two of those questions, from the viewpoint of one who was an operational central banker from 1966 to 1982.

Bagehot's propositions, put forward some 100 years ago, were conditioned by the existence of a privately owned central bank, subject to the statutory restraints of the gold standard and operating in what we would now call a broadly deregulated banking system. In that environment, occasional conflicts were likely to arise between the statutory obligation to maintain the gold convertibility of Bank notes and the implied duty of the central bank to afford the community some substantial degree of protection from disorderly collapse in the banking system. These conflicts could partly be resolved by a prudent build-up or husbanding of gold reserves, despite the expense, and despite the high degree of monetary stringency that could ensue, and partly, if the worst came to the worst, by backing-off from the letter of the gold standard in the interests of averting or dispelling a panic. Pursuit of these activities clearly needed the use of judgement and discretion by the central bank and clearly opened up the risk of misjudgement and error. Accordingly, as I understand it, Bagehot was concerned that the Bank should be equipped both with adequate rationale and adequate expertise; and he made suggestions about both.

All this has some rather special interest today because in many countries, following the monetary disturbance of the past decade or more, there is now a considerably greater emphasis on rules as opposed to discretion in the conduct of monetary policy, and, at least in some countries, a considerably greater emphasis on competitive freedom in banking as opposed to the restrictive regulation and supervision which in many cases resulted from past failure of central banks to avert financial disorder. So there follows some presumption that the nineteenth-century conflicts of objective can again come to the fore, perhaps particularly during a transition to much lower levels of inflation and a concurrent steep reduction in inflationary expectations. This may lead some people, including some economists, to worry lest central banks are so concerned to avert disorder that they back off too readily, and thereby seriously weaken the force of their counter-inflation strategy. The same people worry further lest these risks are made the more serious by the vulnerability of central banks in many countries to transitory pressures of public opinion which could cause long-term objectives to be sacrificed to short-term needs. Associated with these worries is a concern about moral hazard, namely, that central banks, together with the governments with which they are associated, may over the past decades of regulation have come to assume, or be thought to have assumed, such a degree of de facto responsibility to bail out banks in a crisis as positively to encourage or promote imprudent behaviour both by banks and by depositors in a newly deregulated system.

It is not for me to pronounce on whether these worries are well founded in respect of the UK and of the British monetary authorities. But we certainly recognise the problems to which they draw attention and are probably content to be judged by our behaviour in meeting them. By way of illustration let me draw on an at times defective memory, combined with the published record, of some of the events of recent years.

First, let me refer to the secondary banking crisis of 1973–4 and its treatment by the device known as the Lifeboat. As you know, what happened was that deposits of the general public with the so-called secondary banks were indeed all met on maturity, with funds provided as required by the Bank and by the clearing banks. The proprietors of the secondary banks, and depositors directly connected with those banks, were, of course, not similarly rescued and lost a lot of money, though they may in some cases have benefited from the careful management put in by the Lifeboat banks. So being 'bailed out', as the phrase goes, is far from painless and it would be surprising if anyone in the business of banking in the UK now thought it was.

But we did indeed realise the awkward precedent created by our appearing, with the clearing banks, to be prepared to stand behind the ordinary depositors at some rather extraordinary institutions. Isolated episodes in the fifties and sixties had in fact *not* met with a similar response. The upshot of the awkward precedent was the provision made in the subsequent Banking Act for a Deposit Protection Fund financed by the banking system (broadly defined) and guaranteeing 75 per cent of deposits up to £10 000. In the view of the Government and of Parliament this, together with the licensing and supervisory provisions in the Act, provided an adequate degree of guaranteed consumer protection: without encouraging the belief that *all* deposits with all licensed institutions were de facto riskless.

The message would therefore seem to be that bailing out of depositors is not guaranteed but that if it occurs, in the interests of the stability of the whole system, it will not be painless for the proprietors of the institution concerned. I suggest that this may have got the balance about right for the present; and that the solution to the problem of moral hazard lies in a proper balance of partial guarantee of deposits, pain for proprietors where bailing out does occur, and special supervision.

But what about monetary policy 'backing off' too soon, out of undue or exaggerated concern for the health of financial institutions whose ill health would damage the economy more generally? Here, the episode that comes to my mind is the conduct of policy during the winter of 1974–5 when inflation was accelerating to 20 per cent. The broad money supply (*M*3) was only growing at around half that rate but the narrow money supply (*M*1) was growing considerably faster. Yet we exploited an opportunity provided in the main by a fall in US interest rates very early in 1975 and we backed off. Short-term interest rates were allowed to fall by some 2 percentage points and, rather more importantly, the emphasis of debt management was sharply altered so as to encourage a fall in long-term rates and a recovery in long-term asset values. The yield on long-dated Government bonds had reached a peak of around 18 per cent late in 1974 and fell to 13½ per cent by the end of March 1975. Our *Quarterly Bulletin* of March 1975, in referring to this adjustment of policy said, 'Private industry had in many cases become overdependent on short-term borrowing at high rates of interest, and the fall in the capital value of assets, resulting in part from the earlier sharp rise in rates, threatened to create balance sheet problems for some financial institutions; high interest rates and low equity prices had also severely hampered the new issue market.' Somewhat later our Annual Report for the year ending February 1975 remarked, 'The pressing need in the closing months of 1974 seemed to be the restoration of confidence to financial markets, and this underlay the official response to the revival in the gilt-edged market which began early in the New Year.'

In Bagehot's terminology, we had by the end of 1974 reached a condition of generalised apprehension with some flavour of incipient panic. Using a somewhat free adaptation of Anna Schwartz's illuminating terminology, I think we had at least run into a real pseudo-crisis. But I do not recall it being thought subsequently, by any notable body of opinion, that we were misinformed, that our response was wrong, or that we backed off too soon, or that we had fallen victim to transient or myopic political pressures. Rather we had been criticised earlier, in the summer of 1974, for not backing off sooner.

However, it could be argued that steering a successful course through episodes like the one I have just described places altogether too heavy a burden of judgement on a small band of fallible central bankers dealing with infrequent situations, each of which may well be outside the experience of the ruling generation of officials. So I would agree that any means of lightening that burden would be useful. Since 1974, and especially during the difficult period of 1980–2, I believe one way of reducing the burden has been further developed. I am referring to the work of the Industrial Finance Division of the Bank as developed in the first instance by Lord Benson, who became our Industrial Adviser in 1975. This work has not involved the Bank in lending money to anybody; but it has facilitated a process whereby the various bankers, managements, and sometimes also the principal shareholders, of large companies facing severe difficulties, can effect in collaboration such necessary changes of management, asset realisations, and liability-reconstructions as are required to overcome such difficulties without resort, in most cases, to the procedures of sudden bankruptcy with their associated financial alarms and apprehensions. Perhaps there is some echo here, but an industrial echo, of the Bank's approach to the Baring crisis. Be that as it may, it seems that this industrial finance activity can help very considerably, in periods of stress, to reduce the level of apprehensiveness, to avert the onset of incipient panic, and therefore reduce both the chances of having to back off and the associated burden on central banking judgement.

So I am suggesting that both in respect of the moral hazard problem and of the main Bagehot dilemma, of which Hugh Rockoff reminds us, some ways have been developed through which their practical importance can be effectively diminished, or limited. Perhaps this is the most one should expect.

6 Financial Crises, Banking Crises, Stock Market Crashes and the Money Supply: Some International Evidence, 1870–1933[1]

MICHAEL D. BORDO

INTRODUCTION

Recent concern over the threat to the solvency of major commercial banks in the US and other advanced countries posed by potential defaults on the outstanding debts of a number of developing countries has led to widespread interest in the topic of 'financial crises'. This chapter attempts to examine both theory and some limited historical evidence for a number of countries on the impact of financial crises on economic activity and on the international transmission of crises.

Definition of Financial Crises

At the outset it would be useful to define a financial crisis. However, the numerous and often conflicting approaches to this subject in the literature make this a difficult task. Rather than attempt a definition, I briefly list what I believe to be the key elements of a financial crisis.

The key elements or links in the process referred to as a financial crisis are:

(a) a widespread change in expectations associated with fear of a change in the economic environment. Such a change in expectations was often triggered in the past by some real event such as a war or a harvest failure, but also by monetary events, such as the fear that a particular country would leave the gold standard;
(b) fear of solvency of some financial institution(s). Insolvency could stem from mismanagement, lack of foresight, a fragile debt structure but also from a systemwide shortage of liquidity;
(c) an attempt to convert real as well as illiquid financial assets into money, which in turn would raise interest rates and lower asset prices – a liquidity crisis;
(d) threats to the solvency of otherwise sound commercial banks and other financial institutions because of a decline in the values of their portfolios as a consequence of the forced sale of assets;
(e) bank runs precipitated by such threats to solvency. Runs on particular banks in turn could lead to a general banking panic, where the public at large, fearful of suffering severe losses on their deposits should the banks fail, or of paying a premium on currency in the event of a suspension of payments, attempts to convert deposits into currency;
(f) a reduction in the money supply produced in turn by banking panics. The public's deposit–currency ratio falls and the banks reduce their deposit–reserve ratio (by reducing their loans) in an attempt to improve their liquidity positions. In addition, bank failures of themselves destroy deposits;
(g) both real economic activity and the price level fall as a result of the fall in the money supply or a fall in velocity caused by hoarding;
(h) a decline in profits and net worths, and a rise in bankruptcy follow;
(i) a 'debt crisis' produced by both the decline in asset prices associated with liquidation and the decline in the price level. The possibility exists of a (Fisherian) debt deflation process whereby the decline in prices reduces the value of loan collateral and net worths of firms, households and banks, leading to widespread bankruptcies, further bank runs, bank failures, and further declines in the money supply;
(j) the whole process arrested at the outset by the timely intervention of some authority (the lender-of-last-resort) that lends freely at a penalty rate or engages in open market operations.

Different writers have focused on different aspects of the list in their treatment of financial crises. Sinai (1976) and Carron (1982) stress the liquidity aspects. According to Carron (p. 395), in 'a financial crisis . . .

some borrowers face a premium arising from financial developments elsewhere that are unrelated to their own outlook. Such an excess premium can take the form of exceptionally high interest or of credit rationing that effectively precludes borrowing'.

Some writers focus on lack of information in their treatment of financial crises. Wachtel (1982, p. xi), following Meltzer (1982), views a financial crisis as a consequence of Knightian uncertainty – 'a crisis may emerge when there is a shift in the underlying distribution of outcomes of economic events'. Garber (1981) and Flood and Garber (1981) view a financial crisis in a world of rational expectations as a consequence of a predictable change in fixed price regimes. Real activity would only be affected if there were uncertainty on the timing of the change in regime.

Kindleberger (1978), following Fisher (1932; 1933) and Minsky (1957; 1963; 1977; 1980; 1982 a, b), views financial crises as a key element of the upper turning point in the business cycle and as the inevitable consequence of the preceding boom. He stresses the role of adverse expectations, forced liquidation and debt deflation. Without a lender-of-last-resort the capitalist system is doomed to financial crises and instability.

Goldsmith (1982, p. 42) defines a financial crisis as 'a sharp, brief, *ultracyclical* deterioration of all or most of a group of financial indicators – short-term interest rates, asset (stock, real estate, land) prices, commercial insolvencies and failures of financial institutions'.

Bernanke (1983) makes the distinction between a 'banking crisis' involving a run on commercial banks and bank failures and a 'debt crisis' precipitated by a decline in the price of assets. Each type of crisis has serious effects on the economy.

Finally Griffiths (1983), following the monetarist approach of Friedman and Schwartz (1963a), focuses on the meaning of a banking crisis, distinguishing between systemwide illiquidity which threatens the solvency of all banks and the insolvency of particular institutions due to mismanagement. The former threat should be offset by lender-of-last-resort intervention. Mismanaged banks should be encouraged to liquidate.

The Importance of Financial Crises

Why should a financial crisis matter? One answer is that it matters if it has an effect on the level of economic activity.

Within a simple quantity theory of money framework we can isolate three possible channels by which a financial crisis affects economic activity. First, by causing a reduction in the money supply. This occurs if a banking panic causes the public to reduce its deposit–currency ratio, which in turn causes the commercial banks to reduce their deposit–reserve ratio, or if the liquidity crisis *per se* causes commercial banks to reduce their deposit–reserve ratio in order to strengthen their liquidity position.

Second, by reducing velocity. This occurs if the threat to the liquidity and solvency of non-bank financial institutions leads to an increase in the demand for money or if the crisis produces such adverse expectations (as a consequence of widespread bankruptcies) to produce hoarding.

Third, by directly reducing real output. This occurs if a debt deflation process leads to bankruptcies in the non-financial sector or, alternatively, if bank failures reduce the services of financial intermediation.[2]

International Transmission of Financial Crises

Many financial crises in the past 200 years have occurred worldwide (see Kindleberger, 1978) although they have differed markedly in degree of severity. Monetary and real channels have been emphasised in two leading approaches to international transmission.

According to the monetarist approach, financial crises (and also business fluctuations) are transmitted internationally primarily through the monetary standard.[3] Under a fixed exchange rate, such as the classical gold standard, a financial crisis in one country by reducing the money supply or velocity in that country will attract gold flows from other countries. These countries will in turn suffer a contraction in their money supplies and a reduction in economic activity. Transmission can also occur through short-term capital flows, changes in real income, and commodity arbitrage, but the way in which these channels affect activity is primarily through monetary change. By contrast, under flexible exchange rates, according to the monetarist approach, one would expect the transmission of financial disturbances to be considerably muted.

According to the real approach, financial crises are transmitted primarily through non-monetary channels such as linked portfolios of financial institutions, capital flows, commodity arbitrage, and changes in the balance of trade. Monetary factors are treated as of secondary importance.

In some detail the second section examines the two main approaches to the role and importance of financial crises as disturbances to domestic and international economic activity: the monetarist approach and the Fisher–Minsky–Kindleberger real approach. The two approaches yield a number of testable implications. The third section then examines historical evidence for some countries on the links between key real, financial, and monetary variables in periods marked by financial crises. The fourth section examines crude evidence pertinent to the two approaches on the international transmission of financial crises. Finally, the fifth section presents a brief conclusion.

THEORETICAL APPROACHES TO FINANCIAL CRISES

Of two main approaches to understanding the role and importance of financial crises, the approach of Friedman and Schwartz (1963a) and Cagan (1965) identifies financial crises with banking panics. Banking panics in turn may be a source of monetary contraction or may aggravate the effects of monetary contraction on economic activity.[4] The second approach, following the seminal work of Fisher (1932), views financial crises as part of the normal functioning of the business cycle, and explains them as a natural consequence of 'financial fragility' and 'overindebtedness'.

The Monetarist Approach to Financial Crises

In their monumental *A Monetary History of the United States, 1867–1960*, Friedman and Schwartz devote considerable attention to the role of banking panics in producing monetary instability in the United States. For Friedman and Schwartz, banking panics are important because of their effects on the money supply and hence on economic activity. Over the approximate 100-year span studied, the United States had six severe contractions, of which four were marked by major banking or monetary disturbances (Friedman and Schwartz, 1963a, p. 677). Indeed, banking panics 'have greatly intensified (severe) contractions if indeed they have not been the primary factor converting what would otherwise have been mild contractions into severe ones' (1963a, pp. 441–2).

According to Friedman and Schwartz, banking panics arise out of the loss of confidence by the public in the ability of banks to convert deposits into currency. A loss of confidence is typically precipitated by the failure of some important financial institution (e.g. as in 1873,

1893). Attempts by the public to increase the fraction of its money holdings held in currency in a fractional reserve banking system can only be met by a multiple contraction of deposits. A banking panic in turn, if not allayed by the suspension of convertibility of deposits into currency and the issuance of clearing house certificates (as was often the case before the establishment of the Federal Reserve in 1914) or by early intervention by the monetary authorities, will produce massive bank failures. Such failures will be the consequence of otherwise sound banks being forced into insolvency by a fall in the value of their assets induced by a mass scramble for liquidity.

Banking panics leading to widespread bank failures, such as occurred in the 1929–33 period, primarily by reducing the money stock through a decline in both the deposit–currency and deposit–reserve ratios, have deleterious effects on economic activity.

Friedman and Schwartz make an important distinction between the arithmetic and the economic aspects of a banking panic. In their discussion of the panic of 1893 they state

> the panic had important effects on the banking structure ... and it undoubtedly affected the detailed timing, form, and impact of the economic adjustment. At the same time, it was at bottom simply the way in which an adjustment, forced by other considerations, worked itself out. The price declines abroad and the distrust of the maintenance of the gold standard by the United States meant that there were only two alternatives: (1) a sizeable decline in US prices and a decline or a reduced rate of rise in money income; or (2) the abandonment of the gold standard and the depreciation of the dollar relative to other currencies. Given the maintenance of the gold standard, the adjustments in prices and income were unavoidable. If they had not occurred through the banking panic and the accompanying deepening of the recession underway, they would have taken place in some other way (Friedman and Schwartz, 1963, pp. 110–11).

Indeed the peculiarities of the US banking system as it developed in the nineteenth century with its unit fractional reserve banking system and reserves pyramided in New York made it highly susceptible to banking panics. This vulnerability was finally ended by the introduction of federal deposit insurance in 1934 which served to remove the public's fear for its ability to convert deposits into currency.

Friedman and Schwartz highlight the importance in the pre-FDIC system of strong and responsible leadership exercising timely judgement in intervening to allay the public's fears. Before the advent of the

Fed, such intervention by the New York clearing banks in suspending convertibility and issuing clearing house certificates and, on occasion, in conducting open market purchases by the Treasury was generally successful, although not sufficient to prevent severe monetary contraction. The Federal Reserve System established in part to provide such leadership failed dismally in the 1929–33 contraction.

According to Friedman and Schwartz, had the Fed conducted open market operations in 1930 and 1931 to provide the reserves needed by the banking system, the series of bank failures producing the massive unprecedented decline in the money stock would have been prevented.

Finally, according to these authorities, economic disturbances are spread internationally by the monetary standard. US monetary disturbances during the1929–33 contraction quickly spread abroad to other gold countries through the gold exchange standard. Only countries on flexible exchange rates with the US, such as China and Spain, escaped its ravages.[5]

Cagan (1965), in *Determinants and Effects of Changes in the Stock of Money, 1875–1960*, carefully analysed the role of banking panics in the cyclical behaviour of the US money supply. He, like Friedman and Schwartz, explained the incidence of panics by events such as the failure of prominent financial institutions or railways. The resulting decline in the public's confidence in the banks, by raising both the public's currency–money ratio and the banking system's reserve–deposit ratio, led to a contraction in the money supply.[6] Cagan attributed the high incidence of banking panics in the US experience 'to the pre-World War I banking system with its inverted pyramid of credit resting on New York City banks and the absence of emergency reserves provided by a central bank' and to 'sharp outflows of gold which sometimes forced banks to contract credit too fast' (Cagan, 1965, pp. 226–7).

Finally, Cagan presented strong evidence that panics in the US experience did not precipitate cyclical downturns since they all followed peaks in economic activity. Moreover, though panics were important in several cycles in reducing money growth more than would otherwise have happened and in converting mild contractions into severe contractions, he concluded, based on the evidence of two severe cyclical downturns not associated with banking panics – 1920–1 and 1937–8 – and two mild cyclical downturns that were associated with panics – 1890 and 1914 – that panics were neither a necessary nor sufficient condition for producing a severe contraction.

Huffman and Lothian (1984) focus on the international transmission of business cycles under the pre-1933 gold standard. They view monetary shocks as the key sources of cyclical fluctuations, with the fixed-exchange-rate gold standard the primary mechanism for transmission of shocks abroad. An unexpected decline in the money supply in one country (say, the United States) will reduce income and prices and raise interest rates in that country, leading to a balance of payments surplus and a gold and capital inflow from another (say, Great Britain). In Great Britain, the gold outflow will reduce the money supply, prices and real output and raise interest rates, leading to a new equilibrium. Empirical evidence based on Granger–Sims causality tests provides support for the paramount role of specie flows and money supplies in the pre-1933 gold standard transmission mechanism.

Since financial crises are important only to the extent that they affect the money supply, they should not be a crucial part of the transmission mechanism. In a comparison of common cycles in the United States and Great Britain, 1830–1933, Huffman and Lothian found panics in only three of twelve common cycles. This leads them to conclude that little importance should be attached to panics as a direct channel of international transmission of cyclical fluctuations.

The Fisher–Minsky–Kindleberger Approach

In contrast to the monetarist approach which regards financial crises as important via their influence on monetary aggregates, a tradition going back to the nineteenth century regards financial crises as an essential part of the upper turning point of the business cycle – as a necessary consequence of the 'excesses' of the previous boom. The modern proponents, Minsky and Kindleberger, basically extend the views Irving Fisher expressed in *Booms and Depressions* (1932).

According to Fisher (1932) and (1933) the business cycle is explained by two key factors: overindebtedness and deflation.

'Disturbances in these two factors – debt and the purchasing power of the monetary unit – will set up serious disturbances in all, or nearly all, other economic variables. On the other hand, if debt and deflation are absent, other disturbances are powerless to bring on crises comparable in severity to those of 1837, 1873, or 1929–33' (Fisher, 1933, p. 341).

The upswing in the cycle is precipitated by some exogenous event that provides new, profitable opportunities for investment in key sectors of the economy. Such 'starters' can be new inventions, gold discoveries or wars. The exogenous shock encourages new investment in those sectors that increase output and prices. Rising prices, by raising profits, encourage more investment but also encourage speculation for capital gain. The whole process is debt financed, primarily by bank loans, which in turn, by increasing deposits and the money supply, raises the price level. An overall sense of optimism will raise velocity, fuelling the expansion even further. Moreover, the rising price level, by reducing the real value of outstanding debt more than the increase in nominal debt, encourages further borrowing. The process continues until a general state of 'overindebtedness' – defined as 'whatever degree of indebtedness multiplies unduly the chances of becoming insolvent' – is reached (Fisher, 1932, p. 9). A state of overindebtedness exists when individuals, firms, and banks have insufficient liquid assets to meet their liabilities. In such a situation a crisis can be triggered by errors in judgement by debtors or creditors. Debtors, unable to pay debts when due and unable to refinance their positions, may be forced by creditors to liquidate their assets.

Such 'distress selling' if widespread then triggers a 'liquidity crisis' that could in turn lead to a 'debt crisis,' a 'banking crisis', and a deep depression unless the process is averted by intervention by the monetary authorities. Distress selling if engaged in by the whole community produces a decline in the price level because, as loans are extinguished and not renewed, bank deposits decline. As the price level falls the real value of outstanding debt rises and, according to Fisher, based on the assumption of money illusion both by debtors and creditors, it rises faster than nominal debt is extinguished. Thus creditors see the nominal value of their collateral declining with the price level and hence continue to call their loans, while the real debt burden of debtors rises so they continue to liquidate. A fallacy of composition takes over, each individual joining the liquidation to avoid being worse off, while the community as a whole by reducing the price level actually becomes worse off. The process can proceed to involve bank runs as fears for their solvency rise, and to raise the demand for money as a sense of pessimism spreads.

Real economic activity is affected by falling prices that reduce net worth and profits leading to bankruptcy. Both factors contribute to a decline in output and employment. In addition, while nominal interest rates fall with deflation, real rates are increased, worsening the situation. The process can continue until either widespread bankruptcy has eliminated the overindebtedness, or at any stage a reflationary monetary policy is adopted. However, once recovery begins, the whole process will repeat itself. Finally, depressions are transmitted from country to country by the monetary standard.[7]

Minsky, in a series of articles since 1957, has elaborated and extended Fisher's theory.[8] Basically Minsky has extended the notion of overindebtedness and the processes which produce it by his concept of fragility.

According to Minsky, as the economy proceeds through the upswing of the business cycle, the financial structure becomes more fragile. A crisis occurs when a fragile financial structure is shocked by some event that triggers a sell-off of assets in a thin market producing a sharp decline in asset prices (Minsky, 1977, p. 140). The fragility or robustness of a financial structure is determined by three factors: (a) the mix of hedge, speculative, and Ponzi finance; (b) the liquidity of the portfolio; (c) the extent to which ongoing investment is debt financed.

Minsky's terms are defined as follows: 'if a unit's cash flow commitments on debts are such that over each significant period the cash receipts are expected to exceed the cash payments by a significant margin, the unit is said to be engaged in hedge financing'. Speculative financing is defined as 'cash flow payments over some period – typically near term – that exceed the cash flows expected over this period'. A Ponzi finance unit 'is a speculative unit for which the interest portion of its cash payment commitments exceeds its net income cash receipts. A Ponzi unit has to increase its debt in order to meet its commitments on outstanding instruments' (1977, p. 143). The importance of speculative and Ponzi finance is that a rise in the interest rate can convert a positive into a negative present value, precipitating insolvency.

According to Minsky's approach, in the upswing of the cycle, the demand for new investment in response to improved profit opportunities leads to a demand for finance. Part of the new investment is directly financed by short-term banks loans, part by equity, and part by long-term debt. As the economy expands it generates an excess demand for finance, raising interest rates. However, the excess demand is partially and temporarily offset by financial innovation, which in turn fuels the finance of further investment.[9] Thus, the investment boom is fuelled both by an endogenous (elastic) money supply and elastic velocity.

As interest rates rise, four factors work to create a fragile financial environment:[10]

(a) an increase in debt finance;
(b) a shift from long-term to short-term debt;
(c) a shift from hedge to speculative to Ponzi finance;
(d) a reduction in financial institutions' margin of safety.

Once a fragile environment is in place, a further rise in interest rates by shifting hedge to speculative to Ponzi financing can precipitate a refinancing crisis where firms are unable to 'roll over' their debt. In that situation Fisher's 'distress selling' process can be generated with all the attendant consequences. The crisis can be aborted, however, by the central bank acting as lender-of-last-resort to the money markets.[11]

Finally, Minsky's thesis can also explain the international transmission of crises. Commercial banks lending abroad face additional risks. The risks include greater economic and political uncertainty that increase the likelihood of default and capital losses from unexpected changes in exchange rates.[12, 13]

Kindleberger (1978) follows Minsky and Fisher, embellishing the story with pages of anecdotes from history. Basically some displacement which improves profit opportunities leads to an investment boom, fuelled by bank money and rising velocity. This in turn produces a 'speculative mania' involving a shift from money to goods, 'overtrading' and then 'distress'. At that point some event triggers a massive shift from goods to money and a 'panic' results (Kindleberger, 1978, p. 5).

Kindleberger expands on the international transmission mechanism. In addition to the traditional links of gold flows, the balance of trade, and capital flows, he stresses the importance of psychological factors, commodity arbitrage and interest arbitrage which, by linking the banking systems of different countries directly, can offset the normal operations of the classical price–specie–flow mechanism.

> Although Minsky's model is limited to a single country, overtrading has historically tended to spread from one country to another. The conduits are many. Commodity prices may rise and so may the prices of securities that are traded internationally. Speculation in exports, imports, or foreign securities furnishes direct links between markets of countries. By these means euphoria and overtrading in one country can be fed by capital inflows from foreign purchases of particular goods and assets. And if these capital flows lead to inflows of gold or silver, monetary expansion in the original country is enhanced as the boom is fuelled by additional supplies of money on which higher pyramids of credit can be supported. In an ideal world, of course, a gain of specie for one country would be matched by a corresponding loss for another, and the resulting expansion in the first case would be offset by the contraction in the second. In the real world, however, while the boom in the first country might gain speed from the increase in the supply of reserves, or 'high-powered money', it might also rise in the second despite the loss in monetary reserves,

> as investors respond to rising prices and profits abroad by joining in the speculative chase. In other words, the potential contraction from the shrinkage on the monetary side might be overwhelmed by the increase in speculative interest and the rise in demand. For the two countries together, in any event, the credit system is stretched tighter. (Kindleberger, 1973, p. 119)

Kindleberger views a flexible exchange rate as an important conduit for the international transmission of financial crises – 'exchange appreciation and deflation, or exchange depreciation and inflation . . . can be connected with bankruptcies, bank suspensions and changes in the money supply' (p. 119).

Finally, as do Fisher and Minsky, Kindleberger assumes a role to a lender-of-last-resort to abort the crisis but, with his additional emphasis on the international nature of financial crises, he stresses the need for an international lender-of-last-resort.[14]

Testable Implications

The two main approaches to the role and importance of financial crises yield a number of testable implications. The first concerns the importance of monetary change as the primary conduit through which financial crises affect economic activity. According to the monetarist approach, it is primarily by reducing money growth more than otherwise that the banking system, when affected by a crisis, has an impact on the economy. By contrast, the Kindleberger–Minsky approach sees financial crises as being important independent of effects on the money supply.

A second implication concerns the importance of monetary factors in the international transmission of financial crises. According to the monetarist approach, transmission should occur primarily via the monetary standard by precipitating gold flows (or changes in international reserves) between countries that affect monetary bases and hence money supplies. Under flexible exchange rates, transmission would be muted. By contrast, in the Kindleberger–Minsky approach, transmission can occur through a wide variety of channels including the monetary channel. One key channel stressed by Kindleberger and Minsky is the direct link between the banking systems of different countries. Moreover, flexible exchange rates may serve to accelerate transmission.

SOME DESCRIPTIVE EVIDENCE ON FINANCIAL CRISES AND MONETARY, REAL, AND FINANCIAL VARIABLES

Table 6.1 presents evidence for six countries in the period 1870–1933 on the behaviour of key real, financial, and monetary variables during cyclical contractions marked by financial crises. Because of data limitations for the majority of countries much of the focus is on annual data. The use of annual data, though the best available, makes it more difficult to discuss the influence of a phenomenon such as a banking panic or a stock market crash than would be possible with monthly or weekly data.

Six countries are included. The United States, Great Britain, Germany and France were the 'core' countries in the period, with virtually all of the 'crises' either originating in them or greatly amplified by them. The four countries were linked over much of the period by the gold standard and gold exchange standards as well as by close real trade and financial links. Unfortunately, reliable monetary data are available over the entire period for only two of the countries – the United States and Great Britain. For Germany coverage is limited to the pre-First World War period and for France to the post First World War period, and even then the data are spotty. Two 'peripheral' but important countries with reliable data were chosen in addition to the four core countries – Canada (for the period 1900–33) and Sweden (over the whole period). The two were closely linked to the 'core' countries – Canada to the US, and Great Britain; Sweden to Great Britain and Germany.

Real Variables

Twelve 'common international' reference cycles are isolated by picking turning points in the NBER reference cycle chronology for each country that corresponded as closely as possible to the British reference cycle pattern. Thus, for example, the second cycle for Great Britain has a peak in 1883 and a trough in 1886, the comparable cycle for the United States has a peak in 1882 and a trough in 1885. Moreover, the five other countries (in fact) had more (the USA had 16) or fewer reference cycles (Germany had 11) than Great Britain, but all these deviations in dating occurred within or very close to the British cycle. These deviations are characterised as subcycles to the common international cycle and the dates are presented in parentheses under the common international cycle dates.[15] Thus, for example, in the third cycle Great Britain has a peak in 1890, a trough in 1894, while the comparable 'common' US cycle is designated as having a peak in 1890 and a trough in 1894. This dating involved combining for the USA three NBER reference cycles designated here as subcycles – taking the peak from the second NBER reference cycle and the trough from the third.

In addition, following Burns and Mitchell (1946), six cyclical contractions are designated as severe denoted by (S) – cycles (1), (2), (3), (7), (9), and (12). Column (1) presents the annual, and the monthly, displayed in [ ], 'common international' reference cycle chronology, for the peaks and troughs in business cycle contractions. Both annual and monthly data exist for all countries except Sweden, for which only annual data is available. Cyclical contractions are focused on since most financial, banking and stock market crises have occurred at or shortly after the reference peak and have been associated with the severity of the ensuing cyclical contraction.

Column (2) presents a measure of the severity of decline in real economic activity during cyclical contractions in each country – the deviation of the average annual percentage change in real output from the long-run trend growth rate.

In general, the severity of contractions differed considerably across countries in the 'common cycles' although the six NBER designated severe cyclical contractions had the greatest declines in real activity in all the countries.

Financial Variables

Columns (3) to (7) for the four core countries present 'financial' variables. For the two peripheral countries, only minimal comparable evidence was available, shown in two columns for Canada, one for Sweden. Columns (3), (4) and (5) for the core countries show the incidence, based on various sources, of crises. Three definitions reflecting the literature are used.

Column (3) cites the presence of 'financial crises' according to Kindleberger's (1978) chronology of international financial crises.[16, 17] Column (4) cites the presence of stock market crises according to Morgenstern's (1959) chronology. In addition, following Morgenstern, superscripts indicate whether a crisis was major or minor, and international or local in scope. Finally, column (5) cites, based on Thorp (1926), Friedman and Schwartz (1963a) and other sources, the presence of banking crises, classified by superscripts as banking panics (runs,

TABLE 6.1A THE UNITED STATES

Common international reference cycle (trough to trough)	(1) Annual [monthly] reference cycle contractions (subcycles) Peak		Trough	(2) Deviations from trend of average annual real output growth[1] peak to trough	(3) Financial crises	(4) Stock Market crises	(5) Banking crises	(6) Monthly specific cycle long-term short-term interest differential Trough	Peak	(7) Monthly specific cycle stock price index Peak	Trough
	Real variables				*Financial variables*						
								9/73	8/78		
1. 1868–1879	1873	(S)	1879	0.5	9/73	73[c], 75[b], 79[a]	9/73[c]	9/73	8/76	5/72	6/77
	[10/73		3/79]					10/77	8/78		
2. 1879–1886	1882	(S)	1885	−3.2		80[a], 81[a], 82[b],	5/84[f]	6/83	9/85	6/81	1/85
	[3/82		5/85]			84[a]					
3. 1886–1894	1890	(S)	1894	−2.6				12/90	10/94	5/90	3/95
	[7/90		6/94]					7/87	11/88	5/87	6/88
	1867		1888	−6.7		37[b], 89[a]		12/90	6/92	5/90	12/90
	[4/87		4/88]					7/93	10/94	8/93	3/95
	1890		1891	.78		90[c], 91[b]	1890[f]				
	[7/90		5/91								
	1893	(S)	1894	−9.5	5/93	93[a]	7/93[c]				
	[1/93		6/94]								

4. 1894–1901	1899		1900	.03				3/00	11/00	4/99	9/00
	[6/99		12/00]					10/96	1/99	{9/95	8/96
	{1896		1897	6.0				3/00	11/00	4/99	9/00
	[12/96		6/97]								
	1899		1900	.03		99[a], 1900[b]					
	[6/99		12/00]								
5. 1901–1904	1903		1904	−5.4		1901[a], 1904[a]		8/03	1/05	9/02	10/03
	9/02		8/04]								
6. 1904–1908	1907	(S)	1908	−14.7	8/07	1907[c]	10/07[e]	12/07	7/09	9/06	11/07
	[5/07		6/08]								
7. 1908–1914	1913		1915	−6.9		1912[b], 1914[c]	8/14[f]	6/13	N/A	12/09	12/14
	[1/13		12/14]					{6/10	11/11	{12/09	7/10
	1909		1911	−1.5				6/13	N/A	9/12	12/14
	[1/10		1/12]								
	1913		1915	−6.9	8/14[s]						
	[1/13		12/14]								
8. 1914–1919	1918		1919	6.8				N/A	N/A	N/A	N/A
	[6/18		3/19]								
9. 1919–1921	1920	(S)	1921	−7.6	Spring 1921			10/20	8/22	7/19	8/21
	[1/20		7/21]								
10. 1921–1926	1923		1924	−0.4				5/23	10/24	3/23	10/23
	[5/23		7/24]								
11. 1926–1928	1926		1927	−2.2							
	[10/26		11/27]								
12. 1928–1932	1929	(S)	1932	−16.7	10/29, 3/38	1929[c], 1931[c]	1930[f], 1931[f]	8/29	9/34	9/29	6/32
	[8/29		3/33]				1933[e]	8/29	9/31		
								11/31	9/34		

TABLE 6.1A THE UNITED STATES – *cont.*

Common international reference cycle (trough to trough)	(8) Annual [monthly] Specific monetary growth cycle contractions (subcycles) Peak	(8) Trough	(9) Deviation from trend of average annual monetary growth rate² peak to trough	(10) High powered money	(11) Deposit reserve ratio	(12) Deposit currency ratio	(13) Percentage change in monetary gold stock	(14) Percentage change loan earning asset ratio	(15) Exchange rate regime
	Monetary variables — Percentage change in M if determinants indicated alone had changed								
1. 1868–1879	1871 [7/71	1878 5/77]	−4.7	−1.9	4.2	2.7	64.9	1.7	Flexible
2. 1879–1886	1880 [5/81	1884 12/83]	2.6	23.8	2.8	5.2	45.7	7.2	Fixed
3. 1886–1894	1890 [12/89	1893 12/92]	−2.6	11.6	−3.8	0.5	−21.0	−1.4	Fixed
	1886 [12/85	1888 12/87]	−.78	8.3	0.6	0.3	18.5	5.8	
	1890 [12/89	1891 12/90]	−1.4	5.0	−1.4	0.5	−8.6	0.3	
	1892 [12/92	1893 12/93]	−9.3	1.8	−1.5	−4.3	−14.2	−1.2	
4. 1894–1901	1899 [12/98	1900 12/99]	2.6	7.5	1.3	−0.8	6.4	−1.7	Fixed
	1895 [12/94	1896 12/95]	−7.8	−3.25	1.2	0.2	−8.6	−1.1	
	1899 [12/98	1900 12/99]	2.6	7.5	1.3	−0.8	6.4	−1.7	
5. 1901–1904	1901 [12/00	1903 12/03]	2.0	8.3	4.5	1.9	11.4	0.1	Fixed

7. 1908 – 1914	1912 [11/11	1913 6/13]	−1.5	2.2	1.6	0.1	2.9	0.9	Fixed
	1909 [10/08	1910 4/10]	−.33	1.65	1.8	1.6	−0.4	2.3	
	1912 [10/11	1913 6/13]	−1.5	2.2	1.6	0.1	2.9	0.9	
8. 1914–1919	1916 [12/16	1918 5/18]	7.0	39.3	−14.8	3.7	25.9	−4.5	Fixed
9. 1919–1921	1919 [12/18	1921 1/21]	−2.5	−1.35	4.2	2.8	4.6	8.6	Fixed
10. 1921–1926	1923 [4/22	1924 6/23]	−.13	2.7	−0.2	2.8	10.5	−0.1	Fixed
11. 1926–1928	1925 [7/24	1927 12/26]	−2.3	1.6	1.6	2.9	4.8	−0.8	Fixed
12. 1928–1932	1928 [11/27	1932 10/32]	−11.7	8.1	−8.3	−27.4	−6.3	−15.0	Fixed

Data sources: See Data Appendix.

Notes: [a]Crises affecting the U.S. and other countries.

[b]U.S. not affected but major.

[c]Major international crisis sharply affecting the U.S.

[d]U.S. affected alone.

[e]Banking panic—runs, failures, suspension of payments.

[f]Banking crisis—runs and/or failures.

[s]Sprague (1915).

(s)Severe cycle contraction.

[1]The trend growth rate in real output was 3.22 per cent over the perid 1870–1941. It was calculated as the difference between the natural logs of real output between initial and terminal year divided by the number of years.

[2]The trend monetary growth rate was 5.40 per cent over the period 1870–1941. It was calculated as in [1] above.

TABLE 6.1B GREAT BRITAIN

Common international reference cycle (trough to trough)	Real variables				Financial variables						
	(1) Annual [monthly] reference cycle contractions (subcycles)			(2) Deviations from trend of average annual real output growth[1] peak to trough	(3) Financial crises	(4) Stock Market crises	(5) Banking crises	(6) Monthly specific cycle long-term short-term interest differential		(7) Monthly specific cycle stock price index	
	Peak		Trough					Trough	Peak	Peak	Trough
1. 1868–1879	1873 [9/72	(S)	1879 6/79]	0.9	7/70[T]	73[a], 75[a], 78[d]		11/73 {N/A 11/73 8/78	9/79 8/71 10/76 9/79	10/73	7/79
2. 1879–1886	1883 [12/82	(S)	1886 6/85]	−1.2		80[a], 82[a], 84[a]		7/83	6/85	1/80	11/87
3. 1886–1895	1890 [9/90	(S)	1894 2/95]	−.19	11/90	87[a], 90[c], 92[a]		7/90 {7/90 8/93	10/94 9/92 10/94	10/89	4/92
4. 1895–1901	1900 [6/00		1901 9/01]	2.5		95[c], 1900[a]		12/99	10/01	2/00	—

5. 1901–1904	1903 [6/03		1904 11/04]	−.65		01[a], 04[a]	5/03	10/04	—	8/04
6. 1904–1908	1907 [6/07	(S)	1908 11/08]	−4.7		07[b]	11/07	4/09	2/07	3/09
7. 1908–1914	1913 [12/12		1914 9/14]	−1.1	1914[T,S,B]	12[a], 14[c]	7/13 4/10 7/13	N/A 3/11 —	4/11	6/14
8. 1914–1919	1917 [10/18		1919 4/19]	−8.9			N/A	N/A	—	1/19
9. 1919–1921	1920 [6/20	(S)	1921 6/21]	−6.9	Spring 1921		5/20	5/23	1/20	10/21
10. 1921–1926	1924 [11/24		1926 7/26]	−0.9			5/25	—	6/23	7/24
11. 1926–1928	1927 [5/27		1928 9/28]	.46			—	7/28	—	—
12. 1928–1933	1929 [7/29	(S)	1932 8/33]	−3.7	9/31	29[a], 31[c]	10/29 {10/29 { 1/32	7/33 9/20 7/33	2/29	5/32

TABLE 6.1B GREAT BRITAIN – *cont.*

	Monetary variables								
		Percentage change in M if determinants indicated alone had changed							
Common international reference cycle (trough to trough)	(8) Annual [monthly] Specific monetary growth cycle contractions (subcycles) Peak	Trough	(9) Deviation from trend of average annual monetary growth rate[2] peak to trough	(10) High powered money	(11) Deposit reserve ratio	(12) Deposit currency ratio	(13) Percentage change in monetary gold stock	(14) Percentage Change loan earning asset ratio	(15) Exchange rate regime
1. 1868–1879	1872	1878	−3.12	7.1	4.8	5.2	N/A	N/A	Fixed
2. 1879–1886	1881	1886	−2.77	2.4	−0.2	2.3	−15.8	−4.1	Fixed
3. 1886–1895	1891	1893	−2.51	2.7	−0.1	−2.2	7.9	−0.9	Fixed
4. 1895–1901	1900	1901	−3.70	0.5	1.9	0.4	7.2	−1.2	Fixed
	1894	1897	.09	5.6	0.5	−2.3	3.7	1.0	
	1900	1901	−3.70	0.5	−1.9	0.4	7.2	−1.2	
5. 1901–1904	1902	1903	−4.02	0.5	2.2	−3.8	−3.4	0.7	Fixed
6. 1904–1908	1906	1907	−1.57	2.3	0.1	−1.0	4.4	−0.1	Fixed

7. 1908–1914	1910	1912	.89	3.1	−0.1	4.2	5.0	2.4	Fixed
8. 1914–1919	1917	1919	14.25	35.5	2.5	−3.9	44.7	6.2	Pegged/ Controls
9. 1919–1921	1919	1922	−5.06	−13.7	2.0	4.5	0.2	−1.6	Flexible
10. 1921–1926	1924	1925	−3.72	0.0	−1.8	7.8	1.7	4.1	Fixed*
11. 1926–1928	1926	1928	−.49	−2.2	2.9	3.6	9.0	1.9	Fixed
12. 1928–1933	1928	1931	−4.27	−4.1	0.6	−1.3	−15.4	−6.1	Fixed†
	{1928	1929	{−4.20	{−2.1	{0.7	{−0.2	{−10.6	{−0.1	
	{1930	1931	{−8.95	{−0.8	{−1.7	{−3.7	{−10.2	{−3.0	

Data sources: See Data Appendix.

Notes: [a] Affecting G.B. and other countries.
[b] G.B. not affected but major.
[c] Major international crisis sharply affecting G.B.
[d] G.B. affected alone.
[T] Thorp (1926).
[S] Sprague (1915).
[B] Brown (1940).
* G.B. returned to gold in April 1925.
† G.B. left gold in September 1931.

[1] The trend growth rate in real output over the perid 1870–1939 was 1.48 per cent. It was calculated as described in Table I.A.

[2] The trend monetary growth rate over the period 1870–1939 was 2.71. It was calculated as in [1] above.

TABLE 6.1C GERMANY

Common international reference cycle (trough to trough)	Real variables: (1) Annual [monthly] reference cycle contractions (subcycles) Peak		(1) Trough	Real variables: (2) Deviations from trend of average annual real output growth[1] peak to trough	Financial variables: (3) Financial crises	(4) Stock Market crises	(5) Banking crises	(6) Monthly specific cycle long-term short-term interest differential Trough	(6) Peak	(7) Monthly specific cycle stock price index Peak	(7) Trough
1. 1870–1878	1872	(S)	1878 [2/79]	−.48	5/73	73[c]		—	5/79	11/72	6/77
2. 1878–1886	1882 [1/82	(S)	1886 3/86]	.27		80[a], 82[c], 87[a]		2/82 {2/82 4/85	9/86 2/84 9/86	8/81	1/85
3. 1886–1894	1890 [1/90	(S)	1894 2/95]	−.55		90[c], 91[a], 93[a]		2/90 {2/87 2/90 8/93	12/94 1/88 5/92 12/94	12/89	11/91

4.	1894–1902	1900 [1/00		1902 3/02]	−2.04	1901[c,T]	95[c]	1901[e]	3/00 {8/96 {3/00	7/02 5/97 7/02	5/99	10/01
5.	1902–1904	1903 [8/03		1904 2/05]	2.5		00[a], 04[a]		8/03	4/05		
6.	1904–1908	1907 [7/07	(S)	1908 12/08]	−2.2		07[c]		7/07	11/08	9/05	8/08
7.	1908–1914	1913 [4/13		1914 8/14]			12[a], 14[c]		2/13 8/10 2/13	—	9/12	12/13
8.	1914–1919	1918 [6/18		1919 6/19]						7/11		
9.	1919–1923	1922 [5/22	(S)	1923 11/23]								6/24
10.	1923–1926	1925 [3/25		1926 3/26]						7/26	1/25	12/25
11.												
12.	1926–1932	1929 [4/29	(S)	1932 3/32]		6/31	29[a], 31[c]	1931[f]	5/29 {3/28 {5/29 {7/31	6/32 1/29 8/30 6/32	4/27	4/32

TABLE 6.1C GERMANY – *cont.*

Common international reference cycle (trough to trough)	(8) Annual [monthly] Specific monetary growth cycle contractions (subcycles) Peak	Trough	*Monetary variables* — *Percentage change in M if determinants indicated alone had changed* (9) Deviation from trend of average annual monetary growth rate[2] peak to trough	(10) High powered money	(11) Deposit reserve ratio	(12) Deposit currency ratio	(13) Percentage change in monetary gold stock	(14) Exchange rate regime
1. 1870–1878	1872	1877	−2.9	−9.8	5.5	14.0	6.5	Fixed*
	{1872	1875	{−0.6	{0.1	{3.4	{9.6	{15.3	
	{1876	1877	{−8.5	{−8.3	{0.9	{4.1	{−10.2	
2. 1878–1886	1881	1885	−1.7	−2.0	−0.9	17.4	−2.9	Fixed
	{1879	1880	{−2.6	{2.0	{−0.1	{3.0	{−0.7	
	{1881	1882	{−4.1	{−5.9	{−1.1	{−3.0	{−1.0	
	{1884	1885	{−2.5	{−3.5	{−0.1	{6.7	{−0.5	
3. 1886–1894	1889	1893	−2.5	4.3	−0.7	7.4	4.5	Fixed
	{1886	1887	{−2.6	{−0.4	{−0.3	{3.4	{1.7	
	{1889	1890	{−3.4	{−1.5	{−0.3	{3.8	{−1.6	
	{1892	1893	{−2.5	{−0.1	{−0.2	{3.4	{−0.7	
4. 1894–1902	1898	1900	0.45	8.2	−6.0	3.8	7.2	Fixed
	{1895	1896	{−1.5	{−0.3	{−3.1	{7.5	{−1.9	
	[illegible]	[illegible]	[illegible]	[illegible]	[illegible]	[illegible]	[illegible]	

6. 1904–1908	1906 {1908	1907 1910	−17.1 {2.1	−0.2 {3.2	−0.3 0.1	−8.7 { 4.3	−2.6 {1.1	Fixed
7. 1908–1914	1910							Fixed
8. 1914–1919								Flexible
9. 1919–1923								Flexible
10. 1923–1926								Fixed†
11.								Fixed
12. 1926–1932								Fixed

Data sources: See Data Appendix.

Notes: [a]Crisis affecting Germany and other countries.

[b]Germany not affected but major.

[c]Major international crisis sharply affecting Germany.

[d]Germany alone.

[e]McGouldrick (1983) p. 19.

[f]Kindleberger (1973).

[T]Thorp (1926).

*Germany was on a silver standard until 1873, on gold thereafter.

†Germany stabilized the mark in 1924.

[1]The trend growth rate in real output over the period 1870–1913 was 8.01 per cent. It was calculated as described in Table 1.A.

[2]The trend monetary growth rate over the period 1870–1913 was 5.24 per cent. It was calculated as in [1] above.

TABLE 6.1D FRANCE

	Real variables				*Fin*		
	(1)			*(2)*	*(3)*	*(4)*	*(5)*
Common international reference cycle (trough to trough)	*Annual [monthly] reference cycle contractions (subcycles)* Peak		Trough	*Deviations from trend of average annual real output growth*[1] *peak to trough*	*Financial crises*	*Stock market crises*	*Banking crises*
1. 1868–1879	1873	(S)	1879		1871[T]	73[a], 75[a]	
	[8/73		9/79]			79[d]	
	1869		1871				
	[8/70		2/72]				
	1873		1876				
	[9/73		8/76]				
	1878		1879				
	[3/78		9/79]				
2. 1879–1887	1882	(S)	1887		1/82	8[a], 82[c]	1882[e]
	[12/81		8/87]				
3. 1887–1984	1890	(S)	1894			87[a], 89[d],	1889[f]
	[1/91		1/95]			90[c], 91[a],	
						95[c]	
4. 1894–1902	1900		1902			00[b]	
	[3/00		9/02]				
5. 1902–1904	1903		1904	6.43		04[a]	
	[5/03		10/04]				
6. 1904–1908	1907	(S)	1908	−.64	8/07	07[a]	
	[7/07		2/09]				
7. 1908–1914	1913		1914		1914[T]	12[a], 14[c]	
	[6/13		8/14]				
8. 1914–1918	1917		1918				
	[6/18		4/19]				
9. 1918–1921	[9/20	(S)	7/21]	−9.1			
10. 1921–1925	1924		1925	−.58	1926[Y]		
	[10/24		6/25]				
11. 1925–1927	1926		1927	−4.9			
	[10/26		6/27]				
12. 1927–1932	1930	(S)	1932	−7.2		29[a], 31[a]	1930[g]
	[3/30		7/32]				

Data sources: See Data Appendix.

Notes: [a] Crises affecting France and other countries.
[b] France not affected but major.
[c] Major international crisis, sharply affecting France.
[d] France alone.
[e] Failure of Union Generale. Source Kindleberger (1978).
[f] Suspension of payments—Comptoir D'Escompte. Clapham (1966) p. 384.
[g] Bank failures in Paris, Kindleberger (1978), pp. 136—137.

ʼariables	Monetary variables					
(6) hly specific long-term ort-term nterest ferential	(7) Monthly specific cycle stock price index		(8) Annual [monthly] specific monetary growth cycle contractions (subcycles)		(9) Deviation from trend of average annual monetary growth rate[2] peak to trough	(10) Exchange rate regime
Peak	Peak	Trough	Peak	Trough		
6/79						Fixed*
6/86						Fixed
8/95		1/98				Fixed
2/89						
6/92						
8/95						
9/01	4/00					Fixed
8/04		2/04	1904	1905	−3.1	Fixed
5/09	2/07	10/07	1906	1907	−3.4	Fixed
N/A	9/12	7/14	1911	1912	−4.6	Fixed
			1908	1910	4.1	
			1911	1912	4.6	
		3/19				Flexible
	4/20	4/22	1920	1921	−7.1	Flexible
11/25	10/24	5/25	1923	1924	−3.9	Flexible
10/27	9/26	12/26	1925	1926	2.8	Flexible†
6/33	2/26	5/33	1928	1929	−4.6	Fixed

Thorp (1926).
Yeager (1976).
* France was on a bimetallic silver standard until 1878, although gold was de facto the standard after 1872.
† France restored de factor gold convertibility at the end of 1926.
The trend growth rate in real output over the period of 1900–1939 was 1.36 per cent. It was calculated as described in Table 1.A.
The trend monetary growth rate over the period 1900–1939 was 7.34 per cent. It was calculated as in [1] above.

TABLE 6.1E CANADA

	Real variables			Financial variables		Monetary variables							
								Percentage change in it if determinants indicated alone had changed					
	(1)		(2)	(3)	(4)	(5)		(6)	(7)	(8)	(9)	(10)	(11)
Common international reference cycle (trough to trough)	Annual [monthly] reference cycle contractions (subcycles) Peak	Trough	Deviations from trend of average annual real output growth peak to trough	Financial crises	Banking crises	Annual [monthly] specific monetary growth cycle contractions (subcycles) Peak	Trough	Deviation from trend of average annual monetary growth rate² peak to trough	High powered money	Deposit reserve ratio	Deposit currency ratio	Percentage change in monetary gold stock	Exchange rate regime
1.													
2.													
3.													
4.													
5. 1901–1904	1903	1904	1.7	1902[T]		1901	1903	2.8	21.8	−6.6	1.5	38.4	Fixed
	[12/02	6/04]				[4/01	8/02]						
6. 1904–1908	1907 (S)	1908	−6.7	1907[T,J]		1906	1907	9.7	4.0	−6.5	−1.8	11.7	Fixed
	[12/06	7/08]				[1/06	10/07]						

7. 1908–1915	1913		1915	−7.5			1911	1914	−1.1	21.6	−10.3	2.1		Fixed
	[11/12		1/15]				[4/12	5/13]						
	{ 1910		1911	{ 2.5	1910[T]		{ 1909	1910	{ 2.8	{ 7.8	{ 0.1	{ 0.4	11.8	
	[3/10		7/11]				[12/08	10/10]						
	1913		1915	−7.5	1914[J]	1914[a]	1911	1914	−1.1	21.6	−10.3	2.1		
	[11/12		1/15]				[4/12	5/13]						
8. 1915–1919	1917		1919	1.25			1917	1918	0.8	13.9	−5.4	−2.2		Flexible
	[3/17		4/19]				[10/17	4/18]						
9. 1919–1921	1920	(S)	1921	−16.8	1921[T]		1919	1921	−7.1	−14.3	5.8	4.9		Flexible
	[6/20		9/21]				[9/21	9/22]						
10. 1921–1924	1923		1924	−6.9		1923[a,b]	1922	1923	−4.5	−9.1	−2.5	−20.0	−6.6	Fixed*
	[6/23		8/24]				[9/22	9/23]						
11.														Fixed
12. 1924–1933	1929	(S)	1932	−10.9	1931[J]		1927	1931	−7.8	−20.6	9.1	2.0	−35.1	Flexible†
	[4/29		3/33]				[10/27	11/31]						

Data Sources: See Data Appendix.

Notes: [a] Minor bank runs.

[b] Major bank failure.

[J] Jamieson (1959).

[T] Thorp (1926).

* Canada returned to gold de jure 1926.

† Canada left gold de facto in 1929, de jure 1931.

[1] The trend growth rate in real output over the period 1900–1939 was 3.10. It was calculated as described in Table 1.A.

[2] The trend monetary growth rate over the period 1900–1939 was 5.49 per cent. It was calculated as in [1] above.

TABLE 6.1F SWEDEN

Common international reference cycle (trough to trough)	Real variables (1) Annual [monthly] reference cycle contractions (subcycles Peak		Trough	(2) Deviations from trend of average annual real output growth[1] peak to trough	Financial variables (3) Financial crises	Monetary variables: Percentage change in M if determinants indicates alone had changed (4) Annual [monthly] specific monetary growth cycle contractors (subcycles) Peak	Trough	(5) Deviation from trend of average annual monetary growth rate[2] peak to trough	(6) High powered money	(7) Deposit reserve ratio	(8) Deposit currency ratio	(9) Exchange rate regime
1. 1868–1878	1872	(S)	1878	−1.1		1876	1878	−8.4	−11.8	−8.0	15.2	Fixed
	{1872		1875	{−1.3							[−250.4]	
	{1876		1878	{−5.0								
2. 1878–1886	1883	(S)	1886	−1.4		1880	1886	−1.8	1.9	18.1	3.7	Fixed
						1880	1882}	{−1.3	{−7.0	{14.5	{0.6	
						1883	1886}	{−2.3	{8.2	{0.9	{0.3	

3.	1886–1895	1889	(S)	1895	−0.6		1891	1894	−2.9	9.4	−1.0	0.8	Fixed
		1889		1890	−1.5		1889	1890	−3.5	−0.1	1.7	0.4	
		1891		1892	−3.7		1891	1892	−5.1	−1.0	0.4	0.9	
		1894		1895	−5.6		1893	1894	−3.2	5.1	−1.1	−1.7	
4.	1895–1902	1900		1902	−3.3		1899	1902	2.7	36.4	5.4	−16.7	Fixed
5.	1902–1905	1903		1905	−1.4		1903	1904	−1.5	9.0	0.5	−5.6	Fixed
6.	1905–1907	1906	(S)	1907	−2.7	1907[T]	1907	1910	−1.2	1.1	3.6	7.6	Fixed
7.	1907–1914	1913		1914	−5.2	1914[T]							
8.	1914–1917	1916		1917	−11.9								Flexible
9.	1917–1921	1920	(S)	1921	−15.4		1918	1923	−5.3	−19.1	2.6	16.6	Flexible*
10.													
11.	1921–1928	1925		1928	.22								
12.	1928–1931	1929	(S)	1931	−6.1	1931, 1932[J,k]	1930	1932	−6.2	8.7	−11.0	0.8	Fixed

Data Sources: See Data Appendix.

Notes: [k] Kreuger collapse.

[T] Thorp (1926).

[J] Jonung (1981).

*Sweden returned to gold de facto in 1922, de jure in 1924.

†Sweden left gold in 1931.

[1] The trend growth rate in real output over the period 1871–1939 was 2.77. It was calculated as described in Table 1.A.

[2] The trend monetary growth rate over the period 1871–1939 was 5.39 per cent. It was calculated as in [1] above.

failures, and suspension of payments) and banking crises (runs and or failures). Most banking crises and virtually all banking panics were confined to the USA in this period.

Columns (6) and (7) show the peaks and troughs on a monthly basis for the four core countries in movements of two key financial variables – the long-term/short-term interest rate differential, and Morgenstern's index of stock prices. The interest differential chronology is reversed, reflecting financial pressure at the specific cycle trough and ease at the peak. In general, the troughs in this series are very close to the corresponding reference cycle peaks, tending to follow them by only a few months. In addition, as discussed in detail in Morgenstern (1959), the troughs in this series are more closely related between countries than are the peaks, and closer links are found between the three European countries than between any of them and the USA. In addition, Morgenstern demonstrates that movements in the differential are largely explained by movements in short-term interest rates. The behaviour of this series according to Morgenstern is evidence for a tightly linked European short-term capital market. Morgenstern's evidence, as well as that of Lindert (1969) on the relative pulling power of the discount rate in different financial centres, suggests that in time of financial pressure, securities markets were especially closely linked.

The dating of Morgenstern's stock price index column (7) has a number of important features. First, peaks in the series tend to precede reference cycle peaks, reflecting the stock market's role as a frequent leading indicator of real activity. Second, the turning points in the series are very closely related between the four countries, although the links between the European countries are closer than those between the US and Europe.[18] A comparison of the peaks in this series and Morgenstern's chronology of stock market crises, shown in column (4), shows a remarkable coincidence for major crises that are international in scope. Such crises often originated in the USA and then spread quickly to Europe.

Finally, a comparison of the turning points in the two financial variables in columns (6) and (7) with the chronology of financial, banking, and stock market crises in columns (3), (4) and (5) suggests that crises in the gold standard era often tended to be international in scope, but the way in which they manifested themselves in different countries differed considerably, especially comparing the response of the banking system in the US to that of the other countries.

Monetary Variables

Columns (8) to (13) for the three core countries except France, and column (14) for the US and Great Britain display monetary variables. Monetary variables for Canada appear in column (5) to (10) and for Sweden in columns (4) to (8). Figures 6.1 to 6.5 display for each country on a logarithmic scale the money supply and its determinants: high-powered money, the deposit–reserve and deposit–currency ratio; for the US and Great Britain also the loan-earning asset ratio, and for four countries the monetary gold stock.

Column (8) for the core countries, columns (5) and (4) for Canada and Sweden, respectively, present a chronology of peaks and troughs of specific cycles in monetary growth corresponding to the reference cycle chronology of column (1). Annual or monthly (depending on the frequency of the available data) turning points were derived following procedures developed by Friedman and Schwartz (1963b).

For the US turning points in money growth generally precede those in business by a calendar year. However, as can be seen from the monthly series in brackets, the use of annual averaged data greatly distorts the true measure of the lead. Nevertheless, since monthly data are available only for Canada besides the US, the annual data is used as a crude measure of timing.

For the other countries, the turning points in money growth generally precede but in numerous cases coincide with the turning points in business.[19]

Column (9) shows the deviations from a long-run trend of the average rate of money growth between peaks and troughs as a measure of the severity of monetary contraction. Figures 6.1 to 6.5 plot the money supply for the different countries on a logarithmic scale. In virtually every case, with the principal exception of the First World War in Great Britain, declines in money growth below trend are associated with declines in economic activity in the corresponding reference cycle contraction. Indeed, the greater is the deviation of money growth from trend, the greater the decline in economic activity. The most severe declines in both money and real output occur in severe cycles characterised in many instances by financial and stock market crises. However, the greatest declines of the countries examined here (with the exception of the 1920–1 episode) occurred in the US in contractions associated with banking crises.

Columns (10) to (12) for the three core countries (excluding France), column (7) to (9) for Canada and (6) to (8) for Sweden show the

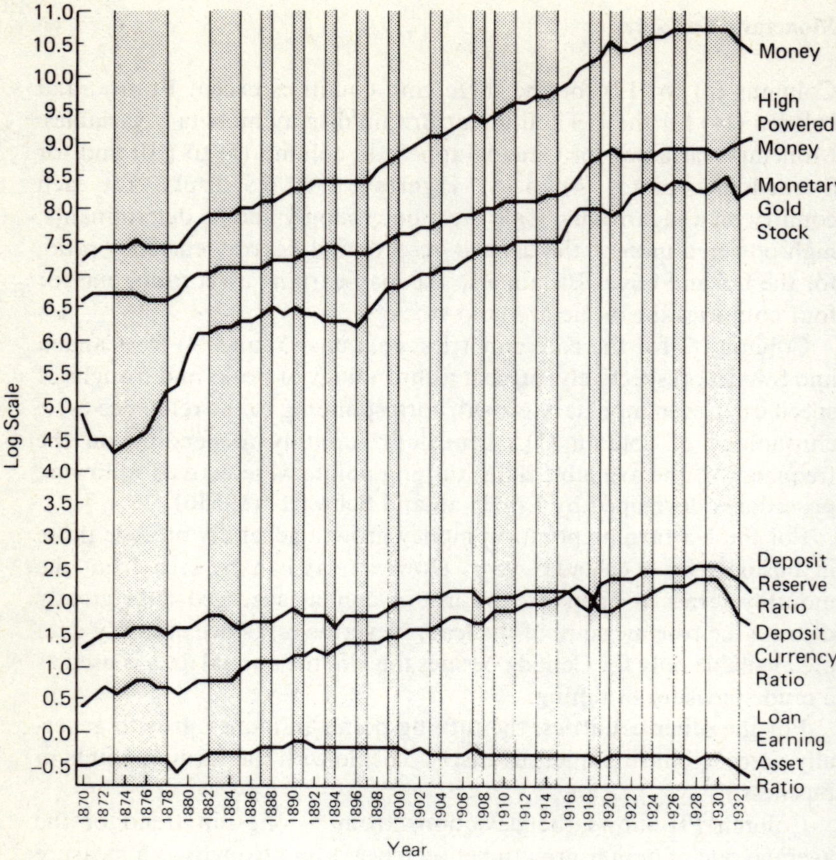

Shaded area represents NBER reference cycle contractions.

FIG. 6.1 The United States

contributions to the specific cycle contractions in monetary growth of the three determinants of the money supply: high-powered money; the deposit–currency ratio; and the deposit–reserve ratio. These series are plotted in the accompanying figures.

Cagan (1965), in his pioneering study for the USA, found the currency–money ratio to be the key determinant of cyclical movements in the money supply with high-powered money and the reserve ratio each having about one half of the influence of the currency ratio. For severe cycles, the order of magnitude remained the same but the

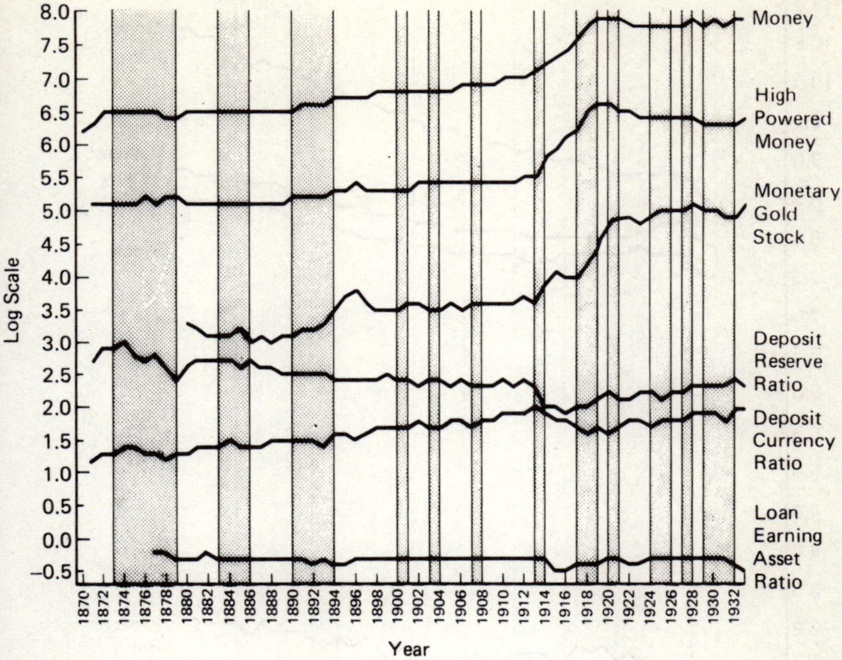

Shaded area represents NBER reference cycle contractions.

FIG. 6.2 Great Britain

influence of the currency ratio increased.[20] Both Cagan and Friedman and Schwartz present evidence for the USA that in severe cycles characterised by banking panics, declines in the deposit–currency ratio and hence in the deposit–reserve ratio on several occasions led to declines in money growth sufficient to produce a severe contraction in economic activity. Such results for the US can be clearly seen in column (12) for the banking panics of 1893, and the great contraction of 1929–33.

For Great Britain, in contrast to the US, high-powered money was the key determinant of cyclical contractions in money, followed by the deposit–currency ratio and the deposit–reserve ratio.[21] For Great Britain, again in contrast to the US, there were no banking crises in the period under consideration, yet the two ratios acting alone or jointly produced significant declines in money in several severe contractions

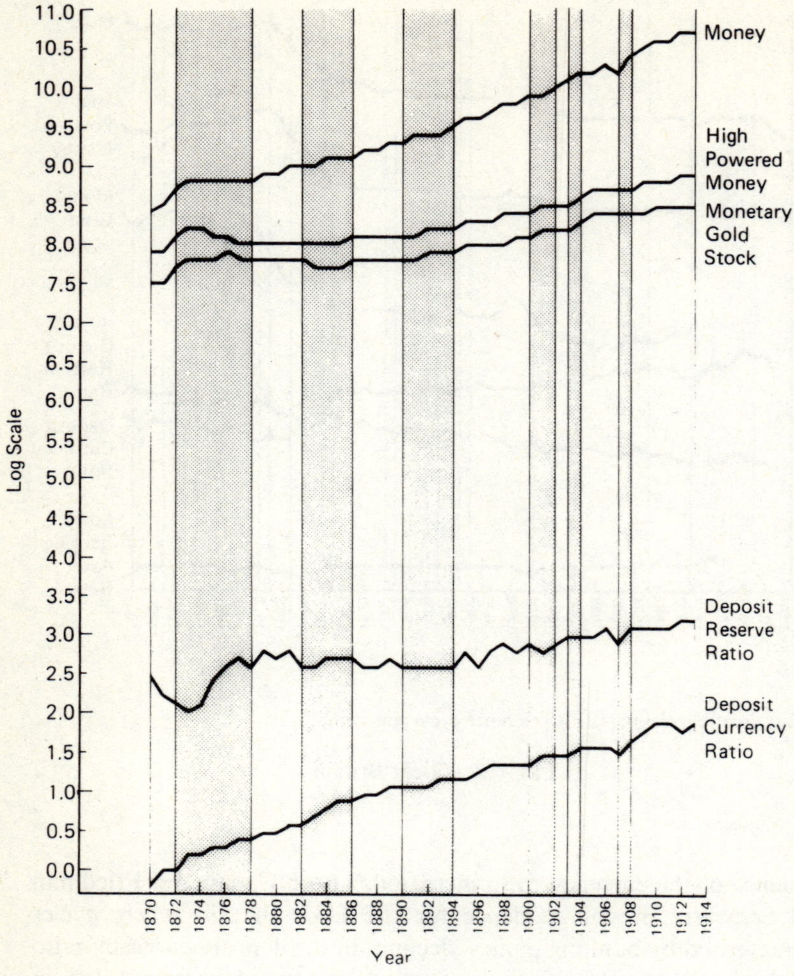

Shaded area represents NBER reference cycle contractions.

FIG. 6.3 Germany

associated with major stock market crises: 1872–8; 1890–3; 1900–1; 1902–3; 1907–8; and 1928–31. However, none of the declines of the ratios, with the exception of 1930–1, were comparable to those observed in the US case.

For Germany, the deposit–currency ratio was the most important determinant of cyclical changes in money in specific cycle contractions.

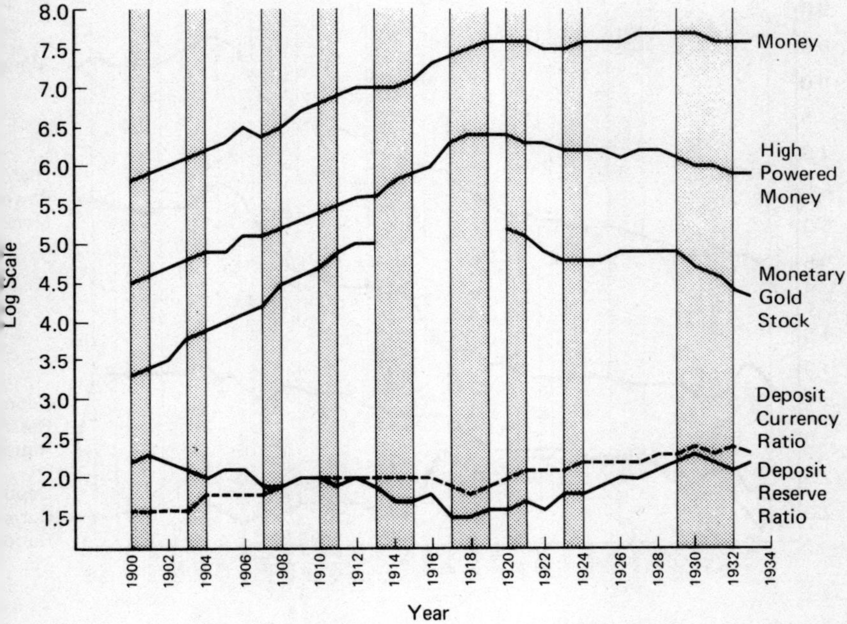

Shaded area represents NBER reference cycle contractions.

FIG. 6.4 Canada

However, in contrast to other countries, money only declined in one specific cycle contraction – 1906–7. With the exception of that episode where a decline in D/C produced a decline in M, the Reichsbank caused H to vary countercyclically to offset the procyclical behaviour of the ratios.[22] Similar to Great Britain, German experience was characterised by the absence of banking crises (with the exception of a mild crisis associated with several bank failures in 1901). Yet the decline in the ratios, especially the D/R, seemed to coincide with major stock market crises.

In both Canada and Sweden, H and D/R were the key determinants of changes in M in cyclical contractions,[23] with D/C playing a minor role. Also both countries were characterised by stable banking systems and the absence of panics. In the Canadian case, the banking system's D/R declined significantly in three severe contractions associated with financial crises abroad: 1877–8; 1894–5; and 1927–31.

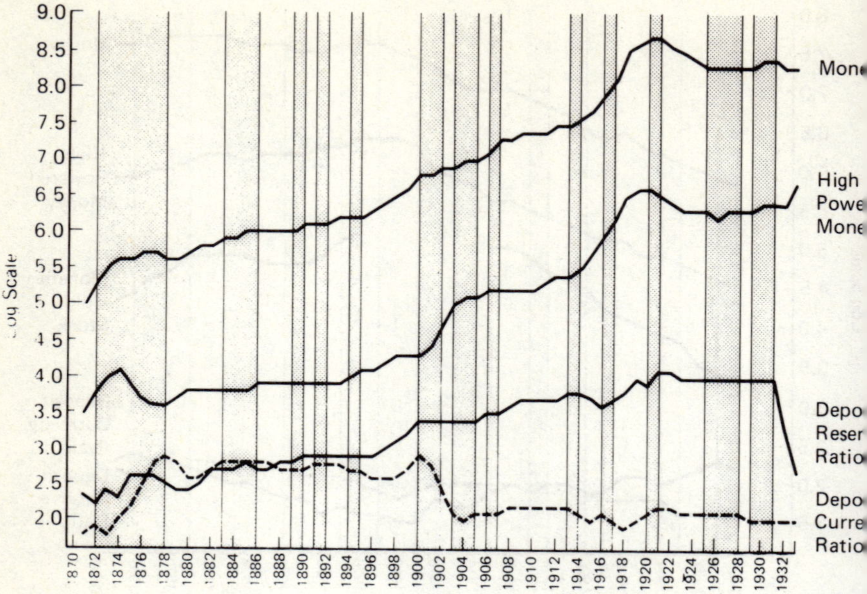

Shaded area represents NBER reference cycle contractions.

FIG. 6.5 Sweden

Column (13) for the US, Great Britain and Germany, and column (10) for Canada show the percentage change in the monetary gold stock between the specific cycle peaks and troughs. These series are also plotted in Figures 6.1, 6.2, 6.3 and 6.5. Under the gold standard, which characterised much of the period for all the countries (see the last column of each table for a chronology of the monetary standards by cycle), one would expect changes in the monetary gold stock to be the key source of change in high-powered money over the cycle unless significant sterilisation is occurring. Under perfectly flexible exchange rates no such link should prevail.

For the USA, for every specific cycle contraction, except that of 1871–8 under flexible exchange rates, there is a close correlation between changes in the monetary gold stock and changes in high-powered money; however, the link is far from one-to-one, reflecting periodic sterilisation especially of gold outflows during contractions.

For Great Britain, the association though positive is much weaker, in accordance with the evidence of Bloomfield (1959) and others that the Bank of England engaged in active sterilisation.

For Germany, the association, though positive, is also weak. According to McGouldrick (1984), this reflects the deliberate policy of the Reichsbank to shield the domestic money market from external influence.

Finally, for Canada, for the few observations we have, the association is positive and quite strong. During this period, Canada did not have a central bank and with the exception of the operation of the Finance Act in the interwar period (see Shearer and Clark, 1984) did not engage in extensive intervention.

Such evidence, though rough, shows, in agreement with Huffman and Lothian (1984), linkages between the money supplies of the different countries through gold flows and high-powered money.

Column (14) for the US and Great Britain presents the loan-earning asset ratio. This ratio reflects, in periods of financial stringency, the banking system's desire for liquidity. Thus in a severe contraction in an effort to increase liquidity, banks will convert loans into (primarily) government securities in order to reduce the ratio. As can be seen in the table, in both countries the ratio declined during several severe cycles characterised by crises.

Finally, the last column in each table distinguishes between periods of fixed and flexible exchange rates. There are too few degrees of freedom to make other than very casual comparisons. The two significant periods of floating: 1862–78 for the USA and the early 1920s for all countries except the US provide some ground for comparison of the insulation properties of fixed and flexible rates. Thus, for example, in the 1873–9 contraction we observe both the interest differential and stock price index cycles for the USA to be more out of phase with those of the European countries than in the rest of the period, and the US contraction to be considerably milder than its European counterpart. However, the USA was affected by various European crises. Similarly, in the 1920s, where both France and Germany floated much of the period, we can observe more cycles for France and fewer for Germany than for other countries. Also France in 1926 experienced a major financial crisis that was not transmitted abroad.

The descriptive evidence in Table 6.1 accordingly suggests a number of conclusions on the relationships between money, financial crises, and real activity in the different countries.

First, severe declines in economic activity in all countries are associated with (prior) declines in money growth. Second, most severe cyclical contractions in all the countries examined are associated with stock market crises but not, with the exception of the US, with banking crises. Third, the junior partners to high-powered money as determinants of change in money – the deposit–reserve and deposit–currency ratios – played an important role in reducing money growth in all countries but not to the extent they displayed in the US experience, especially the role played by the deposit–currency ratio in reducing the money supply during contractions involving banking panics.

Why was monetary contraction associated with financial crises more severe in the US experience than in other countries? One explanation is the greater instability, compared to that of the five other countries, of the US banking system – a system composed largely of unit fractional reserve banks with reserves pyramided in the New York money market. Though numerous institutional reforms were devised to strengthen the system in the period 1862–1934, none, until the advent of federal deposit insurance in 1934, removed the basic instability associated with potential threats to convertibility. Bank runs and panics occurred whenever a shock threatened the solvency of a few key banks or other financial institutions.

In contrast with the US experience, the five other countries in the same period all developed nationwide branch banking systems consolidated into a few very large banks. The system of bank branching, first successfully developed in Scotland in the eighteenth century and emulated by other countries including Canada and Sweden,[25] represented a method of pooling risks which proved quite effective in guarding against the type of 'house of cards' effects common to the US (and early nineteenth-century British) banking system.

A second explanation for the relatively poor performance of the US – stemming from the massive literature on the development of central banking and especially of the Bank of England[26] – is the absence of an *effective* 'lender-of-last-resort'. Four of the six countries in our sample had central banks, which by the beginning of period had (in various degrees) learned in the face of a crisis to follow Bagehot's rule 'to lend freely but at a penalty rate', and to a certain extent to co-operate amongst themselves in times of severe international crisis, such as the Baring crisis of 1890.[27] One exception, Canada, did not have a central bank until 1936, but the chartered banks had, by 1890, with the compliance of the Government, established an effective self-policing agency, the Canadian Bankers Association, which acting *in loco parentis* successfully helped insulate the Canadian banks from the deleterious effects of US banking panics in 1893 and 1907.[28] The existence of such a mechanism, whether provided by the Government or by the private market, once it proved effective would educate and instil a sense of confidence in the public sufficient to prevent incipient crises.[29]

Another contrast with the USA is the greater relative importance of the deposit–reserve ratio in producing cyclical contractions in the money supplies in the four countries–Great Britain, Germany, Canada and Sweden. The apparent association between declines in the D/R ratio and the incidence of stock market crises suggests a possible additional channel of influence whereby financial crises link money supplies between countries. The evidence indicates a link between turning points in money growth and stock price indexes (see for the US monthly data in Table 6.1A by comparing columns (8) and (7)).[30] The link, in turn, may reflect early signs of the effects of changes in money growth on real economic activity. In combination with the evidence on the D/R, the link suggests the following purely hypothetical scenario. A sharp decline in the money stock in one country, e.g. the USA, produced initially by, say, a gold outflow, leads to a sharp decline in stock prices (a 'crash'). The stock market crash in turn could produce, as described in the first-two sections above, in the absence of intervention, both a liquidity crisis and a banking panic, resulting in declines in the deposit–currency and deposit–reserve ratios. Concurrently, reflecting the tight linkage between stock exchanges in different centres shown by Morgenstern, e.g. through a decline in the prices of US securities traded in foreign markets, the decline in securities' prices of the initiating country are transmitted to the stock market of other countries. The decline in securities' prices in these countries could impact quickly on commercial banks that have extended call loans and brokers' loans to the stock market and attempt to strengthen their liquidity by calling these loans and thus reducing the loan earning asset ratio. At the same time, they increase their precautionary reserves, hence lowering the deposit–reserve ratio.

In other words, arbitrage in stock market securities may link national money supplies directly via their effects on commercial bank reserve ratios. Such effects may occur before the monetary shock has had time to spread its influence abroad via the traditional price flow mechanism.[31]

INTERNATIONAL LINKAGES: THE MONETARIST AND KINDLEBERGER–MINSKY APPROACHES

In this section some suggestive evidence on the international transmission of financial crises is offered. As discussed in the second section above, the two approaches to the role and importance of financial crises suggest different ways in which crises may be transmitted abroad. The monetarists stress the role of monetary variables such as gold flows and changes in international reserves as the vehicle by which crises (and business fluctuations) are transmitted abroad. Moreover, the extent to which monetary disturbances associated with possible crises affect economic activity in different countries depends on the nature of the link between money and economic activity in each country, which in turn is determined by the nature of the banking structure, the money holding habits of the public, and the conduct of monetary policy. By contrast, in the 'realist' view of Minsky and Kindleberger the money supply in each country is basically endogenous – determined by the demand for the finance of investment activity. Thus financial crises are a necessary consequence of the boom phase of the cycle. Such crises can be transmitted between countries in many ways, including arbitrage in commodities and capital markets, psychological links, and through foreign securities holdings in the portfolios of commercial banks. The role of monetary variables, such as gold flows and high-powered money, would be secondary. Moreover, the nature of the monetary standard would be secondary – crises would be transmitted under fixed or flexible rates.

In this section the evidence distinguishing between the two approaches is based on correlations between successive pairs of countries, in periods characterised by severe cyclical declines in economic activity, of the year-to-year rates of changes of money, high-powered money, the monetary gold stock, the deposit–reserve, deposit–currency, and loan-earning asset ratios.[32]

On first glance it would appear that strong, significant correlations between monetary gold stocks, high-powered money, and the money supply and less so for the ratios would be evidence for the monetarist approach under fixed rates. Strong correlations between the ratios, less so for the aggregates, would be evidence for the Kindleberger–Minsky view. However, on closer examination a number of qualifications must be made before we can meaningfully interpret such correlations.

First, according to the Kindleberger–Minsky view, to the extent that common, international, real factors affect the D/R and D/C ratios in each country, they would also affect the money supplies. Hence observed correlation between money supplies may be consistent with causality running from real forces to money in each country rather than a connection through the balance of payments.[33] However, evidence based on Granger–Sims causality tests by Huffman and Lothian (1984) for the US and Great Britain in the period 1830–1933, and by Schwartz (1981) for the US in the 1929–33 Great Depression indicates causality runs primarily from monetary to real variables.[34]

Second, under the classical gold standard which prevailed throughout much of the period under consideration, commercial banks in many countries (especially the peripheral countries such as Canada and Sweden) held bankers' balances with commercial banks (and central banks) in the key financial centres of the core countries – especially in London, Paris and Berlin.[35] Indeed, in the Canadian case, the chartered banks held most of their reserves in the New York money market.[36] Thus a direct channel of transmission via the D/R ratios of the commercial banks between countries under the gold standard would also be consistent with the monetarist approach.

Third, to the extent that correlation exists within each country between high-powered money and the ratios, a clear-cut distinction between the two views, holding the other qualifications constant, would be difficult to make.[37]

Fourth, in the light of the above qualifications, the most clear-cut distinction between the two approaches would be the correlations of the monetary gold stocks and of high-powered money between successive countries. Such correlation would be a direct implication of transmission for the monetarist view, but not necessarily for the Kindleberger–Minsky view.[38]

Finally, the use of annual data may be too crude to pick up the influence of phenomena as ephemeral as financial crises.

Given the above qualifications, Table 6.2 presents the correlations for the six variables on a country-by-country basis, with the data set decomposed into: the full period; reference cycle contractions; reference cycle expansions; and severe reference cycle contractions.

The correlations presented for all the countries except France over the periods for which the data are available are limited to those at the 10 per cent or lower level of significance. The evidence in Table 6.2 is generally in favour of the monetarist hypothesis. Significant correlations between money and between H are detected in the majority of pairwise comparisons over the whole period and in reference cycle contractions and expansions. Moreover, though correlations between the D/R ratios are also significant in a number of periods, such results are consistent with both views. Only the evidence of a few significant correlations between the D/C ratios and between the loan-earning asset is consistent with the alternative view.

TABLE 6.2 CORRELATION COEFFICIENTS (DEGREES OF FREEDOM) BETWEEN MONETARY AND FINANCIAL VARIABLES. FIVE COUNTRIES, 1870–1933

A. The Whole Period 1870–1933

	Year to year percentage changes in:					
	(1) Money supply	*(2) High powered money*	*(3) Monetary gold*	*(4) Deposit reserve ratio*	*(5) Deposit currency ratio*	*(6) Loan earning asset ratio*
1. US–GB	.31*(53)	.38*(62)	−.34*(53)			.34*(56)
2. US–Germany			−.34*(43)			
3. US–Canada	.69*(34)	.62*(33)		.46†(33)		
4. US–Sweden	.41*(62)	.51*(62)		.36*(62)		
5. GB–Germany	.31*(43)			−.33*(42)		
6. GB–Canada	.40*(34)	.56*(33)	.53*(13)		.42*(33)	
7. GB–Sweden	.70*(62)	.48*(62)				
8. Germany–Canada	.75*(14)				.79*(13)	
9. Germany–Sweden	.38*(42)	.60*(42)				
10. Canada–Sweden	.48*(34)	.62*(33)				

*Statistically significant at the 5 per cent level.
†Statistically significant at the 10 per cent level.

B. Reference Cycle Contractions[1]

	Year to year percentage changes in:					
	(1) Money supply	*(2) High powered money*	*(3) Monetary gold*	*(4) Deposit reserve ratio*	*(5) Deposit currency ratio*	*(6) Loan earning asset ratio*
1. US–GB						
2. US–Germany		.58*(14)				
3. US–Canada	.68*(10)	.65*(10)				
4. US–Sweden	.56*(17)			.67*(17)		
5. GB–Germany						
6. GB–Canada	.67*(10)			.64*(10)	.73*(10)	
7. GB–Sweden	.48*(20)					
8. Germany—Canada						
9. Germany–Sweden	.52*(16)	.71*(16)				
10. Canada–Sweden	.74†(6)	.80†(6)				

[1] Years contained in common international reference cycles as defined in Table 6.1.

C. Reference Cycle Expansions[1]

	Year to year percentage changes in:					
	(1) Money supply	*(2) High powered money*	*(3) Monetary gold*	*(4) Deposit reserve ratio*	*(5) Deposit currency ratio*	*(6) Loan earning asset ratio*
1. US–GB	.40*(32)		−.49*(28)			.42*(29)
2. US–Germany						
3. US–Canada	.63*(20)	.60*(20)		.41*(20)		
4. US–Sweden	.39*(27)	.50*(27)		.60*(27)		
5. GB–Germany	.40†(24)					
6. GB–Canada	.69*(19)	.58*(18)				
7. GB–Sweden	.78*(28)	.48*(28)		.35*(27)	.47*(28)	
8. Germany–Canada	.88*(10)			.64†(9)	.65†(9)	
9. Germany–Sweden	.66*(20)	.50*(20)				
10. Canada–Sweden	.69*(15)					

[1] Years contained in common international reference cycle as defined in Table 6.1.

D. Severe Reference Cycle Contractions[1]

	Year to year percentage changes in:					
	(1) Money supply	*(2) High powered money*	*(3) Monetary gold*	*(4) Deposit reserve ratio*	*(5) Deposit currency ratio*	*(6) Loan earning asset ratio*
1. US–GB		.45†(16)				.51†(12)
2. US–Germany		.53†(13)				
3. US–Canada		.91*(5)		.82*(5)		
4. US–Sweden		.49*(14)		.72*(14)		
5. GB–Germany						
6. GB–Canada						
7. GB–Sweden	.61*(15)					
8. Germany–Canada						
9. Germany–Sweden	.57*(13)	.79*(13)				
10. Canada–Sweden						

[1] Six cycles: 1873–9; 1883–7; 1890–5; 1907–8; 1920–1; 1929–33.

Finally, in severe reference cycle contractions – periods which contain financial crises – there is strong evidence for the monetarist approach. Though few money supply links are detected, correlations between high-powered money were significant in five comparisons. Moreover, though correlations between the D/R ratios were significant in two cases, one of them, Canada–US, reflects the direct links between the reserves of commercial banks in the two countries, a result consistent with the monetarist approach.

The significance of the D/R ratio, and in one case the loan-earning asset ratio, in addition to that of high-powered money, suggests that links through bank portfolios in times of crises may be a possible additional channel of transmission.[39]

CONCLUSION

This paper has surveyed the theory and provided some historical evidence on financial crises and their relationship to the money supply, the financial system, and real activity over the period 1870–1933 in six countries. The evidence, though highly suggestive, yields the following conclusion.

The first is the important role of monetary institutions, particularly the banking system, in explaining why some countries had more serious monetary and real contractions in the face of crises. The absence of a nationwide branch banking system in the United States compared to the five other countries examined, and the less effective role played by the US monetary authorities in acting as a lender-of-last-resort may explain why the USA experienced banking panics in a period when they were a historical curiosity in other countries.

The second is an apparent connection in all the countries examined between crises in the stock market and a decline in the commercial banking system's deposit–reserve ratio. Such a relationship may provide an alternative link between the money supplies of different countries in addition to the traditional linkages through gold flows and the balance of payments. A possible avenue for fruitful further research might be to examine, using monthly data and time-series analysis, the timing of the relationship between different international monetary linkages – on the one hand, between the stock market and other asset markets and commercial bank portfolios, and on the other hand, between gold and international reserve flows and the monetary base.

Finally, correlations between countries of annual changes in both monetary aggregates and asset ratios provides support for the monetarist theory to the international transmission of financial crises, although evidence for linkages through bank portfolios in times of crises stressed by the real approach was also found.

APPENDIX: DATA SOURCES

A. **United States** 1870–1933

Reference cycle turning points: Burns and Mitchell (1946), table 16, p. 78.
Real output: NNP Variant III in 1929 prices. Friedman and Schwartz (1982), table 4.8, p. 121.
Money supply and determinants: M_2 definition. Friedman and Schwartz (1982), table 4.8, p. 121.
Long-term, short-term interest differential: Morgenstern (1959), table 125, p. 501.
Stock price index: Morgenstern (1959), table 132, p. 531.
Monetary gold stock: Cagan (1965), table 5–7, p. 340.
Loan earning asset ratio: Ratio of loans to loans plus investments, Federal Reserve Board (1944), p. 20.
Federal Reserve Board (1955), pp. 35–6.

B. **Great Britain** 1870–1933

Reference cycle turning points: Burns and Mitchell (1946), table 16, p. 78.
Real output: NNP in 1929 prices. Friedman and Schwartz (1982), table 4.9, p. 130.
Money supply and determinants: M_2 definition. Friedman and Schwartz (1982), table 4.8, p. 30 and data supplied by A. J. Schwartz.
Long-term, short-term interest differential: Morgenstern (1959), table 125, p. 501.
Stock price index: Morgenstern (1959), table 132, p. 531.
Monetary gold stock: Bordo (1981), table 4; Sheppard (1971), table A 1.12.
Loan earning asset ratio. Ratio of loans plus discounts to loans plus discounts plus investments: Bordo (1977) and Sheppard (1971), table A 1.1.

C. **Germany** 1870–1913

Reference cycle turning points: Burns and Mitchell (1946), table 16, p. 78.
Real output: NNP in 1913 prices. Hoffman (1965), table 249.
Money supply and determinants: M_2 definition. Tilly (1973), table 5, p. 347.
Long-term, short-term interest differential: Morgenstern (1959), table 125, p. 501.
Stock price index: Morgenstern. (1959), table 132, p. 513.
Monetary gold stock: Tilly (1973), Appendix 1, p. 359.

D. **France** 1900–33

Reference cycle turning points: Burns and Mitchell (1946), table 16, p. 78.

Real output: GNP in 1938 prices. Sauvy (1954).
Money supply: M_2 INSEE (1966).
Long-term, short-term interest differential: Morgenstern (1959), table 125, p. 501.
Stock price index: Morgenstern (1959), table 132, p. 531.

E. **Canada** 1900–33

Reference cycle turning points: Hay (1966), table III, p. 362.
Real output: GNP in 1949 prices. Data used in Bordo and Jonung (1977).
Money supply and determinants: M_2 definition. Data used in Bordo and Jonung (1981).
Monetary Gold Stock 1900–13: Rich (1980), tables 2.1 and 2.2, 1920–33. Data supplied by R. A. Shearer.

F. **Sweden** 1870–1933

Reference cycle turning points: Calculated from turning points in annual rates of change of real GNP.
Real output: Real GDP in 1913 prices. Data used in Bordo and Jonung (1981).
Money supply and determinants: M_2 definition. Jonung (1975), table A-1.

NOTES

1. For helpful comments and suggestions I would like to thank: Ehsan Choudhri, Steve Easton, Lars Jonung, John McDermott, Jim Lothian, and Anna Schwartz. For excellent research assistance I am indebted to Fernando Santos.
2. See Bernanke (1983) and Diamond and Dybvig (1983).
3. See Fisher (1935) and Huffman and Lothian (1983).
4. A recent approach taken by Bernanke (1983) and Diamond and Dybvig (1983) argues that financial crises including bankruptcies have direct effects on economic activity over and above their effects on the money supply. To the extent that financial crises produce losses in the financial sector of the economy, this raises the cost of financial intermediation and hence reduces the efficiency of resource allocation.
5. See Choudrhi and Kochin (1980) for evidence of the insulation properties of flexible exchange rates in the Spanish case, and Jonung (1981) on Sweden.
6. According to Gorton (1983) banking panics are not a unique event but represent a rational response by depositors wishing to smooth out their consumption flows over time. Rational depositors wish to dissave in

periods of expected low consumption such as business cycle troughs but, since the likelihood of suspensions of convertibility also would be highest at the trough, they will rush to convert their deposits to currency when they expect a trough to occur.

7. See Fisher (1935) for evidence on the transmission of economic disturbances in the Great Depression.
8. See Minsky (1957), (1963), (1977), (1979), (1980), (1982a, b, c).
9. Minsky (1957).
10. Minsky (1982a).
11. Ibid.
12. Minsky (1979).
13. Minsky's thesis has been criticised by Sinai (1977) for not yielding any testable hypotheses, and by Goldsmith (1982) on the ground that the evidence of history is against a key implication of Minsky's view – that financial development and financial fragility are positively correlated. Melitz (1982) argues that Minsky's thesis is inconsistent with evidence on the behaviour of the term structure of interest rates and the experience of countries with universal lenders-of-last-resort such as Sweden. Finally, Flemming (1982) argues that one implication of Minsky's thesis – that the boom lulls economic agents into taking a risky financial position conducive to a crisis – leads to the implausible suggestion that central banks should increase the amount of risk in the economic system.
14. In his discussion of the 1873, 1920–1 and 1931 crises, Kindleberger (1978) and (1973) argues that the crises could have been aborted by the effective operation of a supernational monetary authority. However, Moggridge (1982) effectively argues that in the case of 1920–1, there was no crisis hence no need for the lender-of-last-resort and in 1931 that, though there was a considerable amount of international co-operation, the fundamental disequilibrium of the international monetary system could not have been alleviated by an international lender-of-last-resort.
15. The use of the common international cycle is purely descriptive to facilitate international comparisons. The discussion which follows for each country alone is based on the NBER reference cycle chronology.
16. Also included are a number of extra 'financial crises' based on Thorp (1926), Yeager (1976), and others.
17. This demarcation of crises begs the question of whether all these events really were crises. On this point, see Schwartz (1983).
18. Morgenstern's indices include many securities which today would be called bonds. Also a significant fraction of the securities in the samples underlying the indexes for the European exchanges were foreign securities (both government and private). See Morgenstern (1959), pp. 507–28 for an extensive discussion of the several direct linkages between stock exchanges in the gold standard era.
19. The observed lead from the turning points in money growth to the reference cycle for the US has been widely cited as an important piece of evidence for 'causality' from money to business. See Friedman and Schwartz (1963b), Poole (1975). For a counterview, see Tobin (1970) and Friedman's (1970) reply. Recent advances in the methodology of testing 'for causality' Sims (1972) confirm Friendman and Schwartz's evidence for

a US monetary cycle (the traditional quantity theory approach) but the case is mixed for other countries. Mills and Wood (1978) and Williams, Goodhart and Gowland (1976) provide evidence for the UK of 'Causality' running from business to money in both the gold standard and subsequent Bretton Woods eras. These authors explain reverse causality by arguing that the UK under fixed exchange rates operated as a small open economy, according to the monetary approach to the balance of payments, with changes in its money supply via reserve flows caused by changes in money demand which in turn effect changes in economic activity. This is compared to the US, viewed essentially as a closed economy in this period, in which changes in the money supply interact with a stable money demand to produce changes in activity according to the traditional quantity theory approach. However, Cassese and Lothian (1982) present convincing evidence for a number of countries under fixed exchange rates consistent both with a dynamic stock adjustment version of the monetary approach to the balance of payments and a monetary theory of the cycle.

20. For the sixteen reference cycles displayed here, the relative contributions of the determinants to cyclical contractions were: H, 67.6; D/R, 3.9; and D/C 30.1. For six severe cycles, it was H, 38.7; D/R, 16.2; and D/C, 47.6.
21. Over the twelve British cycles the relative contributions of the determinants to cyclical contractions were: H, 79.3; D/C, 18.9; and D/R, 9.1. For severe contractions, they were: H, 109.0; D/R, 19.7; and D/C, −28.7.
22. See McGouldrick (1984).
23. See Hay (1968), and Jonung (1976).
24. In the gold standard period, the Canadian chartered banks kept a large proportion of their gold reserves in the New York and, to a lesser extent, London money markets. These outside reserves provided a direct link between financial conditions in these countries and Canada through the D/R ratio. See Hay (1967, 1968) and Rich (1983).
25. For the Scottish banking experience, see Cameron (1967) and White (1981); for Canada, see Jamieson (1959); for Sweden, see Jonung (1977). For a comparison between the US and Canadian experiences, see White (1982).
26. See e.g. Sayers (1957).
27. See Sayers (1936) and Pressnell (1968).
28. This was done by quickly arranging mergers between sound and failing banks, by encouraging co-operation between strong and weaker banks in times of stringency, and by establishing a reserve fund to be used to compensate deposit holders in the event of failure. Friedman and Schwartz (1963) argue that the New York Clearing House performed a somewhat similar role in stemming incipient crises before 1914 through the issue of clearing house certificates and by arranging for syndicates of strong banks to assist those in trouble. As Schwartz (1983) argues, in most cases the system worked but in two important exceptions, 1893 and 1907, it did not. These may be explained, she argues, by bad timing of relief in 1907 and public misinformation in 1893.
29. See Schwartz (1983).
30. See Sprinkel (1971) for additional US evidence.
31. Or even possibly before raising short-term interest rates and causing short-

term capital to flow. This would be consistent with Morgenstern's finding that peaks in the short-term interest rates cycle tended to follow peaks in business whenever the stock market index would precede it.

32. It would also be of interest to compare the transmission mechanisms under fixed and flexible exchange rates. However, the sample of countries and years does not contain enough observations to make any inferences on transmission under flexible rates. As it stands, the sample from 1870 to 1933 contains observations under both fixed and flexible rates which would distort the results. Correlations for periods of fixed rates alone – the vast majority of years for all the countries – turned out to be almost identical to those for the whole period.
33. See e.g. Temin's (1976) 'realist' explanation for the Great Depression in the USA.
34. Also see Gandolfi and Lothian (1977).
35. See e.g. Lindert (1969) and Bloomfield (1959).
36. See Viner (1924) and Rich (1984).
37. Correlations (not presented here) between (rates of change of) H and the ratios were on the whole weak for most of the countries for each of the periods covered in Table 6.2, with the notable exceptions of a strong negative correlation between H and D/R for Germany in periods of severe contraction; and of a strong negative correlation between H and D/C for Sweden for similar periods.
38. However, the absence of correlation between the monetary gold stocks and between high powered money could also reflect the operation of a successful sterilisation policy rather than the influence of non-monetary factors. As discussed in the third section above sterilisation of gold flows was widespread but by no means universal under the classical gold standard but pretty well universal in the interwar period.
39. However, because the D/R ratio normally displays a procyclical pattern, such an inference would require accounting for the common 'normal' cyclical movements in each country.

REFERENCES

Bernanke, B. S. (1983) 'Non monetary effects of the financial crisis in the propagation of the Great Depression', *American Economic Review* 73, no. 3 (June): 257–76.

Bloomfield, A. (1959) *Monetary Policy Under the International and Gold Standard* (New York: Federal Reserve Bank of New York).

Bordo, M. D. (1977) 'The income effects of the sources of new money: a comparison of the United States and the United Kingdom, 1870–1913', *Explorations in Economic History* 14: 20–47.

Bordo, M. D. (1981) 'The UK money supply', *Research in Economic History* 6: 107–25.

Bordo, M. D. and Jonung L. (1981) 'The long-run behavior of the income velocity of money in five advanced countries, 1870–1975: an institutional approach', *Economic Inquiry* XIX (January): 96–116.

Bouvier, J. (1973) *Un Sìecle de Banque Francaise* (Paris: Hachette).
Brown, W. A. Jr. (1940) *The International Gold Standard Reinterpreted, 1914–1934*, vol. 1 (New York: NBER).
Burns, A. F. and Mitchell, W. C. (1946) *Measuring Business Cycles* (New York: NBER).
Cagan, P. (1965) *Determinants and Effects of Changes in the Stock of Money, 1875–1960* (New York: Columbia University Press).
Cameron, R. (1967) *Banking in the Early Stages of Industrialisation* (New York: Oxford University Press).
Carron, A. S. (1982) 'Financial crises: recent experience in US and international markets', *Brookings Papers on Economic Activity* 2: 395–418.
Cassese, A. and Lothian, J. R. (1982) 'The timing of monetary and price changes and the international transmission of inflation', *Journal of Monetary Economics* 10: 1–23).
Choudhri, E. U. and Kochin, L. A. (1980) 'The exchange rate and the international transmission of business cycle disturbances: some evidence from the Great Depression', *Journal of Money, Credit and Banking* XII, no. 4, Part 1 (November): 565–74.
Diamond, D. W. and Dybvig, P. H. (1983) 'Bank runs, deposit insurance and liquidity', *Journal of Political Economy* 91, no. 3 (June): 401–19.
Federal Reserve Board (1944) *Banking and Monetary Statistics.*
Federal Reserve Board (1955) *All Bank Statistics.*
Fisher, I. (1932) *Booms and Depressions* (New York: Adelphi).
Fisher, I. (1933) 'The debt deflation theory of great depressions', *Econometrica* Vol. 1: 337–57.
Fisher, I. (1935) 'Are booms and depressions transmitted internationally through monetary standards?' *Bulletin of the International Statistical Institute* 28, no. 1: 1–29.
Flemming, J. (1982) 'Comments on Minsky . . .', in C. P. Kindleberger and J. P. Laffargue.
Flood, R. P. Jr. and Garber, P. M. (1981) 'A systematic banking collapse in a perfect foresight world', NBER working paper no. 691.
Friedman, M. (1970) 'Comment on Tobin', *Quarterly Journal of Economics* Vol. 84.
Friedman, M. and Schwartz, A. J. (1963a) *A Monetary History of the United States 1867–1960* (New York: NBER).
Friedman, M. and Schwartz, A. J. (1963b) 'Money and business cycles', *Review of Economics and Statistics* 45, no. 1, part 2/supplement.
Friedman, M. and Schwartz, A. J. (1982) *Monetary Trends in the United States and the United Kingdom: Their Relation to Income, Prices, and Interest Rates, 1867–1975* (Chicago: University of Chicago Press).
Gandolfi, A. and Lothian J. (1977) 'Did monetary forces cause the Great Depression? A review essay', *Journal of Money, Credit and Banking* (November): 679–91.
Garber, P. M. (1981) 'The lender of last resort and the run on the savings and loans', NBER working paper no. 823.
Goldsmith, R. W. (1982) 'Comment on H. P. Minsky, "The financial instability hypothesis"', in C. P. Kindleberger and J. P. Laffargue (eds).
Gorton, G. (1983) 'Banking panics and business cycles' (mimeo.) *Federal Reserve Bank of Atlanta.*

Griffiths, B. (1983) 'Banking in crisis', *Policy Review* 25 (Summer): 28–35.
Hay, K. A. J. (1966) 'Early twentieth century business cycles in Canada', *Canadian Journal of Economics* XXXII no. (3): 354–61.
Hay, K. A. J. (1967) 'Money and cycles in post confederation Canada', *Journal of Political Economies* 75 (2): 263–73.
Hay, K. A. J. (1968) 'Determinants of the Canadian money supply', Carleton University (mimeo).
Hoffman, W. (1965) *Das Wachstum der deutschen Wirtschaft seit der Mitte des 19 Jahrhundart* (Berlin: Springer Verlag).
Huffman, W. E. and Lothian, J. R. (1984) 'US–UK business cycle linkages under the gold standard, 1834–1933', in M. D. Bordo and A. J. Schwartz (eds) *A Retrospective on the Classical Gold Standard, 1821–1931* (Chicago: University of Chicago Press).
INSEE (1966). *Annuaire Statistique*, tableau I: 515.
Jamieson, A. B. (1959) *Chartered Banking in Canada* (Toronto: Ryerson Press).
Jonung, L. (1975) 'Studies in the monetary history of Sweden', unpublished Ph.D dissertation, UCLA.
Jonung, L. (1976) 'Sources of growth in the Swedish money stock, 1871–1971', *Scandinavian Journal of Economics* 78: 611–27.
Jonung, L. (1977) 'The legal framework and the economics of private bank notes in Sweden, 1831–1902', in G. Skogh (ed.) *Law and Economics* (Lund: Juridiska Foreningen Studentlitteratur).
Jonung, L. (1981) 'The Depression in Sweden and the United States: a comparison of causes and policies', in K. Brunner (ed.) *The Great Depression Revisited* (Boston: Martinus Nijhoff).
Kindleberger, C. P. (1973) *The World in Depression 1929–1939* (Berkeley: University of California Press).
Kindleberger, C. P. (1978) *Manias, Panics, and Crashes: A History of Financial Crises* (New York: Basic Books).
Kindleberger, C. P. and Laffargue, J. P. (ed.) (1982), *Financial Crises: Theory, History, Policy* (Cambridge, Cambridge University Press).
Lindert, P. H. (1969) *Key Currencies and Gold, 1900–1913*, Princeton Studies in International Finance, no. 24 (Princeton: Princeton University Press).
McGouldrick, P. (1984) 'Operations of the German central bank and the rules of the game, 1879–1923', in M. D. Bordo and A. J. Schwartz (eds) *A Retrospective on the Classical Gold Standard, 1821–1931* (Chicago: University of Chicago Press).
Melitz, J. (1982) 'Comments on H. P. Minsky . . .', in C. P. Kindleberger and J. P. Laffargue.
Meltzer, A. (1982) 'Rational expectations, risk, uncertainty, and market responses', in P. Wachtel (ed.) *Crises in the Economic and Financial Structure* (New York: Lexington Books).
Mills, T. C. and Wood G. E. (1978) 'Money income relationships and the exchange rate regime', *Federal Reserve Bank of St Louis Review* 60 (August): 22–9.
Minsky, H. P. (1957) 'Central banking and money market changes', *Quarterly Journal of Economics* LXXI (2): 175–87.
Minsky, H. P. (1963) 'Comment on Friedman and Schwartz's "Money and Business Cycles"', *Review of Economics and Statistics*, vol. 30.

Minsky, H. P. (1977) 'A theory of systematic fragility', in E. J. Altman and A. W. Sametz (eds) *Financial Crises: Institutions and Markets in a Fragile Environment* (New York: Wiley): 138–52.

Minsky, H. P. (1979) 'Financial interrelations, the balance of payments and the dollar crisis', in Jonathan Aron (ed.) *Debt and the Less Developed Countries* (Boulder, Col.: Westview Press).

Minsky, H. P. (1980) 'Finance and profits: the changing nature of business cycles', Joint Economic Committee of the United States Congress, *The Business Cycle and Public Policy, 1929–1980*.

Minsky, H. P. (1982a) 'Debt deflation processes in today's institutional environment', *Banca Nazionale Del Lavoro Review* 143 (December): 375–93.

Minsky, H. P. (1982b) 'Financial innovations and financial instability: observations and theory', *Seventh Annual Policy Conference of the Federal Reserve Bank of St Louis* (October).

Minsky, H. P. (1982c) 'The potential for financial crises', Washington University, St Louis Working Paper 46.

Moggridge, D. E. (1982) 'Policy in the crises of 1920 and 1929', in C. P. Kindlegerger and J. P. Laffargue (eds) *Financial Crises: Theory, History, and Policy* (New York: Cambridge University Press).

Morgenstern, O. (1959) *International Financial Transactions and Business Cycles* (New York: NBER).

Poole, W. (1975) 'The relationship of monetary decelerations to business cycle peaks: another look at the evidence', *Journal of Finance* (June): 697–712.

Pressnell, L. S. (1968) 'Gold reserves, banking reserves, and the Baring crisis of 1890', in C. R. Whittlesey and J. S. G. Wilson (eds) *Essays in Money and Banking in Honour of R. S. Sayers* (Oxford: Clarendon Press).

Rich, G. (1980) 'The cross of gold: money and the Canadian business cycle', unpublished manuscript.

Rich, G. (1984) 'Canada without a central bank: operation of the price specie flow mechanism, 1872–1913', in M. D. Bordo and A. J. Schwartz (eds) *A Retrospective on the Classical Gold Standard, 1821–1931* (Chicago: University of Chicago Press).

Sauvy, A. (1954) 'Rapport sur le revenu national', *Journal Official. Avis et Rapports du Conseil Economique*.

Sayers, R. S. (1936) *Bank of England Operations, 1890–1914* (London: P. S. King).

Sayers, R. S. (1957) *Central Banking After Bagehot* (Oxford: Clarendon Press).

Schwartz, A. J. (1981) 'Understanding 1929–33', in K. Brunner (ed.) *The Great Depression Revisited* (Boston: Martinus Nijholf).

Schwartz, A. J. (1986) 'Real and pseudo-financial crises', in F. Capie and G. E. Wood (eds) *Financial Crises and the World Banking System* (Macmillan).

Shearer, R. A. and Clark C. (1984) 'Canada and the interwar gold standard, 1920–1935: monetary policy without a central bank', in M. D. Bordo and A. J. Schwartz (eds) *A Retrospective on the Classical Gold Standard, 1821–1931* (Chicago: University of Chicago Press).

Sheppard, D. K. (1971) *The Growth and Role of UK Financial Institutions, 1880–1962* (London: Methuen).

Sims, C. A. (1972) 'Money, income, and causality', *A.E.R.* (September), vol.

LXII, (4): 540–52.
Sinai, A. (1976) 'Credit crunches – an analysis of the postwar experience', in Otto Eckestein (ed.) *Parameters and Policies in the US Economy*, Data Resources Survey, vol. 2 (Amsterdam: North-Holland): 244–74.
Sinai, A. (1977) 'Comment on Minsky', in D. Altman and A. W. Sametz (eds) *Financial Crises: Institutions and Markets in a Fragile Environment* (New York: Wiley).
Sprague, O. M. W. (1915) 'The crisis of 1914 in the United States', *American Economic Review* V, no. 3 (September): 499–533.
Sprinkel, B. W. (1971) *Money and Markets: A Monetarist View* (Chicago: Richard D. Irwin).
Temin, P. (1976) *Did Monetary Forces Cause the Great Depression?* (New York: W. W. Norton).
Thorp, W. (1926) *Business Annals* (New York: NBER).
Tilly, R. H. (1973) 'Zeitreihen Zum Geldumlauf in Deutschland, 1870–1912', *J. für Nationalekonomie und Statistik* 87: 360–3.
Tobin, J. (1970) 'Money and income: post hoc ergo propter hoc', *Quarterly Journal of Economics* Vol. 84.
Viner, J. (1924) *Canada's Balance of International Indebtedness 1900–1913* (Cambridge, Mass.: Harvard University Press).
Wachtel, P. (1982) 'Introduction', in P. Wachtel (ed.) *Crises in the Economic and Financial Structure* (New York: Lexington Books).
White, E. M. (1982) *The Regulation and Reform of the American Banking System, 1900–1929* (Princeton, NJ: Princeton University Press).
White, L. H. (1981) 'Free banking in Britain: theory, experience and debate, 1900–1945', unpublished Ph.D. dissertation, UCLA.
Williams, D., Goodhart, C. A. E. and Gowland, D. H. (1976) 'Money, income and causality: the UK experience', *American Economic Review* 66, no. 3 (June): 417–23.
Yeager, L. (1976) *International Monetary Relations: Theory, History, and Policy*, 2nd edn (New York: Harper & Row).

Comment on 'Financial Crises, Banking Crises, Stock Market Crashes and the Money Supply: Some International Evidence 1870–1933'

ALEC G. FORD

In my comment on Professor Bordo's contribution I would first wish to pay tribute to his careful presentation and the thorough underlying work, and to say that in the main my suggestions are intended to supplement, rather than supplant, his approaches. In particular they centre on the economic analysis used in the various approaches to the internal and external transmission mechanisms for both cycles and crises, as well as in considering the role of the gold standard and the nature of the pre-1939 (international) trade cycle.

Recent work in these areas has seemed to be marked by some reluctance to stress the role of effective demand variations in such transmission mechanisms, and Professor Bordo's paper is no exception. It does not appear to use, at least explicitly, any Keynesian style of economic analysis with emphasis on the roles of direct changes in effective demand to add to supply-side effects. It is true that he presents and compares the monetarist and the Kindleberger–Minsky approaches which seem to exhibit the same omission – and perhaps I am really grumbling at these – but I consider a rewarding addition would be the more explicit mention of the roles of direct (autonomous) spending collapses, expectational changes (the 'animal spirits' point), and international capital flow changes which affected spending directly in borrowers and provoked crises (for example, Argentina in 1890). In my work on the pre-1914 gold standard and trade cycles, and in looking more specifically at particular crises (the Baring crises of 1890) I have found such an approach both instructive and valuable.[1]

To illustrate these points and particularly elements in the transmission mechanisms let us look at key features in the international trade cycle before 1914 from the British point of view. How far can it be said that the international trade cycle – if, indeed, there was such a thing pre-1906–7 other than a *European* cycle – was a monetary affair and that fluctuations were transmitted (as suggested on p. 193) by gold movements and their effects on money stocks and economic activity? It may well be questioned whether enough gold moved and whether the central banks had enough power or will to influence the money supply, particularly in the British or French cases. Indeed, there is a high degree of cyclical parallelism between Britain, France and Germany over the period 1879 to 1914, being in the same phase of the cycle in 83 per cent of all months,[2] but a very different pattern in their net gold imports, especially at crisis periods.[3]

In contrast, I would wish to stress the vital role of trade flows with changes in exports influencing incomes and imports in providing a rapid 'pass-on' to others of cyclical influences, the whole process being reinforced by contagious changes in confidence, especially in Europe before 1914 and in the world in the interwar period. Secondly, I would emphasise the part played by British overseas lending (as measured by overseas issues on the London Stock Exchange) in the cycles particularly before 1900. For British overseas lending which was essentially developmental in character and provided much of the social overhead capital of some borrowers, *leads* the European cycle by one to two years. Such lending was spent by the recipients and stimulated directly and indirectly the borrowers' purchases of European exports while in addition the same factor abroad (booming prospects) might well be attracting both lending and exports from Europe. When loans dried up, so activity collapsed in the borrowers and European exports fell, thereby provoking depression and, on occasions, crises in both borrowers and lenders (for example, 1873 and 1890). However, *why* British overseas issues dried up could well be a monetary point and needs more attention (see pages 49–54 for a view of 1890).

In Figure 6.6 are presented the main elements of the British trade cycle before 1914 in terms of absolute deviations from nine-year

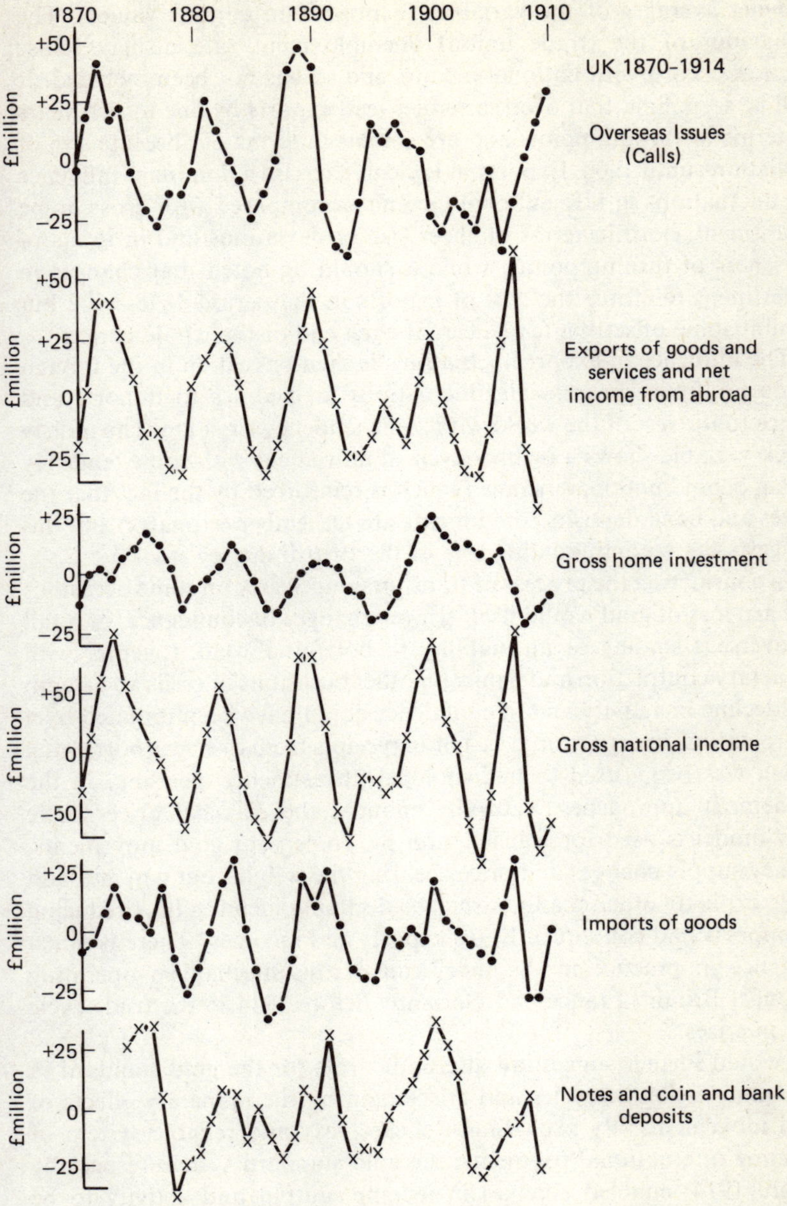

FIG. 6.6 Deviations from nine-year moving averages (all current values).

moving averages of the variables (expressed in current values). The behaviour of the (trade union) unemployment rate displays close cyclical accord with national income and so has not been included. It will be seen, first, that overseas issues lead exports by one to two years in terms of turning points and are similar in terms of absolute size of deviations until 1900. Exports, it is clear, exercise a dominant influence on fluctuations in UK national income as compared with gross home investment, both in terms of sheer size of deviations and in terms of closeness of turning points, while it should be noted that changes in investment reinforce the role of exports in the period 1878–1902 but exhibit some offsetting tendencies at each end of the whole period.

The influence of export fluctuations is then passed on in the foreign trade multiplier process via fluctuations in incomes to imports and hence to the rest of the world with some tendency for a lag. The money stock variable shows a distinct cyclical movement with some tendency to lag behind national income (which is reinforced by the fact that the notes and bank deposits components are December estimates) and this suggests the accommodating role of the British money stock.[4]

In considering the process of transmission, clearly on some occasions a sharp loss of gold would itself trigger changes in confidence, or a fall in overseas lending or an inability to borrow abroad, together with monetary contraction and panic: on other occasions of crisis and slump the decline in activity and in confidence could have been initiated by a sharp decline in export proceeds or in receipts from overseas borrowing which was being used to finance local (investment) spending. In the monetarist approaches, naturally enough, the classical price–specie flow model is used for transmission purposes with gold movements, money supply changes and prices bearing the weight, but why not add more explictly other channels such as declining incomes in *A* reducing its imports and consequently *B*'s exports and incomes? There is much evidence in practice in the short run of this mechanism operating amongst Britain, France and Germany before 1914 in the trade cycle and in crises.

I would further suggest an alternative role for the gold standard in the transmission of cycles and crises than by the monetary effects of gold movements. By providing a cheap, easy and reliable system of effecting international payments, the gold standard system (especially before 1914) enabled changes in income, output and activity to be spread rapidly by trade movements – a fall in exports in one country reducing its activity and imports and so passing on the depressive disease to others. Under flexible exchange rates such trading effects might be damped somewhat by the offsetting relative price changes (although Argentine economic activity in the period 1888–92 did not seem to be particularly insulated by its flexible paper peso).

Hence I would allot much lower emphasis to gold movements in the international transmission process of economic fluctuations, and would suggest the same for financial crises and their transmission, with more emphasis on the role of changing trade and capital flows. More generally, how far should we seek regularity in explanations of financial crises (as with economic fluctuations)? There do seem common patterns and common elements of institutional weakness but also unique features in each – for example, the external source of 1890 is very different from 1866 or 1907. There is value in both the monetarist and the Fisher–Kindleberger–Minsky approaches, as Professor Bordo's interesting paper demonstrates, but I would like to suggest supplementation of each on the lines sketched out above.

NOTES

1. See for example, A. G. Ford, *The Gold Standard 1880–1914: Britain and Argentina* (Oxford: Clarendon Press, 1962) and chapter 2, 'The Trade Cycle in Britain 1860–1914', in R. Floud and D. McCloskey (eds) *The Economic History of Britain since 1700*, vol. II (Cambridge, Cambridge University Press, 1981). See also pp. 41–76 in this volume.
2. See O. Morgenstern, *International Financial Transactions and Business Cycles* (New York: BNBER): 43.
3. See A. G. Ford, *The Gold Standard 1880–1914*, pp. 36–42.
4. For a fuller account see A. G. Ford, 'The Trade Cycle in Britain 1860–1914', in R. Floud and D. McCloskey, *The Economic History of Britain since 1700*, especially pp. 42–8.

REFERENCES

Sources of statistics underlying Figure 6.6.

Overseas Issues: M. Simon, 'The Pattern of New British Portfolio Investment, 1865–1914', in A. R. Hall (ed.) *The Export of Capital from Britain 1870–1914* (London: Methuen, 1968).

Money Stock: F. Capie and A. Webber, 'Bank deposits and the quantity of money in the UK 1870–1921', Discussion Paper 3, Centre for Banking and International Finance (London: The City University, 1982).

Other variables: C. H. Feinstein, *National Income, Expenditure and Output of the UK, 1855–1955* (Cambridge: Cambridge University Press, 1972).

International Financial Crisis and the Swedish Economy 1857–1933[1]

LARS JONUNG

'The London money market is the biggest in the world, the smaller exchanges rotate around its axis as the planets around the sun, and it is no wonder that the phenomena, which appear simple and easy to understand from the center, appear mysterious and complicated, when regarded from the periphery.'

Quoted from I. Heckscher: 'Om växelkurserna i Sverige' (On foreign exchange rates in Sweden). Postscript to the Swedish translation of G. Goschen, *Läran om utländska växelkurser*, Stockholm, Nordstedt, 1892.

INTRODUCTION

How were financial crises transmitted from one country to another in the period 1870–1933? What were the effects of financial crises on economic activity? Michael Bordo answers these two questions by making a distinction between two approaches to the international transmission of financial crises: (a) the monetary approach and (b) the Fisher–Kindleberger–Minsky 'real' approach. A number of testable implications are derived and examined by studying the international covariation between various monetary and financial aggregates and ratios during the whole period 1870–1933, during NBER reference cycle contractions, and during NBER reference cycle expansions. Six countries are included in this very ambitious investigation, namely the United States, Great Britain, Germany, France, Canada and Sweden.

Canada and Sweden are viewed as countries on the periphery of the world financial centres of London, New York, Paris and Berlin.

My comment is based on an examination of the Swedish record focusing on Swedish–British developments. My aim is to study how and to what extent foreign financial crises influenced the Swedish economy. First, I describe the Swedish institutional setting. Then I study the domestic impact of a large number of international financial crises. Finally, I compare my conclusions with those of Bordo.

THE INSTITUTIONAL SETTING

An account of how Swedish monetary and financial markets were linked to international ones during the pre-1914 gold standard may throw light upon the international transmission mechanism of financial crises.

International Financial Connections

The histories of Sweden's major commercial banks during the gold standard (*the Stockholms Enskilda Bank, Skandinaviska Kreditaktiebolaget* and *the Handelsbank*) show that these banks had very close international connections. They held accounts (credit lines) with major banks or bankers in a number of foreign financial centres, in particular in London, Hamburg, Berlin and Paris. Another commonly used way of obtaining reserves from abroad was by the discounting of bills, both foreign and domestic. Major commercial banks also held bonds which were easily saleable on foreign financial markets. They were active in long-term borrowing from abroad as middlemen between foreign investors and the Swedish Government, Swedish local authorities and Swedish companies. Financial institutions other than commercial banks were also engaged in international financial intermediation. To sum up, Swedish money and capital markets were closely tied to the English, French and German markets.

While London and Paris were reserve centres for the major Swedish commercial banks, they in turn functioned as lenders-of-last-resort for regional domestic banks. Furthermore, the *Riksbank* and the National Debt Office were also engaged in international financial transactions. Gradually, these institutions developed into lenders-of-last-resort ready to carry out offsetting operations in case of foreign disturbances.[2]

International Trade

Sweden was tied to the international economy through international trade. Exports and imports represented roughly 20 per cent of GDP in the period 1871–1914. As the Swedish economy was an open one, the international business cycle determined the Swedish one. Table 6.3, displaying the troughs and peaks of the British and Swedish business cycles in 1868–1909, shows a near-perfect cyclical covariation between the two countries. Fluctuations in Swedish exports were thus a most important channel of transmitting foreign cyclical variations.

TABLE 6.3 BRITISH AND SWEDISH BUSINESS CYCLES 1869–1909

		Trough	*Peak*	*Trough*
1.	British cycle	1868	1872	1879
	Swedish cycle	1868–9	1874–5	1878–9
2.	British cycle	1879	1882	1886
	Swedish cycle	1878–9	1884	1887
3.	British cycle	1886	1890	1894
	Swedish cycle	1887	1890	1892–3
4.	British cycle	1894	1900	1901
	Swedish cycle	1892–3	1900	1901
5.	British cycle	1901	1907	1908
	Swedish cycle	1901	1907	1909

Source: British cycles dated by Burns and Mitchell (1946). Swedish cycles dated by Jörberg (1961) using the NBER reference cycles method. His dating is based on the cyclical behaviour of between 96 and 180 time series combined with non-statistical information on the activity of Swedish industry. Jörberg is more certain about the dating of troughs than of peaks.

To the extent that a British financial crisis influenced the British economy, reducing real activity, there are reasons to believe that a British contraction would reduce Swedish exports and thus reduce real output in Sweden.

A foreign financial crisis could thus be transmitted to Sweden in two major ways:

(a) through financial markets, directly reducing the supply of foreign finance, and thus the Swedish monetary base and money supply, as well as raising interest rates;
(b) through markets for goods and services reducing the demand for Swedish exports.

DOMESTIC EFFECTS OF FOREIGN FINANCIAL CRISES

To investigate the domestic effects of foreign financial crises, I have used the crisis chronology found in Åkerman's (1944) account of business cycles in the United States, Britain, Germany and France between 1820 and 1940. By combining his narrative with other evidence for Sweden, the following general picture emerges.

Pre Gold Standard Period 1857–72

Prior to the introduction of the gold standard in Sweden, three major foreign financial panics occurred, that is in 1857, 1864 and 1866. They caused rises in interest rates in Sweden and reduction in the money supply, in particular in 1857–8 as the *Riksbank* responded by calling in loans when its silver holdings were reduced due to foreign demand. There were no major effects on domestic economic activity during these crises, the main reason being that Sweden was primarily an agricultural economy. The monetary sector and the export sector encompassed such a small share of the domestic economy that the aggregative effects of the financial disturbances were minor.[3]

The Gold Standard 1873–1914

A foreign financial panic generally had the following two effects on Swedish money and capital markets: interest rates tended to rise and commercial banks experienced 'difficulties' in obtaining foreign finance. Commercial banks compensated for the reduction in foreign reserves in various ways; by borrowing from the *Riksbank*, by selling bonds and by discounting bills abroad. The monetary authorities usually took measures to offset the drain on foreign reserves by borrowing from abroad and by lending at home.

This stylised description holds good for the 1890 Baring Brothers crash and the 1907 crisis. It does not hold for all foreign panics. Several of them did not have any noticeable impact on Swedish money and capital markets, for example the 1873 crises in Austria, Germany and the USA, the 1882 crisis in France, and the stock market crash in Paris 1889 (see Table 6.4).

Considering the impact of financial crises on domestic economic activity, it is difficult to separate the effects of such crises from the effects of the general business cycle. One financial crisis occurred during a recession, i.e. in 1878–9. Others took place in the midst of or at the end of a boom, i.e. in 1873 and 1907, having practically no impact on Swedish developments (see Table 6.4).

The evidence suggests that foreign financial crises had as a rule no significant separate and lasting effects on the Swedish economy during the gold standard prior to 1914. These crises were of short duration, thus not reducing the domestic activity in the country of origin to such an extent that Swedish exports were critically reduced. Furthermore, the *Riksbank* engaged in offsetting operations reducing the impact of foreign monetary disturbances. Nor were financial crises prior to 1914 a major threat to the international financial system.

The gold standard before 1914 was thus associated with such stability, including expectations of stability, that financial panics tended to be of fairly short-lived and consequently of minor economic importance compared to the experience of the post-First World War gold standard.

Interwar Period 1919–33

The interwar period was drastically different from the pre-1914 gold standard. Long-lasting deep depressions with large unemployment characterise the 1920s and 1930s. The world financial system functioned badly. There was general uncertainty about the workings of the monetary regimes and the exchange standards compared to the situation prior to the First World War.

To the extent that the depressions of the 1920s and 1930s were caused by monetary and financial disorder, one can argue that domestic activity was influenced by international financial problems. However, there were no specific foreign financial crises that spread to Sweden. Notably, the stock market crash of 1929 in the US did not influence Sweden directly. Rather, the international downturn in economic activity exerted a strong influence on the domestic economy starting in late 1931.

The policy of the *Riksbank* played a much larger role in determining economic outcomes in the interwar period than during the pre-1914

TABLE 6.4 FOREIGN CRISES AND DOMESTIC DEVELOPMENTS 1857–1932

Date *(1)*	*Foreign crises* *City (Countries)* *(2)*	*Domestic developments* *(3)*
Oct–Dec 1857 Nov 1857	Britain Germany, Continent	– trade crises, default of merchant houses,[1] increase in interest rates, Swedish government borrows in Hamburg,[2] no major effect on Swedish economy.
May 1864	Paris,[3] London	– increase in interest rates, "lack of money", no major effect[4]).
May 1866	London, Overend, Gurney crash	– no crisis in Sweden, increase in domestic interest rates.
May 1873 Sept 1873	Germany/Austria USA	– no crisis in Sweden, boom in export industries.
Jan 1882	Lyon, Paris bank defaults	– no crisis in Sweden[5]
Spring 1889	Paris, Panama Company crash.[6]	– no effect on Sweden.
Nov 1890	London, Baring crash	– no crisis in Sweden, interest rate increases.
May 1893	USA	– no crisis in Sweden.
Aug 1907 Oct 1907	France, Italy US Bank runs	– no financial crisis in Sweden, increase in interest rates, depression.
Aug 1914	outbreak of war	– Sweden leaves the gold standard.
1920–1	post-war depression	– post-war depression, financial 'distress', default of some minor banks, no panics, large unemployment.
Oct 1929	US stock market crash	– no crisis in Sweden, 1929 a boom year.
May–June 1931	Austria–Germany bank panics	– no financial crisis in Sweden.
Sept 1931	Britain leaves gold	– Sweden leaves gold.
1932–3	worldwide depression	– death of Ivar Kreuger, financial 'distress', large unemployment.

Source: Åkerman (1944: 247–552)
Kindleberger (1978: 253–9)

Notes: [1] Hedlund–Nyström (1970).
[2] Åkerman (1944: 318) notes that the crisis of 1857 is the first 'modern' international crisis, in the sense that the industries of the Continent were now linked to UK and US business cycles through the rise of an international money market.
[3] Minor stock exchange crises.
[4] Hedlund–Nyström (1970: 190).
[5] Åkerman (1944: 368).
[6] Åkerman (1944: 387).

gold standard. Basically, the monetary authorities had the choice of maintaining a fixed exchange rate for the *krona* to gold (or to any other international reserve currency) or of allowing the exchange rate to fluctuate. In the first case, foreign disturbances were directly imported through the fixed rate. In the second case, flexible rates could insulate Sweden from foreign disturbances, at least partially.

In the early 1920s, the *Riksbank* decided to return to gold at the pre-war parity. This decision caused a large deflation and as a consequence widespread unemployment, actually larger than in the 1930s. The depression of the 1920s was thus to a large extent caused by domestic measures. Sweden was the first country in Europe to return to the gold standard after the First World War.

Sweden remained on gold until the early 1930s. The *Riksbank* decided to leave the gold standard in September 1931, shortly after the Bank of England had taken the same step, and devalued the Swedish currency substantially. Domestic price stabilisation was announced as the official goal of Swedish monetary policy. This monetary regime managed to isolate Sweden from the depression compared to the case of countries that stayed on a fixed rate to gold longer than Sweden.[4]

Crises of Domestic Origin

A few crises originated primarily within Sweden during the period covered. One such crisis occurred in 1868–9 due to harvest failures. The death of Ivar Kreuger in 1932 started a domestic financial crisis. However, the Government, the *Riksbank*, and other banks intervened, thus mitigating the effects of the default of the Kreuger empire. Generally, the Swedish monetary sector displayed considerable stability during the period 1856–1933. The sources of disturbances were as a rule of foreign – not of domestic – origin.

Conclusions

The above account of the transmission and effects of foreign financial crises suggests the following conclusions.

1. Foreign financial crises did not have any major and lasting influence on the Swedish economy prior to 1914. One reason was that they were of a short-run character. Another was that the pre-1914 gold standard regime functioned such that financial crises did not develop into major international disturbances.

2. The international business cycle exerted the major influence on domestic economic events.
3. The initial impacts of foreign financial crises were registered on Swedish financial markets, raising interest rates and reducing lending from abroad. These effects, however, did not spread to such an extent that they exerted by themselves a significant influence on the domestic economy.
4. The experience of financial as well as of real disturbances in the 1920s and 1930s is radically different from the experience of the pre-1914 gold standard. The disturbances emanating from abroad were much larger in the interwar period than before 1914. These differences were due to the absence of a stable international monetary regime. The occurrence of financial instability in this period was a reflection of this state of affairs.[5]

A COMPARISON WITH BORDO'S RESULTS

Bordo presents three conclusions. First of all, he stresses the 'important role of monetary institutions'. I am in complete agreement with him on this account. The conduct of monetary policy, in particular the existence of a lender-of-last-resort, determined to what extent foreign financial disturbances were transmitted into Sweden. The stability of the monetary regime should also be stressed. The pre-1914 gold standard was associated with a stable international financial system compared with the post-1918 experience. Within Sweden, the legal framework of the commercial banking system fostered stability and public trust in the solvency of the banks. As rightly pointed out by Bordo, the US experience of banking panics appears as 'an historical curiosity in other countries'.

Secondly, Bordo concludes that movements in the deposit–reserve ratio of the commercial banking system may have been important in the international transmission of crises. He suggests a link between the stock market and the commercial banking system. The Swedish stock market, however, was not well developed prior to 1914. Rather, I should like to stress another link involving the commercial banking system – that is the link between commercial banks in the periphery borrowing from the reserve centres in London, Paris and Berlin in a way similar to the US system, where regional banks were financially connected to the New York banks.

Let me develop this view further. Bordo presents a domestic and an international version of the monetarist approach to the transmission of financial crises. The domestic version stems from US monetary history where New York City banks were the reserves for US regional banks. When facing bank runs and panics, regional banks were dependent on financial support from the centre. Movements in the reserve ratios of the US commercial banking system thus reflected financial crises and the conduct of monetary policy. According to Bordo, the international version of the monetarist approach stresses gold and capital flows as the primary mechanism for transmitting crises internationally. Thus, he tests for cross-country covariation between money supply and gold stocks to investigate the explanatory power of the monetarist approach. In my opinion, the international version of the monetarist approach should be closely combined with the domestic version when examining how financial crises spread internationally.

Bordo's third and final conclusion is that the cross-country correlations 'provides support for the monetarist theory of the international transmission of financial crises although evidence for linkages through bank portfolios in times of crises stressed by the real approach was also found'. I have a few comments on these tests. It is difficult to separate the influence of general business cycle developments from the effects of financial crises. The empirical results tends to be tests of the international transmission of the business cycle, in particular as some financial crises did not spread internationally.

The spread of financial crises through the balance of trade is not explicitly dealt with in the tests. Bordo's comparison between two approaches, the monetarist and the 'real' view, focuses most of his interest upon monetary and financial variables possibly at the expense of the role of the balance of trade. Judging from the Swedish experience, its seems promising to explore how a financial panic spreads (a) through money and capital markets and (b) through 'real' channels. My preliminary conclusion is that the initial impact came through financial channels and the second-round effects through the balance of trade, in particular in the case of a serious foreign financial crisis.

Furthermore, I am of the opinion that it is difficult to find readily testable implications of the 'real' approach of Fisher–Kindleberger–Minsky. Kindleberger's (1978) description is on such a general level that I do not perceive any clear testable implications. I suspect that Bordo has tried hard to construct a 'worthy' counter-hypothesis to the monetarist interpretation. In the process, the Kindleberger approach is made a stronger challenger than it actually deserves to be. In any case, I think the term 'real' should be used for the transmission of financial crises through international trade, not through financial markets.

Let me sum up my reading of the Swedish record and of Bordo's results. International financial panics under a fixed and stable system of exchange rates, as the case was during the pre-1914 gold standard, did not cause *per se* major domestic disturbances. They spread initially through financial markets (money and capital markets). When they were severe, generally in connection with a downturn of international economic activity, the domestic economy may also have been influenced. These crises were often mitigated by an offsetting domestic monetary policy.

During the interwar period, two deep depressions influenced the world economy. They were associated with a general uncertainty concerning the prevailing monetary regime as well as with large financial disturbances. Eventually, the international financial system broke down. The interwar period should be classified as a crisis for the international financial system.

A comparison between the pre-1914 gold standard and the interwar period suggests that financial panics occurring in one or several countries do not cause major problems in a stable monetary system. However, a crisis for the whole monetary system, 'the whole regime', threatens the foundations of international finance and trade and thus of economic growth and prosperity. This seems to be a valuable lesson for today.

NOTES

1. I have received valuable comments from Michael Bordo, Lennart Jöberg and Torun Hedlund-Nyström. Richard Brooks improved my English.
2. The offsetting policy of the *Riksbank* is described in Jonung (1984).
3. On this point see Hedlund-Nyström (1970).
4. See Jonung (1979).
5. This argument is forcefully presented by Cassel (1936).

REFERENCES

Åkerman, J. (1944) *Ekonomisk teori II* (Lund: Gleerups).

Burns, A. and Mitchell, W. (1946) *Measuring Business Cycles* (New York: NBER).

Cassel, G. (1936) *The Downfall of the Gold Standard* (Oxford: Clarendon Press).

Hedlund-Nyström, T. (1970) *Svenska kriser och internationella konjunkturer* (Lund: Studentlitteratur).

Jonung, L. (1979) 'Knut Wicksell's norm of price stabilisation and Swedish monetary policy in the 1930's', *Journal of Monetary Economics* 4.

Jonung, L. (1984) 'Swedish experience under the classical gold standard 1873–1913', in M. D. Bordo and A. Schwartz (eds), *The Classical Gold Standard in Retrospective* (New York: NBER).

Jörberg, L. (1961) *Growth and Fluctuations of Swedish Industry* 1869–1912 (Stockholm: Almquist & Wiksell).

Kindleberger, C. (1978) *Manias, Panics, and Crashes* (New York: Basic Books).

Index